French Louisiana Music and Its Patrons

Patricia Peknik

French Louisiana Music and Its Patrons

The Popularization and Transformation of a Regional Sound

palgrave
macmillan

Patricia Peknik
Berklee College of Music
Boston, MA, USA

ISBN 978-3-319-97423-1   ISBN 978-3-319-97424-8   (eBook)
https://doi.org/10.1007/978-3-319-97424-8

Library of Congress Control Number: 2018951604

Cover credit: Cover illustration of Améde Ardoin and Dennis McGee by Pamela Kosin
Cover design by Emma Hardy

This Palgrave Macmillan imprint is published by the registered company Springer Nature Switzerland AG
The registered company address is: Gewerbestrasse 11, 6330 Cham, Switzerland

To the memory of Paul Peknik, who really should be here to read this.

ACKNOWLEDGMENTS

I greatly appreciated the assistance of Greg Adams at the Smithsonian Center for Folklife and Cultural Heritage, and Todd Harvey of the Folklife Center at the Library of Congress, along with Chris Segura at the Archives of Cajun and Creole Folklore at the University of Louisiana at Lafayette, and the archivists at the Research Center at the Historic New Orleans Collection. Charles Larroque and Jean-Robert Frigault offered their insights and enthusiasm at the offices of the Council for the Development of French in Louisiana in Lafayette. Richard DesHotels kindly shared his historic photo collection of Mamou, Louisiana. I owe a special thank you to Frank Tate, who apparently inherited his father's graciousness.

Berklee College of Music's Faculty Development Office funded my research and travel through a fellowship, and Berklee as an institution has been unfailingly generous in supporting this project. I owe a special thanks to Reg Didham and the interlibrary loan office at the Stan Getz Library. Megan Laddusaw and Christine Pardue at Palgrave Macmillan were simply excellent, and I valued the comprehensive feedback of the academic reviewers who contributed their time and professional wisdom to make this a better book.

We academics also have our patrons. They are the parents, siblings, and friends who support us with intellectual companionship and social celebrations as we weather the lonely joy of archival research and travel. I've been lucky to know the best people. I am grateful for the mentorship of Jon Roberts at Boston University and for the example of his intellectual rigor and prodigious curiosity. I first walked into his office as a student of intellectual history eager to have a conversation about scientific and religious ideas in *Moby-Dick*, and for the next ten years, he endured with patience and humor my ramblings on about topics each time farther afield, always helping me to the see the foundational connections between disciplines. I envy his current students the opportunity to learn from him.

This book belongs in a way to Bruce Schulman of Boston University, who had the great kindness to entrust me with the topic, offer exceptionally precise and helpful critical feedback, and guide me through years of reworking and refining my understanding of a complicated narrative. He continually inspired me with his ability to connect trends in music with larger political, social, and cultural conflicts and innovations, and with his knowledgeable passion for American music. I am deeply appreciative to him for having faith in my ability to tell the story.

Un grand merci à ma chère petite famille. Dominique, Madeleine and Maximin, thank you for the magnanimous gift of time you gave me to work on the research and writing, for the editorial assistance with the French, and for patiently believing in the project.

Finally, I must thank my father for instilling in me a love of history and a desire to listen to other people's stories. When I was a teenager sitting on the porch of our family camp on a small lake in upstate New York, he said he thought the most interesting literary form was the American novel, for its lessons in history. I'd like to think that the narratives of history are as strange and compelling as fiction, and that although many of the characters in Southwest Louisiana spoke in a musical language inflected with a disappearing dialect of French, theirs is very much an American story.

Contents

CHAPTER 1

Introduction: "A Wild and Ferocious Waltz"

This book about music is also a story about looking, observing, and perception. It tells the story of the manner in which the collectors, advocates, and patrons of French Louisiana music saw its traditions and performers in the context of social, political, and cultural debates in the United States from the mid-1920s to the early 1970s. It is about the outsider's gaze as it fell on a regional culture, and the insights and misperceptions of ethnomusicologists and commercial promoters as they struggled to understand a regional music that appeared to exist on the outskirts of American musical culture and outside the traditional scope of folk and popular music scholarship. French Louisiana music, a harmonically simplistic, ballad-based music that developed on the bayous and prairies of Southwest Louisiana in the late nineteenth and early twentieth centuries, is dissonant, raucous, exuberant and haunting, and although Southwest Louisianans listened to and performed a whole range of musical genres and styles, including jazz, blues, and country, old-time French-language music was a unique cultural expression of the region and played a powerful and enduring role in rural community life. Folklorists who first documented and recorded it, following the trail of renowned ethnomusicologist John Lomax, painted a portrait of a Southwest Louisiana culture that was largely isolated and insulated from popular music well into the first few decades of the twentieth century, while recent accounts by Cajun music scholar Ryan Brasseaux and French anthropologist Sara Le Menestrel have emphasized the adaptation, innovation, and improvisation of Southwest Louisiana

© The Author(s) 2019
P. Peknik, *French Louisiana Music and Its Patrons*,
https://doi.org/10.1007/978-3-319-97424-8_1

musicians tuned to the sounds of mainstream popular music culture. Yet, to whatever extent French Louisiana musicians were engaged with the larger national and international music culture, the larger music culture was not engaged with French Louisiana music. Then, at three moments of intense sociopolitical and cultural importance in America—the late years of the glimmering, frantic Jazz Age, the anxious, suburbanizing Cold War years that followed World War II, and the liberal, idealistic years that began with the Johnson presidency—distant listeners in Washington, DC, New York, and Paris cocked their ears to listen to an utterly strange and foreign sound: a high-pitched fiddle playing loud and fast above the vibrating bellow of a diatonic accordion, with lyrics about disaster and heartache sung cheerfully in a French dialect.

These early aficionados may have been captivated at first by the sound alone, but their individual aesthetic sensibilities do not account for the determination with which they sought to promote the sound to other outsiders. Political, social, and cultural forces drive and shape the popularization of a genre, and the actors driving popularization in this particular story were local, national, and international elites who succeeded remarkably well at bringing the music onto a larger stage, thereby changing it in fundamental ways. Historians have contextualized the rise to prominence of every other kind of southern music, chronicling the technical and artistic innovations and development of jazz, the blues, and country, and describing the commercial and cultural forces that generated national interest in what began as regional sounds. But French Louisiana music has been left out of histories of folk music, an odd cousin on the family tree of southern musical culture, like a distant relative whose ancestral connectedness to everyone else was somewhat murky, and who was always a little hard to talk to.

French Louisiana music tells the story of people who are constantly looking at each other or being observed. Old-time fiddle and accordion-based French Louisiana songs were passed from grandfather to father to son and, with the exception of the early twentieth-century musician Cleoma Breaux, narrated from the perspective of male suitors. The lyrics captured only the second half of every courtship narrative, the half in which the man laments that the woman who caught his eye has turned her back on him, or the part in which the woman who once looked at him so seductively has abandoned him to stroll around the dance hall on another man's arm. Scenes in which a man waits impatiently for a woman to return his glance, or urges a woman to evade her parents' surveillance, are punctuated with the phrases *"regardez"* [look] and *"tu vois"* [you see], as he implores her to take pity on him, to see things from his perspective, to disregard the neighbors' point of view. Every Saturday night in Southwest Louisiana, communities gathered to drink and dance to songs about men who, scorned in love, stopped to take a good hard look at their prospects, and at their souls, as they contemplated their state of rejection, poverty, and hardship. Some of the songs described the chastising gaze of parents as they watched, and then forbade, the blossoming of a romance. We, as listeners, are locked in a voyeuristic gaze, hearing a singer describe in spare detail, in a lamentatious yell, and to an upbeat melody, the last place he saw the woman who caused his heartbreak. We see him as he watches the woman he loves glance over her shoulder and tell him she's never coming back. We look at him as he sits in the window of his house watching her walk by, or as he takes in the sight of her when she returns to their home at dawn with her hair messed up and her clothes rumpled. To document what ethnomusicologists, folklorists, record collectors, and record label executives found so captivating in French Louisiana music complicates this voyeuristic dynamic by introducing yet another set of observers: readers of this book will be watching those folklorists and commercial promoters from an historical distance, tracking their movements and perceptions as they looked at a musical genre in which people were always—ruefully, skeptically, knowingly—watching each other.

French Louisiana music developed as the common musical genre of impoverished Acadian and Afro-Caribbean settlers in the prairie parishes of nineteenth-century Southwest Louisiana, and its regional practitioners thought of it simply as "French music." The debate over what outsiders would call it—and what they would call it would determine its categorization in music history and its marketability as a cultural product—began in the early twentieth century when ethnomusicologists and folklore collectors began to look closely at the musicians who played it and the communities that danced to it. Collector Harry Oster called it "the music of the Louisiana Acadians"; ethnomusicologist Alan Lomax called it "Cajun and Creole music," and both categorized it as folk music because the genre had developed through informal, face-to-face interaction between members of different generations in the same communities, with social, but not institutional or professional, oversight or support. The way the music was thereafter collected, studied and promoted, not only by scholars and commercial record labels but also by state, national and international government actors, reveals the many interests at work in its popularization. French Louisiana music wasn't seen simply as an unfamiliar musical practice that outsiders recorded out of an aesthetic appreciation for the aural dynamics of the fiddle and accordion; it was used by those outsiders as an instrument that could be made to perform a kind of cultural or political work.

The academic and commercial patrons of French Louisiana music were looking for the oldest sounds they could find: the unaccompanied voice of a ballad singer or the unamplified sound of a couple of fiddles and an accordion. It was important to them that the songs had been passed down through generations (one of their primary inquiries when talking with musicians was how, when, and from whom a song had been learned) and that they were sung in French. They used the terms "folk" and "old-time" to describe the music they were listening to, documenting, recording, and promoting. As commercially ambitious French Louisiana bands broadened their instrumentation, style, and repertoire to get in tune with national pop and country sounds, the patrons of French Louisiana music continued to privilege any music played by musicians in Southwest Louisiana that still included a fiddle or two and an accordion, and was still sung (at least partly) in French. Although some of the ballads can be traced back to medieval France, the French Louisiana music tradition has not been included in most scholarship on American folk music and the folk revival.

Benjamin Filene chronicled the establishment of the American folk music canon in *Romancing the Folk: Public Memory & American Roots Music*, arguing that in their pursuit of folk-crafted American music, ethnomusicologists John and Alan Lomax created a "cult of authenticity" in which the highest fruit was the music of an isolated rural musician who had a sentimental, but not commercial, engagement with music. While this may not have been a true descriptor of the musicians they recorded, this was the sepia-tinged image of Southern musicians the Lomaxes presented to new audiences in their quest not simply to document traditions, but to perpetuate them. Record label talent scouts likewise had their eye on commercial prominence, and the separate categories they established for music—hillbilly and "race" records—concealed the musical interactions between white and black communities, Filene explains: "Even though blacks' songs and whites' songs were often recorded by the same people on the same trips in the same cities, every company in the twenties treated its race and hillbilly selections as completely independent series that had … separate markets." French Louisiana music, on the other hand, was marketed to the totality of the Southwestern Louisiana market, as if it were a kind of hillbilly race music, with black and white musicians playing the same songs, and recording together.

Filene suggests that the term "vernacular" is better than "folk" to describe any musical genre that is "current, familiar, and manipulable by ordinary people" and "demands only minimal formal training and material resources to produce it," and he employs "roots" as the ideal term for the genres out of which contemporary commercial pop music was generated.[1] French Louisiana music cannot be called that sort of antecedent form. Its popularizers, who referred to it as folk music because it didn't fit into the category of popular commercial music played by professional or institutionally trained musicians, didn't want to know, or didn't want to publicize as such, the fact that that some of the French Louisiana musicians they labeled as down-home amateurs playing age-old tunes were really semi-professional musicians who played as often as they could to supplement their wages, experimenting in a variety of genres, and imitating popular commercial styles. Because this book focuses on the patrons of traditional Southwest Louisiana music, I adopt Filene's method of using the terms "folk," and "old-time" as those terms were used by these actors at different historical moments to encompass the body of suppositions, values, and standards all of these patrons brought to their collecting, commercializing and promoting of the music. However contested the term has become as an umbrella category for all sorts of rural, ethnic, and traditional forms of music that developed far from the urban centers of music production and distribution, the phrase "folk music" meant something specific to the original patrons of French Louisiana music—Alan Lomax, Harry Oster, and Ralph Rinzler—and it meant the same thing to all of them. I employ the term to capture their perspective on what the music was (in its earliest stage, acoustic renditions of generations-old ballads) and did (communicate stories about the community). This study is therefore not an interrogation of the integrity of the categories "folk," "roots," or "vernacular" music as those terms are now used in the disciplines of anthropology and ethnomusicology, but an analysis of the perceptions and actions of French Louisiana music's historical advocates, who, without exception, had far more than just music on their minds whenever they promoted that regional sound.

Anthropologists have written engaging studies on the origins and social and creative development of French Louisiana music. Brasseaux has documented the instrumental, stylistic, and perspective shifts that led to the development of the Cajun swing genre, which he calls "an American vernacular music," in the 1940s and 1950s. Cajun musicians sought out and incorporated popular music into a traditional style, Brasseaux argues, innovating, improvising, and creating swinging new sounds from the synthesis. French cultural anthropologist Sara Le Menestrel has also emphasized the way in which Louisiana musicians' adaptation to popular music styles continually and dynamically changed French Louisiana music, and the ways that local definitions of race, ethnicity, and social class have informed the Southwest Louisiana music scene since the late twentieth century. Both ethnographers rule out the use of terms like "folk" and "authentic" in order to create a portrait of the culture as it was understood by its actors and in order to explicate what tradition and innovation meant to cultural insiders who performed the music, and to their local audiences. The musicians themselves, and their regional listeners, would never have used the vocabularies of academics, collectors, and promoters. They called their music "French music" only when it became necessary to distinguish it from the English-language commercial music coming through the radio.

Given that the music's patrons were interested in French Louisiana music precisely because they considered it a folk genre, and that recording label executives recorded it because they saw it as such, this study preserves the use of the term "folk" as a descriptor contemporaneous to the perspective of the genre's patrons. They used the term with earnest intentions in order to generate interest, explain the music's provenance and social function, secure grant funding for fieldwork and concerts, and sell records. To a Depression-era resident of Southwest Louisiana who had grown up listening to the music played by older relatives, dancing to the ballads at Saturday night dance hall socials, and listening to fiddle duets on the living room phonograph, these were the most popular, familiar songs, neither "folk" nor alien. But this is not a study of what the music meant to the musicians and their local audiences, nor does it purport to describe what race, ethnic identity or genre meant to those historical actors themselves; rather, it looks at what outsiders interested in old-time music thought they were seeing when they looked at the facts on the ground in Southwest Louisiana. And there is no doubt that what outsiders saw in the music and in the musicians mattered, and is what drove the national and international popularization of French Louisiana music.

To mid-twentieth century ethnomusicologists Alan Lomax and Ralph Rinzler, who recorded French-language ballads during fieldwork expeditions in the South, French Louisiana music was a pathway into a rural American ethos of communally crafted art and social leisure, an exotic ingredient added to an already-robust mix of collectable American folk material. To post-war modernist Harry Smith, who heard in folk music the voice of democratic pluralism, French-language music could be cited as evidence of a regional vitality and identity that had not disappeared in the face of mass-market suburban American entertainment culture. To sixties generation liberals, the interracially collaborative origins and development of the genre seemed to constitute evidence of a time and place of less fraught and fractious race relations in the rural South. A music once heard only in the rural parishes of Southwest Louisiana's Acadiana region could be heard by its French and French-Canadian promoters as evidence of a vital French Atlantic culture. And for the recording industry executives who scouted the musicians and signed them to labels, the music could sell—regionally, nationally, and internationally. No one was more surprised than the Louisiana musicians when it did.

Regional music can function as an exceptionally condensed and evocative social science text, documenting the geography and history of a landscape, social relationships within families and communities, tragic and comical love stories, the political and economic hardships and resistance of ordinary people, and community-enforced ideals about justice, marriage, and labor. French Louisiana music was a particularly rich text because the music had such a privileged place in the culture of Southwest Louisiana. Among a population that was Catholic but not particularly churchgoing, house dances and dance hall gatherings provided the primary or sole occasion when extended families and rural neighbors could congregate to share news and encourage courtships. The evening family assembly at which parents and children sang and performed music for one another knit the household together.

The subject matter of Southwest Louisiana music was much more circumscribed than much of the rest of the Southern folk canon, and is one reason American historians have neglected a study of the genre. Folk music historians have written extensively about the music of hard labor in the cotton fields and coal mines, tragic ballads about figures like the steel-driving John Henry and textile mill worker Ella Mae Wiggins, whose "Mill Mother's Lament" became a rallying cry for unionization, and the work song canon has been used frequently and well by labor and civil rights activists to historicize calls for economic equality and social justice. But there are few such labor songs in the Southwest Louisiana music tradition. French Louisiana music chronicles leisure: the comforts of home and the dangers of leaving home, the joys and obstacles of courtship, of drinking and wandering. Couples struggle to make the best of domestic life, despite their economic travails, or a husband's drunken absence, or a wife's infidelities, but none of it sounds like grievance sharing. The songs are fast-paced and lively, meant to be danced to—energetic, upbeat-sounding tales, however grave the subject matter. Home is a landscape of fields of corn and sweet potatoes, punctuated by the occasional house with its sagging porch, and it's better to stay there: "*Touche pas ça tu vois*" is a cautionary tale of the seduction and robbery of a Louisiana man in the streets of Port Arthur, Texas. Indeed, many songs warn would-be adventurers about the ill fate that awaits them if they choose to live like orphans on the highway. Everyone who leaves hearth and home is psychologically and socially in peril. During the decades in which Louisianans were increasingly driven, by economic circumstances, to migrate to Texas for work, these songs warned about the danger and solitude that awaited those who would dare leave the French-speaking community behind, pleading with the sons and daughters of Acadiana: *please stay*. In many songs, husbands and wives return home late, or not at all. A husband describes his wife's abandonment of the children as Christmas approaches. There are anxious courtships and sudden betrayals. Willful daughters either tragically heed or tragically ignore their families' advice about whether or not to marry their lovers; a hard-headed son, prison-bound, appeals to his grieving mother to pray for his soul. There is an unforgiving attitude toward broken promises. Grudges are taken to the grave.

Broken promises and the frustration and bewilderment of betrayal were a theme in the history of the region for as far back as memory and myth could reach. The displacement of French-speaking Catholics from the provinces of New Brunswick and Nova Scotia in the decade after the French and Indian War marks the beginning of a story in which exiled Acadians, after first being shipped off to France and the Caribbean, immigrated to Louisiana to settle in the prairie parishes of Southwest Louisiana alongside the exiled, driven-out, uprooted and migrating people of Afro-Caribbean descent. Their shared culture was an island of French language and French traditions in an Anglophone land. Americans are raised on an American narrative in which a polyglot immigrant population assimilated into the mainstream culture of English-speaking Protestant Northern cities, but in Southwest Louisiana, German-speaking, Spanish-speaking, and English-speaking immigrants assimilated into the French-speaking Catholic culture of an impoverished region in the rural South: Irishmen named McCarthy and McGee, and Germans named Foltz and Schexnayder, became as "French" as the Thibodeaus and the Beaumonts.

The French language, and the music that was its most cogent expression, became a means of composing identity across the boundaries not only of ethnicity but also of race. French-speaking Creoles may have felt they had more in common with their Haitian and West Indian ancestors than they did with other Southern blacks, just as French-speaking Cajuns had discovered, painfully, that they had nothing in common with other white French-speaking Louisianans, whose ancestry and historical experiences were products of the cosmopolitan culture of French New Orleans. The fact that Creoles and Cajuns developed a common musical tradition has been well documented by folklorists who have studied the instrumentation, melodies and lyrical content of French Louisiana music and the collaborations and borrowings that resulted from proximity, sympathy and inspiration. That shared musical tradition is an important subject of study for the same reason the study of music within its historical context is important: music is a uniquely accessible forum for the expression and dissemination of social values and personal storytelling, bearing meanings and influences that are not only aesthetic and individual, but also communal and political.

The language we use about race and ethnicity has changed over time, but such semantic variety and fluidity was always the norm in Louisiana, where the term "Creole" as an ethnic descriptor referred in the early French colonial period to white Louisianans of European ancestry, then by the late eighteenth century to free blacks of African descent living in New Orleans, often members of a prosperous merchant class. In the context of traditional French Louisiana music, the term "Creole" denotes people of African and Afro-Caribbean descent, often of mixed African, French, Spanish or Native American ancestry, living in the Acadian-settled parishes of Southwest Louisiana and commonly called black Creoles or Afro-Creoles. Cajuns incorporated the African rhythms and call-and-response forms of the music of their Creole neighbors into their European violin-based waltzes and two-step dances, and Creoles incorporated the harmonic patterns of European dance melodies into their Afro-Caribbean percussion-based chants. These French Louisiana musical forms developed over the century between the first Acadian settlement in Southwest Louisiana and the post-Civil War era. Both groups adopted the accordion, imported into Louisiana by German settlers on the east side of the Mississippi River in the late nineteenth century. Poor white and black Louisianans who worked in the rice and sugar cane fields of Evangeline and Vermilion parishes lived in close proximity to each other, often in the same communities, and spoke the same musical language, revising, refining, and developing a shared repertoire. Given a New Orleans in which race had existed on a continuum and not on a polarity, in which free people of color had attended mixed balls and dances alongside whites from the time of Spanish New Orleans until Reconstruction, the integration of musical groups had a long history in Louisiana, and such collaborations existed in spite of and alongside of histories of racial violence, segregation, and disenfranchisement.

The federal government and the government of the state of Louisiana attempted, in the early years of the twentieth century, to "Americanize" the French-speaking population of Louisiana through English-only educational policies. With compelled change in the structure of communication came social change—the family and immediate neighbors could not retain their status as the highest authorities if they spoke a different language than school teachers and civil servants—and a wave of Texan oil workers migrated to Louisiana with the arrival of the petroleum industry, further Anglicizing social culture. French language music could, as a result, have become as much a regional historical remnant as the culture of the Pennsylvania Germans was also, by then, becoming. But a cohort of Louisiana soldiers returned from World War II determined to sustain the culture of French language music in Southwest Louisiana, just as American folklorists, worried about the disappearance of all forms of traditional cultural practice, set out to document, record and popularize that same music. Then the post-war French government, gazing at its former colonial possessions in Africa, the Caribbean, and North America and determined to reassert the importance of global French culture, took a proprietary interest in old-time French Louisiana music, which although uniquely a product of the complicated historical contingencies of Southwest Louisiana culture, was seen (by the French government) as contributing to the French musical tradition. In the 1960s, as French Louisiana music arrived on the national American recording and festival scene, French governmental entities funded and sponsored programs to rehabilitate the French language and French-language music in Louisiana. Thus local, regional, national, and international forces conspired to create and then benefit from the popularization of a regional Southern music.

Other Southern folk music forms have been successfully historicized. Scholars of the Southern rural blues revival rightly look to race relations in the American South and to black popular culture to ground the discussion of the cultural prominence of black musical forms in the mid-twentieth century, but a study of the French Louisiana music that was performed by Cajun and Creole musicians together, or played by Creole musicians at Cajun dance halls in a segregated South, is absent from otherwise comprehensive discussions of American folk music from the 1920s to the 1970s. The history of country music, the national popularization of hillbilly ballads, the vogue for down-home musicians, and the rise of bluegrass forms have all been the subject of considerable music history scholarship, but the language barrier has been an effective obstacle to an historical study of French Louisiana music's strange mid-twentieth-century popularization. Thus, this genre of regional music has remained "an American musical footnote" within discussions of American folk music traditions.[2]

The study of folk music has been the largest constituent element of folklore studies, a discipline devoted to the study of the customs, culture, crafts, and arts of traditional societies. Folk scholarship gained a firm foundation in American universities after World War II.[3] The need for a category called "folk" was most urgent whenever the moral authority of the dominant urban consumer culture had been undermined by political and social turmoil—after the Civil War, during the Great Depression, after World War II, and during the Vietnam War. Americans recovering from national trauma eagerly turned to the past to look for an imaginary time of social and moral simplicity, to the idea that some constituent part of the American population had been mercifully sheltered from the psychological damages of wartime, the excesses and stresses of consumerism, the anxious shifts in outlook and expectation. Each war prompted metropolitan Americans to look to the country's heartland, south, and farmlands for reassurance that rugged, plain-stock citizens had weathered the country's wars without drifting altogether too far from the particular, peculiar histories and fables that constituted the American narrative. The idea of the folk was no insult to these so-called citizens; rather, it was a symptom of urban Americans' urgent desire to grasp any individual strands that had not yet disappeared entirely into the loomed weave of the giant national flag, and evade a sense of time accelerating too rapidly toward a purely collective, mass-culture future. Ralph Rinzler associated the "city-folk" with that future.

Francophone folklore was among the very first subjects studied by American Folklore Society scholars when that professional organization was founded in 1888. The trauma of the Civil War and the political and economic Reconstruction of the South prompted American intellectuals to engage in a soul-searching interrogation into regional identity and inspired a determination to emphasize not only a common national origin but a characteristically America-within-America set of aesthetics, values, and pragmatic approaches to the problems of human experience. Harvard philosophy professor William Wells Newell, son of a Unitarian minister, worried that the cultures of Native American, African-American and ethnic American populations would not survive in the modern, industrialized, westward-expanding nation. Newell founded the American Folklore Society to bring together an interdisciplinary group of folklore scholars, including anthropologist Franz Boas and Harvard literature professor James Francis Child, who compiled Scottish and English ballads in the seminal collection *Child Ballads*. In its founding year, the American Folklore Society's *Journal of American Folk-Lore* published French Louisiana fairy tales collected by Tulane University literature professor Alcée Fortier, and in 1895, twenty-seven African-derived animal tales and fairy tales appeared as "Louisiana Folk-Tales" in the second volume of the *Memoirs of the American Folk-Lore Society*, with the note that "the study of the Creole dialect is of importance and interest."[4] Even before the AFS emerged, important collections of folksong and regional storytelling had appeared, including the 1867 *Slave Songs of the United States*, compiled by classical literature scholar William Francis Allen, along with Charles Pickard Ware, who had worked with freedmen during the Civil War, and Lucy McKim Garrison, daughter-in-law of William Lloyd Garrison. New Orleans writer George Washington Cable's 1879 *Old Creole Days* depicted the intrigues, injustices, and interconnectedness of antebellum New Orleans's French, Spanish, African and Native American inhabitants. Kate Chopin's short story collections *Bayou Folk* in 1894 and *A Night in Acadie* in 1897 used regional dialects to tell the stories of Cajun and Creole characters, and collecting regional tales and theorizing about folksong became a powerful interest early in the twentieth century as the nation became predominantly urban and scholars focused on the recovery and documentation of the cultural products of rural America. Rapid, efficient manufacturing and mass production for mass consumption compelled scholars to fret about the homogenization of national culture and to argue over whether the folk singer was part of "an unbroken chain of transmission" on the assembly line of past-to-present, or a creative interpreter of culture and an individualistic artist: "The song he sings is not his own by right of authorship … At the same time the folk-singer is equally sure that he sings a song learned from tradition exactly as his predecessors sang it. … A folk song has *texts*, but no *text, tunes* but no *tune* … [The folk singer] is, together with every other folk singer who sings the song in question—past, present or future—, co-author with the author of the text, and co-composer of the air."[5] Urbanization, immigration, and industrialization gave rise to a powerful set of questions about what constituted American national identity and what the role of the individual was in a pluralistic democracy—that is, in a nation that has *texts* but no *text*, *tunes* but no *tune*. What sort of national fabric did the great American immigration machine make out of constituent foreign materials and homespun rural cloth?

Immigrant and rural voices were brought to the forefront of music culture first by the mass production of printed sheet music and then by the phonograph. Sheet music had been described as a both a spoiler of old traditions, since the authority of print would suppress a multitude of other versions of a song, and as a preserver of those traditions, since at least some versions of a song could be captured before they disappeared under the noise of mass culture. Beneath each theory lay the anxious assumption that some form of cultural intervention was needed to "save" traditional music, and that ordinary people didn't have the training, sensibility, or motivation to preserve their own cultural traditions.[6] The ethnomusicologist John Lomax grew up in a country restless with that anxiety, and made it his life's work to record the cowboy ballads and frontier songs of people he idealized as "the plain people, devoid of tinsel and glamour, some base, a few suspicious and surly, many beautifully kind."[7] During the Depression, New Deal projects enlisted Lomax and a cohort of American folklorists to engage in what they saw as cultural rescue and recovery projects to preserve musical traditions that were fading into the past in communities facing outmigration and social change because of the disappearance of jobs in mining and agriculture. Whether or not those musical traditions were still vital cultural practices in any given community mattered less to them than that they were alien practices to urban outsiders. John Lomax's son Alan collected and documented an important cache of traditional French Louisiana songs and inspired later field workers, including Harry Oster and Ralph Rinzler, to follow in his footsteps across the prairies of Louisiana in search of old-time ballads. What they saw as they collected was rural poverty, and they reflexively conflated the categories of poverty and musical isolation.

Rural poverty and old-time musical "authenticity" became linked in the American mind during the Great Depression as southern communities showcased traditional mountain music and dancing at Asheville, North Carolina's Mountain Dance and Folk Festival (1929), the American Folk

Song Festival in Ashland, Kentucky (1932), and the National Folk Festival in St. Louis, Missouri (1934). Eleanor Roosevelt attended the White Top Folk Festival in Marion Virginia in 1933, bringing national publicity to old-time music. French Louisiana musicians, like these other traditional, regional musicians, were recorded by major labels in the 1920s and 1930s, and then experienced a decreased industry demand for their music during World War II, a time in which rural and ethnic Americans were mobilized for the war effort in the all-for-one and one-for-all singular mood of industrious patriotism.

Post-World War II modernism created a new appetite for folk cultures. For American intellectuals and cultural elites, the glamor of European high-art traditions had been challenged by the realities of a catastrophically violent war that undermined the authority of the European cultural inheritance. Hegemonic national traditions had been "implicated in the process by which war and genocide were rationalized,"[8] and the embrace of folk art was conceived of as a potential antidote to xenophobia and racism[9]: the cultural contributions of American ethnic and minority populations could be illuminated, explained, and celebrated. Universities began founding academic programs dedicated to the study of American folkways and the cultural output of the impoverished, the historically marginalized, and the rural isolated, though Southwest Louisiana folklore received scant attention in that era compared to the outpouring of scholarship on Appalachian and rural Southern populations.

Ralph Rinzler was the most successful and avid patron of French Louisiana music, undertaking several important field recording trips to Southwest Louisiana in the 1960s and 1970s, and bringing old-time musicians to the national stage at the Newport Folk Festival and the Smithsonian Folklife Festival, launching them into international recording careers. Rinzler knew that the musicians he found in the rural South weren't necessarily all "active bearers" of the old-time tradition, because by the time he got to them in the 1960s, some had stopped playing the oldest tunes and were experimenting with country music instrumentation and style. But he did wish for the older generation to pass on technique and repertoire to the younger generation so that French Louisiana music could be sustained against the barrage of popular and commercial music.

The historical development of French Louisiana music, its phases, and its resurgence in the 1960s, is coherent with the larger story documented by Richard Blaustein in his survey of the history and popularity of old-time fiddle music in the United States. Blaustein documents old-time fiddle music trends from Arkansas and Missouri to Vermont and North Carolina from the mid-nineteenth century to the early 1970s, beginning in the antebellum South, where a "distinctly indigenous type of instrumental fiddle music and dance, reflecting a high degree of cultural interchange between blacks and whites,"[10] emerged. A canon of tunes developed within and across communities as people heard music at Saturday night community dances: "You hear a tune and you try to remember it. You go off by yourself and play it; you don't remember exactly the way you heard it, so you play it with your idea of how it should sound. ... All done by ear, and somebody would learn a little piece from you and they would start to play a little different from you. ... So that's why you hear that same tune played in all parts of the country in a little different manner."[11] Music was the primary non-laboring social activity: "You went over to the neighbors' and had some music or they came over to your house and had some music. And every night or two you picked up your old banjo or fiddle, and if nobody came in, you'd practice, and if somebody came in, you played an hour or two."[12] During the golden age of recording in the 1920s and 1930s, the fiddle was a highly prominent sound on American records, reflecting the rural preservation movement in an urbanized country. Then, in the 1940s, interest in old-time fiddle music began to taper off: "It persisted, but not to the degree that it was well known. I thought it was gone. I think World War II had something to do with it. ... It seemed we entered an era then that people who loved the music and grew up with the music became ashamed of it."[13] As the music became more scarce, a mid-life cohort of old-time musicians began to recognize anew the value and integrity of traditional genres, and form organizations to preserve and promote the music: "A lot of them had quit playing ... there was a lot of fiddles coming out of the closet."[14] The American Old-Time Fiddlers Association, formed in 1964 and intent on maintaining the tradition in an organized, deliberate fashion by sponsoring public concerts and competitions, succeeded at attracting young musicians into apprenticeships, but then had to contend with a younger generation's interest in musical experimentation and technology. Old-time fiddlers balked at folklorists' tendency to emphasize only "the more archaic and picturesque aspects of the cultural repertories of [old-time fiddlers] ... discounting or neglecting whatever fails to meet their own standards of authenticity or good taste."[15] The popularity of French Louisiana fiddle-based music follows this historical trajectory.

Mid-twentieth century academic and organizational interest in folk music translated into a popular folk music movement as young middle-class urban liberals began to embrace old-time music in the late 1940s, first through the string-band music of Pete Seeger and The Weavers and then, in the 1950s, through commercial folk bands like The Kingston Trio; Harry Smith's *Anthology of American Folk Music*, released on Folkways Records in 1952, baptized a generation of listeners in the roots music of the rural American past. The old-time French Louisiana music featured in Smith's *Anthology* entered the folk music scene as curious evidence of an enduringly foreign version of America preserved within the national culture. Southwest Louisianans, incomprehensible to other Southerners in their attitudes about race, and peculiar in their speech, seemed an exotic incarnation of the American people, folk-like, yet peregrine, strangers. Catholicism and the French tradition in Louisiana had fostered more "easy human relationships and tolerance," a team of Fisk University researchers concluded during their investigation into race relations in Louisiana in the early 1940s, and the region was characterized by acceptance, interdependence, interaction, and civility across racial boundaries.[16] That is not to say that Louisiana was not a racially divided, unjust, rough and hazardous place for people of African descent, but it is to assert that, even in the face of a brutal history of slavery, Jim Crow, and an ever-reanimated and potent racism that sometimes violently, sometimes more subtly and insidiously, informed interactions between blacks and whites in Southwest Louisiana, French Louisiana music was created through dynamic interracial collaboration and exchange. And its patrons understood that. For this reason alone, a narrative account of the music's national popularization is warranted, since the cross-racial collaborations of the genre's history fascinated its collectors and promoters.

Black and white collaboration in the development of this distinct genre of Southern music was, to the musicians who composed and performed together, a fact of history, geography and culture, but to its outside listeners, that collaboration stood in baffling contradiction to the assumptions beneath established categories like bluegrass and blues, which was that each rural genre had developed among a discrete population, and that racial groups stood in propriety relationship to distinct musical forms. French Louisiana music endured as a contradiction and a counterargument for a century. Southwestern Louisianans had historically been good at scoffing at questions about whether the music had been developed first and most consequentially by white musicians or primarily and more influentially by black musicians, because it simply wasn't possible to know, or to care. It was all just French music, the players would say when pressed on the genre's origins and asked about its most influential composers and practitioners.

In his riveting study of Southern music, Karl Hagstrom Miller establishes that many black and white musicians "performed any music they could, regardless of their racial or regional identities," and that musicians across genres were engaged with every kind of "blues, ballads, ragtime, and string band music," as well as popular Tin Pan Alley and Broadway tunes. Academics and commercial promoters categorized and compartmentalized music into folk and pop genres in a way that "did not reflect how generations of southern people had understood and enjoyed music," Miller writes in *Segregating Sound, Inventing Folk and Pop Music in the Age of Jim Crow*. The portrait created by folklorists of "fixed and distinguishable racial cultures deeply rooted in history" does not tell the real story, Miller says, finding it "odd that while the scholarship on segregation chronicles white southerners' obsessive parsing of racial difference and policing of racial distance (the creation of a segregated South), there is little corresponding music literature that moves from racial integration to separation."[17] French Louisiana music was, indeed, one such genre, developed and performed by black and white musicians influenced by Franco-American and Franco-Caribbean traditions and styles. But as a new national audience came to appreciate the music in the 1960s and 1970s, its commercial promoters and some of its performers began to gaze at the music's history through the new lens of the Civil Rights movement and the ethnic revival, and to see the genre in that distorting and refracted light. Just as Louisiana had, as a new US state, transformed from the most racially mixed place in the American South to a segregated and violent land for people of African descent, the events of the late 1960s and early 1970s generated a recapitulation of that dynamic: under the pressures of the French language-reform movement and civil rights and ethnic identity movements, a regional expressive practice that had been the shared property of rural blacks and whites broke apart, splitting into separate genres, one shaped by white identification with a European and Acadian past, the other shaped by black identification with urban African-American culture.

Christopher Waterman has argued that musicians, genres, and songs that do not fit neatly into academic and industry-established categories of black and white folk and popular music have often been "elided from academic, journalistic, and popular representations of American music," and emphasizes the importance of a study of music from "the excluded middle," music that "springs from, circulates around, and seeps through the interstices between racial categories … an outcome and emblem of circulatory patterns that linked … cultures based, in increasingly oppositional fashion, on racial identity." Waterman suggests that the study of such musical forms can help us to understand musicians and audiences not as instances of idealized types, but as "human beings working under particular historical conditions to produce, texture, and defend certain modes of social existence."[18] The patrons of French Louisiana music were not idealized types, but human beings driven not only by an interest in the music itself but also by their ideas about the kinds of people who had created it. Alan Lomax, Harry Oster, Harry Smith, and Ralph Rinzler were agents of change for a genre whose roots and social function they, as outsiders, earnestly sought to understand. They successfully promoted its key performers to a national audience, to the benefit of their own professional reputations, and, more importantly, to the benefit of the musicians, the region, and the genre.

The dominant role traditional music played in the social culture of black and white French-speaking Southwest Louisianans is discussed in Chap. 1, which looks at the lyrical content of French Louisiana dance music and considers early recording stars of the genre. Old-time music was shaped by the collaborative adaptation of French and French-Canadian song traditions by white and black musicians, and a canon developed that would continue to inform French Louisiana music into the following century. Chapter 2 follows Louisianans from rural Acadiana, the name given to the twenty-two parishes in which French-speaking exiles settled in the eighteenth century, to World War II military service, and then back to their local communities, where, with a new perspective on their French heritage after fighting to liberate France, they established venues and events where old-time music could be played. This chapter argues that a reinvigorated identification with France as the ancestral mother country motivated Southwest Louisianans to establish a grassroots preservation movement to showcase regional cultural practices and language, and that this local movement was antecedent to the national "revival" of French Louisiana music.

Chapter 3 provides an overview of the work of the nationally and state-funded folklorists and commercial label scouts who, while doing fieldwork in Southwest Louisiana, found their long-held conceptions about folk music, race, and culture challenged in a less segregated and seemingly more "foreign" part of the American South. Ethnomusicologist Alan Lomax, charged in much contemporary scholarship with having a romantic's tunnel vision perspective on Southern folk music, saw French Louisiana music as the collective cultural expression of French speakers in the region, whereas the folklorist Harry Oster, in the years of heightened tension over race-based categories following *Brown v. Board of Education*, segregated old-time music into the categories "Cajun" and "Negro." Their successor, the Johnson-era liberal Ralph Rinzler, believed that an education in America's old-time music would inspire a public commitment to improved race relations in Civil Rights-era America. Looking at French Louisiana musicians and their predecessors, Rinzler saw a cross-racial artistic rapport that was absent from mainstream American life.

In Chap. 4, the eccentric modernist Harry Smith introduces the music of a vernacular American past to a generation of young, liberal, middle-class music lovers struggling to find ways to believe in the possibilities of a more racially just American future. Harry Smith's *Anthology of American Music* broadly inspires the American folk music revival, and incorporates French-language music into the canon of American folk. In Chap. 5, French Louisiana musicians find themselves on the national stage alongside young urban folk revivalists, prompting debates about "authenticity" and the relationship between regional and national cultures, and inspiring a reinvigoration of traditional music and French language education back in Louisiana.

Chapter 6 traces national and state efforts to suppress French-language education in the early twentieth century, and looks at the central role of the French and French-Canadian governments in funding and promoting French language education programs in Louisiana beginning in the 1960s. Folklorists quickly concluded that the survival of the language and the survival of the music were interdependent, fueling local efforts, funded by the federal government and the state, to raise the profile of old-time music in a changing modern Acadiana. In Chap. 7, the young generation of Louisiana Creole musicians turns to the sounds of urban African-American culture, leaving traditional music, and the black-white collaborations that had created French Louisiana music, in the past, while a new generation of Louisiana Cajun musicians, inspired by their own pilgrimages to France, turn back to the traditions of old-time music. Although black and white composers, lyricists and performers had improvised, interpreted, adapted and performed music together and developed the genre collaboratively over centuries, by the 1960s, cultural politics and stylistic and technological innovations in music divorced Creole culture from its association with Cajun music, and the music culture of

Southwest Louisiana became, like much of American culture in the late 1960s and early 1970s, more fractured and self-conscious.

This study concludes by examining the strong drive, in French Louisiana music, to celebrate a romanticized Acadian heritage, and the concomitant migration of Creole musicians out of a common French Louisiana music culture and into mainstream African-American music culture. The Louisiana tourist industry celebrates the culture of Southwest Louisiana as historically "Cajun," emphasizing the endurance of the French language and rural French Catholic traditions, while Creoles now largely identify as African-Americans who speak Creole African American Vernacular English[19]; likewise, French Louisiana music split into distinct genres, obscuring the proximate experiences, collaborations, and repertoire of old-time musicians during the music's formative decades.

Ralph Rinzler's correspondence with French Louisiana music advocates in Southwest Louisiana, the interviews he conducted with musicians, and fieldwork notes from his recording trips to Mamou, Louisiana, were invaluable to this study. The materials in the Ralph Rinzler Archives and Collections of the Smithsonian Center for Folklife and Cultural Heritage reveal the scope of his interest in music as a form of social-cultural expression that documents a community's values, relationships, and way of life. The field recordings, field notes, and correspondence of Rinzler, Alan Lomax, and Harry Oster in the Louisiana Collections of the American Folklife Center at the Library of Congress American Folklife Center provided a map of their work in Southwest Louisiana. The lyrics of the songs in the French Louisiana repertoire were transcribed from original recordings, and the French-to-English translations of the lyrics are also original to the writing of this book. Spellings have been standardized, with the goal of assuring that the lyrics are readily comprehensible to speakers of French who are outsiders to the traditional Cajun and Creole dialects in which the songs were performed. Government documents, texts of legislative hearings, and the records and correspondence of the Council for the Development of French in Louisiana highlight the controversies surrounding the French language and culture movement. Louisiana folklorists compiled interviews from the 1960s to the 1980s with some of the most celebrated French Louisiana musicians, and these first-hand accounts of the music culture of Southwest Louisiana were highly informative, as were compact disc liner notes. Chris Strachwitz, the founder of Arhoolie Records in El Cerrito, California, contributed important information about his experiences on the trail of French Louisiana music. These scattered materials tell the story of how local activists, folklorists, commercial record labels, and federal, state, and international governmental and cultural organizations all became interested in the old-time music of French Louisiana at the same time, and how their work with the music compelled them to rethink the meaning of cultural identity.

French Louisiana music remained a neglected orphan within music history studies in part because ethnomusicologists and cultural historians have focused their attention on those genres of Southern music that constitute the core of American roots music: blues, bluegrass, gospel, and old-time country. Old-time French Louisiana music is not glorified as one of the "sources out of which the twentieth-century's popular music was created"[20] in the same sense that blues is celebrated as the source of rock and roll, or banjo-centered string bands are considered the foundational sources of country music. Yet, in its origins and development, and its encounter with popular culture and the cultural politics of the mid-twentieth century, it illustrates what Waterman calls "musical circulation, movement, and traversal," and reveals the confluence of historical, social, and cultural circumstances through which regional sounds that are at first peripheral to the national music scene become popularized.

When Alan Lomax set off to record Cajun and Creole singers in Southwest Louisiana, he expected to find "tropical French music," and in a sweeping and humorous summary of the genre's origins, he said in a 1948 radio interview, "The story is that Evangeline and her people came down from Arcadia in the seventeenth century. They moved into this swampy country and they turned kind of tropical. They changed their language, changed their music, and just listen to what happened." Lomax and the patrons of French Louisiana music that followed in his footsteps saw the genre as an art form that needed to be put into the public eye and simultaneously as a folk craft that needed to be protected from the larger public culture, and they promoted the music for reasons that sometimes had a little less to do with the music itself than with sociopolitical idealisms. They also loved the music itself, which was raucous and joyful, beautifully alien to Lomax's outsider ear. "What we're going to find down there," Lomax said, recalling the expectations of his first field recording trip, "is a kind of lazy, wild, and ferocious waltz."[21] The patrons of French Louisiana music choreographed its traversal onto a national, and then an international stage, and their work illuminates the enduring potency of ages-old American arguments about the relationship of the parts of the nation to the whole, of folk form process to manufactured commercial product, and of artifact to art.

NOTES

1. Benjamin Filene, *Romancing the Folk: Public Memory & American Roots Music* (Chapel Hill: The University of North Carolina Press, 2000), 36; 4–5.
2. Ryan André Brasseaux, *Cajun Breakdown: The Emergence of an American-Made Music* (Oxford: Oxford University Press, 2009), 25. Brasseaux argues that Cajun music is not, in any case, folk music (a term Brasseaux finds pejorative and exploitative).
3. Regina Bendix, *In Search of Authenticity, The Formation of Folklore Studies* (Madison: The University of Wisconsin Press, 1997), 122.
4. *Louisiana Folk-Tales, In French Dialect and Translation*, collected and edited by Alcée Fortier, The American Folklore Society (Boston: Houghton, Mifflin and Company, 1895): Preface.
5. Phillips Barry, quoted in Bendix, *In Search of Authenticity*, 144–145.
6. Bendix, *In Search of Authenticity*, 151.
7. Alan Lomax quoted in Bendix, *In Search of Authenticity*, 147.
8. Roger D. Abrahams, "The Public, The Folklorist, and the Public Folklorist" in *Public Folklore*, ed. Robert Baron and Nick Spitzer (Jackson: University of Mississippi Press, 2007), 24.
9. Bendix, *In Search of Authenticity*, 150.
10. Richard J. Blaustein, "Traditional Music and Social Change: The Old Time Fiddlers Association Movement in the United States" (Ph.D. dissertation, Indiana University, 1975), 22.
11. Old-time California fiddler Kelley Kirksey, quoted in Blaustein, "Traditional Music," 86.
12. Missouri fiddler Jake Hughes, quoted in Blaustein, "Traditional Music," 30.
13. Alabama fiddler Bill Harrison, quoted in Blaustein, "Traditional Music," 83.
14. Missouri fiddler Jake Hughes, quoted in Blaustein, "Traditional Music," 66.
15. Blaustein, Traditional Music, 6.
16. Phillip J. Johnson, "The Limits of Interracial Compromise: Louisiana, 1941," *The Journal of Southern History*, Volume LXIX, No. 2 (May 2003): 324.
17. Karl Hagstrom Miller, *Segregating Sound, Inventing Folk and Pop Music in the Age of Jim Crow* (Durham: Duke University Press, 2010), 1–2; 12.
18. Christopher A. Waterman, "Race Music: Bo Chatmon, "Corrine, Corrina" and the Excluded Middle," in *Music and the Racial Imagination*, edited by Ronald Radano and Philip Bohlman (Chicago: University of Chicago Press, 2001), 167–168; 182; 199.
19. Sylvie Dubois and Barbara M. Horvath, "Creoles and Cajuns: A Portrait in Black and White," *American Speech* 78.2 (2003): 197.

20. Benjamin Filene, *Romancing the Folk: Public Memory & American Roots Music* (Chapel Hill: The University of North Carolina Press, 2000), 4.
21. Alan Lomax, quoted in "Lomax in Louisiana: Trials and Triumphs," Barry Jean Ancelet, Folklife in Louisiana, Louisiana's Living Traditions http://www.louisianafolklife.org/LT/Articles_Essays/LFMlomax.html.

BIBLIOGRAPHY

Filene, Benjamin. *Romancing the Folk: Public Memory & American Roots Music.* Chapel Hill: University of North Carolina Press, 2000.

Brasseaux, Ryan André. *Cajun Breakdown, The Emergence of an American-Made Music.* New York: Oxford University Press, 2009.

Bendix, Regina. *In Search of Authenticity, The Formation of Folklore Studies.* Madison: The University of Wisconsin Press, 1997.

Fortier, Alcée, ed. *Louisiana Folk-Tales, In French Dialect and Translation.* Boston: Houghton, Mifflin and Company, 1895.

Roger D. Abrahams. "The Public, The Folklorist, and the Public Folklorist" in *Public Folklore*, ed. Robert Baron and Nick Spitzer. Jackson: University of Mississippi Press, 2007.

Blaustein, Richard J. "Traditional Music and Social Change: The Old Time Fiddlers Association Movement in the United States." Ph.D. dissertation, Indiana University, 1975.

Johnson, Phillip J. "The Limits of Interracial Compromise: Louisiana, 1941." *The Journal of Southern History*, Volume LXIX, No. 2 (May 2003): 319–348.

Lomax, Alan, quoted in "Lomax in Louisiana, Trials and Triumphs," Barry Jean Ancelet, Folklife in Louisiana. http://www.louisianafolklife.org/LT/Articles_Essays/LFMlomax.html.

Miller, Karl Hagstrom. *Segregating Sound, Inventing Folk and Pop Music in the Age of Jim Crow.* Durham: Duke University Press, 2010.

Waterman, Christopher A. "Race Music: Bo Chatmon, "Corrine Corrina" and the Excluded Middle." In *Music and the Racial Imagination*, edited by Ronald Radano and Philip Bohlman. Chicago: University of Chicago Press, 2001.

Dubois, Sylvie, and Barbara M. Horvath. "Creoles and Cajuns: A Portrait in Black and White." *American Speech* 78.2 (2003): 192–207.

CHAPTER 2

French Louisiana Music from Home and Dance Hall to Radio and Fred's Lounge

Fred's Lounge, a tiny, concrete-block bar in the isolated village of Mamou, Louisiana on the southern prairies of Evangeline Parish, seems an unlikely place to be memorialized as the starting point of the "French Renaissance" in America, as the plaque beside its front door reads.[1] The building has the architecture of a bunker and the décor of a juke joint, and although Fred's is a music venue, there is no stage for musicians. A handwritten sign on the wall reads "This is not a dance hall." Its doors are only open on Saturday mornings, when third shift oil refinery workers crowd the bar beside crawfish farmers and men who work in the rice mills. It is not a dance hall, but the men have come to Fred's to two-step and waltz with their wives and girlfriends, and posted signs ask patrons not to stand on the tables or the cigarette machine to get a better view of the dance floor.

Fred's is a place of cigarettes and canned beer. In the summer, the humid darkness indoors provides little relief from the sweltering Louisiana sun, which bakes the streets and sidewalks of downtown Mamou—really just a single street of Depression-era storefronts—with the same intensity as it beats down on the prairie fields and the marshy grasslands of the bayou. In a state world-famous for Dixieland jazz and New Orleans blues clubs, Fred's Lounge is a remote and hard times-looking venue off Louisiana State Highway 13 on 6th Street, but the story the plaque tells is true: In addition to cane sugar and cotton, the Acadian parishes of Southwest Louisiana produced French-language music and culture, exporting it first to the nation and then to an international audience in the

© The Author(s) 2019
P. Peknik, *French Louisiana Music and Its Patrons,*
https://doi.org/10.1007/978-3-319-97424-8_2

decades after World War II. It wasn't far from Fred's that many of the greatest Cajun and Creole fiddlers and accordionists were born, lived and died, some of them uncertain about whether or not they even wanted their music to live on after them.

Ethnomusicologists and folklorists who have written about traditional French Louisiana music—songs played on an accordion and a fiddle or two, with perhaps a triangle to keep time—have argued that the music was on the brink of extinction by the mid-1930s as the new technology of radio, which broadcast string bands, country music and English-language news, drowned out "old home music," and the political and cultural forces of Americanization effaced Cajun and Creole folkways and the Southwest Louisiana French language.[2] In this narrative, there is a *before*, a long interlude, and then an *after*, the *before* captured by the accounts of Works Progress Administration-affiliated ethnographers who recorded their fieldwork observations of Cajun sharecroppers working in grueling conditions in the hot sun, and then living "like medieval troubadours, traveling about the Cajun settlements, living on the bounty of those who enjoy their music."[3] The 1920s and 1930s were marked as the golden age of old-time French-language music in Southwest Louisiana, and then, according to the narrative, for twenty-five years the music lost favor in its indigenous region and was silenced until, in the 1960s, the next wave of folklore scholars "discovered" old-time Louisiana folk music and "initiated a cultural revival"[4] in which local populations were taught to take pride in the music of their French heritage. Fred's Lounge, and the cultural activism of two of Fred Tate's friends in Mamou, Louisiana, Paul Tate and Revon Reed, provides evidence for another version of the story and illuminates the role of the local patrons of French Louisiana music, and of Creole musicians, independent record labels and local radio stations in sustaining, from the mid-1940s on, a traditional music that would come to be recognized nationally as every bit as historically and aesthetically valuable as the more famous old-time folk music of Appalachia and the Mississippi Delta. "We have been fortunate in that we have not had to revive Acadian music traditions,"[5] Paul Tate insisted, explaining that the music was still omnipresent in the community, even while some young musicians were gravitating toward more contemporary popular genres—hardly a novel or exceptional development in American music history. There is much evidence to support the portrait of an older generation of musicians carrying on with the repertoire and styles they had been brought up with, playing for audiences of a similar age and aesthetic sensibility,

while the more well-traveled middle generation experimented with country and swing, and the youngest generation sought out rock and roll and
country pop. This is a classic dynamic in music consumer history. And
Mamou, as a case study, reveals trends at work across Southwest Louisiana:
traditional fiddle-and-accordion groups played at Vidrine's, which
attracted Mamou's older Cajun generation, while country swing bands
performed at Piersall's Cocktail Parlor, a place where young Cajun married couples went to dance, and Creoles went to Papa Paul's Club one
mile away. But it isn't the case that the young generation had entirely
walked away from old-time music by the World War II era. Fred Tate
bought the bar on his twenty-ninth birthday, and Paul Tate, who was a
passionate advocate of French Louisiana music on a global scale, was only
twenty-four, and both spent the next decades promoting fiddle-and-
accordion French-language dance ballads as the foundational musical language of the region.

Fred Tate opened his lounge as a returning GI with the intention of
showcasing French-language music and promoting Mamou, which now
calls itself "The Cajun Music Capital of the World." Tate was an effective
local promoter in a region that would come to draw its share of "cultural
intervenors," a term David E. Whisnant uses in *All That is Native and
Fine, The Politics of Culture in an American Region*, to describe outside
preservationists whose mission is to preserve and revive what they perceive
to be an authentic and endangered folk culture.[6] This is not to say that
old-time music was the single genre performed by or appreciated by
Southwest Louisianans. As French anthropologist Sara Le Menestrel has
documented, a great variety of American popular music was played and
consumed across the region, from jazz and big band orchestra to Tin Pan
Alley and Broadway tunes,[7] and at no time in dance hall or radio history
was old-time music the single soundtrack of Southwest Louisiana. But the
music was the region's signature soundtrack, an expression of the degree
to which the histories and experiences of Southwestern Louisianans were
different from the histories and experiences of other rural southerners.
Mamou attorney Paul Tate, one of the partners in Fred's Lounge, wanted
to keep it that way. Tate, who had a cohort of musicians as clients, was
described by Smithsonian folklorist Ralph Rinzler as wealthy, knowledgeable, and the person most responsible for the latter's understanding of
French Louisiana music and traditions. Tate was a sophisticated anti-
modernist whose interest was not in promoting music for its own sake but
in policing the cultural boundary between rural Southwest Louisiana and

the rest of the state. "I have often remarked that I am in no sense a folk-lorist, but that I am simply 'one of the Acadian folks' interested in preserving our culture and traditions," Tate wrote to Joan Baez after French Louisiana musicians appeared at the Newport Folk Festival. Describing Mamou's Mardi Gras celebration to Ralph Rinzler, Tate stressed that it was not at all like the carnivalesque parade of New Orleans or urban Lafayette's celebration. "It is the only non-commercial festival in Louisiana, has never been subsidized by the State nor anyone else, and is truly a folk institution," he insisted. Fred Tate's bar in Mamou was meant to be a venue where the community could socialize and hear familiar tunes: "At Fred's place, every Saturday morning, all the Louisiana Cajuns come out to sing and dance ... Nowhere else can you hear such lively folk music ... People go to Fred Tate's after stopping by the bank or after going to the barbershop ... The whole family is there .... At Fred's, on Saturday mornings, you are in the heart of French Louisiana."[8] The experience of World War II had deepened and radicalized the nostalgia of a generation who, punished in school for speaking French, had been brought up to think of themselves as strangers in a strange land—Catholic, French-speaking rice and potato farmers and bayou fishermen in an increasingly urban, modernized and English-speaking Protestant America. The campaign to sustain old-time music would take Paul Tate to Paris and then to Niamey, Niger in West Central Africa, Revon Reed to Newport, Rhode Island and Montreal, and the governor of Louisiana to the dance floor of Fred's Lounge, where some of the most talented musicians of twentieth-century Louisiana had played, to declare that the day the bar opened on November 20, 1946, had been a special day in the history of Louisiana, and that its fiftieth anniversary was "Fred's Day," in honor of Fred Tate.[9]

In the Evangeline Parish of Fred Tate's childhood, Cajun and Creole musicians had played the same songs, "the same kind of rhythm," and no one, Leo Soileau remembered, had even called it Cajun or Creole music in those days. "They called it French music," Soileau said.[10] Black and white Southwest Louisianans listened to it without conceiving of it as the cultural product or property of one or the other group, black or white, as the more germane distinction was between local French-language music and the music of the larger national culture. In fact, one Cajun woman was convinced that the "AM/FM" on the radio dial meant "American Music" and "French Music."[11] It was this "French music" that brought Library of Congress ethnomusicologist John Lomax and his son Alan to Southwest

Louisiana in the 1930s, drew song collector Harry Oster to Mamou on behalf of the government of Louisiana in the 1950s, and brought Claudie Marcel-Dubois, a scholar of traditional French dance, to Fred's Lounge in the 1970s on behalf of the *Centre National de la Recherche Scientifique* [French National Centre for Scientific Research]. If there was a joke that began "Three folklorists walked into a bar," that bar was Fred's Lounge.

The fiddle-and-accordion music of the bayou and prairie parishes of Louisiana grew out of the geographical isolation of the impoverished French-speaking settlers, both black and white, who inhabited the region upriver from New Orleans and west to the Texas border, a land that was, for all economic and political purposes, the backyard of empires. Eighteenth-century Louisiana had been governed by Bourbon France as a far-flung colony even more remote than its sugar plantations in Guadeloupe and Martinique, then passed off to Spain after the French and Indian War to serve as the Spanish empire's northernmost guard post, protecting the silver of Mexico against Anglo-American incursion into Spanish territory. The territory was briefly French again before being sold in the Louisiana Purchase, and through its seven governments, from colonial to territorial to state and confederate, it sustained the most diverse population in the South, from French-speaking Houma Indians to German immigrants and free people of African descent. Louisiana is the only US state with a civil law legal system, having inherited the philosophy and practices of French legal tradition, and the only Southern state that was as ethnically diverse as a Northern city, with immigrants from Sicily, Germany, the West Indies, and Spain inhabiting land alongside the Choctaw Indians. But it was under the legal codes of the Spanish empire that a vibrant music culture was able to develop in New Orleans and Louisiana's rural parishes, because the Spanish government, unlike its British and French counterparts, made no attempt to outlaw musical instruments like the drum, nor to suppress African-derived rhythms and dance in public culture.[12]

Jazz music is an instructive example of how ethnic and racial diversity generated new musical forms in Louisiana. Irish soldiers who served as the police force for the Spanish empire in New Orleans brought brass bands to the city, while classically trained musicians, including free men of color, brought African rhythms to the harmonies and syncopation of European music, experimenting with new instrumentation and improvisational styles. In the mid-nineteenth century, German immigrants brought the accordion and polka music to New Orleans, and these urban immigrants then migrated out to the lands west of New Orleans on the east bank of the Mississippi River in an area that came to be called the German Coast. Black and white Francophone musicians living in close proximity in rural areas taught one another to play the German accordion and learned from each other's fiddle-playing style. Such cross-racial collaboration is entirely coherent with the story of the historical and cultural origins of jazz; though stunning in the context of the antebellum and Jim Crow South, such exchanges were not remarkable in Louisiana, where music was not a cultural barrier, but a social incentive.

The music culture of Southwest Louisiana developed in the context of the liberality of cultural expression and cultural mixing that had always characterized Francophone New Orleans. Acadiana was in no sense a geographical extension of cosmopolitan New Orleans French culture, but neither did Southwest Louisiana Francophone culture develop uniquely and independently in an Anglophone, Protestant state. New Orleans and Acadiana shared deep ties to the Catholic church, a strong attachment to the idea of French colonial heritage, and a dynamic tradition of musical performance and consumption. Some of the forms that tradition took shocked outsiders like Benjamin Henry Latrobe, architect of the nation's capitol building, who, on his 1819 visit to New Orleans, stumbled upon a drum circle on a Sunday afternoon stroll around the city. Five to six hundred black New Orleanian men and women had gathered in the city center, vigorously beating drums to accompany the yelling of singers and the strumming of banjos.[13] Latrobe's account was an early contributor to what Bruce Raeburn calls the "environmental thesis," an oversimplified origin story that locates the birthplace of jazz in the particular and exclusively African space of Congo Square. But it is more apt to adopt the metaphor of laboratory than of cradle, with polyphonic New Orleans nurturing a wealth of colliding, colluding sound and rhythm. Ethnomusicologist Matt Sakakeeny emphasizes New Orleans's stature as a music city long before the emergence of jazz, describing the varied and dynamic music culture of New Orleans as the outcome of an expansive "circulatory system" in which Africans, mixed-race Creoles, Anglo-Americans, European immigrants, and Latin Americans were all part of a musical feedback loop vibrating with the sounds of French opera, ballroom dance, brass band military marches, African ring shouts, the French-language work songs of Creole craftsmen, and the melodic yells of Italian produce vendors hawking their wares.[14]

Ambling around the French Quarter on the Fourth of July the same year as Latrobe, Rowley, Massachusetts writer Henry C. Knight captured the dynamism and panoply of the city when he described overhearing

the black-veiled nuns of the Ursuline Convent saying Mass "in their ban-
ishment from the world," and, a moment later, walking along the crowded
and bustling levee, passed Creek and Chickasaw Indians, "strolling and
idling ... half naked ... the chief with tall white feathers in his coarse black
hair"; passing "a drove of forty slaves" and a Scottish Highlander playing
a bagpipe, he stopped to look into the windows of the Museum Coffee-
House, a kind of novelty shop and gaming house, taking in the patrons
and the band: "[The place] is illuminated, and enlivened by a band of
musicians, on every evening. ... Here meet, every night, on the balcony,
or level roof of the piazza, in the open air, behind brilliant transparencies,
hundreds of people, from the novice shop-boy, to the gray man in spec-
tacles .... [Then] on Sabbath evening, the African slaves meet on the
green, by the swamp, and rock the city with their Congo dances."[15]

Like Latrobe, Knight was struck by the novelty, expressiveness, diversity, and intimacy of socializing and spectacle. In the decades that followed, New Orleans streets grew even more crowded with polka music
and parades, Sicilian street vendors and German brass bands, drum circles
and jazz funerals: "Every musician in New Orleans in 1900, white, black,
Creole, was drawing from the same sources," jazz historian Samuel
Charters explains, "the syncopated cakewalks ... the melodies of ragtime
... the popular songs that drifted into town like seeds in the wind with the
traveling vaudeville shows, and the sheet music that was found in nearly
every home in each of the city's social and ethnic groups."[16]

This dynamic of musical exchange was reiterated in the Acadian parishes, where the descendants of the French Catholic settlers driven out of
British Protestant Canada after the French and Indian War lived in a rural
culture of Catholic faith, economic hardship, a devotion to music and
social life, and a habit of co-existence with people of African descent.
Thus, although New Orleans and Southwest Louisiana were economically
and politically sharply distinct from one another, the example of New
Orleans as the state's shining Francophone cultural gem validated and
normalized Southwest Louisianans' focus on the communal ties of language, religion, and music in a racially diverse social landscape.

Entertainment and leisure culture in Acadiana was organized around
four music-based traditions. The *veillée* was an evening gathering of neighbors that featured either a cappella ballad sung by the wife and mother of
the house, or acoustic fiddle and accordion music performed by the men,
accompanied by foot stomping and hand clapping. The *bal de maison* was
a larger gathering of extended families sometimes called a *"fais do do,"*

a French colloquialism meaning "go to sleep," since late-night dancing for adults couldn't begin until the children were asleep. As communities grew and single houses couldn't accommodate every uncle, cousin, and in-law, these dances expanded into larger Saturday night events held in *salles de danse*, or public dance halls, which began to be built in Southwest Louisiana in the mid-to-late nineteenth century. French travelers to Southwest Louisiana would have found the architecture of the dance hall and the accordion-backed ballads reminiscent of the Parisian *bal musette* that developed in Paris in the same period—indoor and outdoor dance halls where couples waltzed to accordion and piano music—and that characterized urban French social life in the interwar years. In "Memory of France: April 1944," the French literature scholar Wallace Fowlie described a typical *bal musette* he visited in 1930s Paris, where couples danced to "a jerky kind of music" featuring the "ever puffing and swelling accordion." Drinks were served with enthusiasm, and the dancers formed "one universe" as young couples courted in the "dream and silence of love in the midst of raucous accordion playing."[17]

In American photographer and writer Carl Van Vechten's account in *Au Bal Musette*, the dance halls, hidden away among the cobblestone streets of Montmartre, were illuminated by globe lights and decorated with brightly painted wall murals, and the music of the accordion droned on until the very late hours of the night. The accordion had replaced the traditional "*musette*," the bagpipe which had been the fashionable instrument of French dance in earlier centuries. Van Vechten's description of a dance hall in post-World War I France could just as well describe a Louisiana dance hall of the same era: rows of long tables with wooden benches in a large hall, a corner of the floor cleared for dancing, and the music of the accordion "both rhythmic and ordered ... but never faster or slower, and never ending. ... [The dancers] whirled to the inexorable music when it was a waltz. ... In the dances in two-four time ... something between a one-step, a mattchiche, and a tango, with strange fascinating steps of their own devising, a folk-dance manner. ... Yes, under their feet, the dance became a real dance of the people." Van Vechten emphasized the role of the accordionist in the dynamism of the scene: "His accordion, manipulated with great skill, was augmented by sleigh-bells attached to his ankles in such a manner that a minimum of movement produced a maximum of effect." The accordionist sat expressionless, like "a static picture," playing "old *chansons de France...*" adding complexity to the sound and rhythm by periodically hitting a cymbal with one of his feet, but never evincing the expressions or gestures of a performer, since the focus was meant to be on the couples whirling and whirling across the dance floor.[18]

Van Vechten had a deep appreciation for being an outside observer immersed in the nightlife of a new or foreign city, neighborhood, or block. A connoisseur of the avant-garde in dance, music, and literature, he began, in Jazz Age New York, to photograph leading Harlem Renaissance artists and intellectuals, then spent twenty-five years documenting creative life in black Manhattan, shooting portraits of Paul Robeson, Bessie Smith, Billie Holiday, W.E.B. Du Bois, Richard Wright, and dozens of other artistic luminaries. As music critic for *The New York Times*, Van Vechten lauded opera and ragtime, jazz and George Gershwin, and as the paper's correspondent in Paris, he sat in the Montmartre dance hall, cocked a well-trained ear to the brash scene, and found the rousing dance and music enchanting.

His descriptions of another Parisian dance hall, with long wooden benches arranged against the walls to make space for dancing to the music of an accordionist and a guitarist, once again sound much like descriptions of the Louisiana version, which featured long wooden benches and bleachers along the wall, and a band composed of an accordionist and either a guitarist or a fiddler. The sign on the wall in Van Vechten's French *musette* asked patrons who were watching the dancers not to stamp their feet in time to the music,[19] but in the Southwest Louisiana setting, the foot stomp became an integral component of the call-and-response pattern of clapping, stomping and yelling that characterized French Louisiana social music. The fast-paced, exuberant drinking song that was sung that night in Montmartre, "*Auprès de ma blonde*," was a seventeenth-century antecedent to French Louisiana songs like "*Ma blonde est partie*" and "*Jolie blonde*," which also lamented, in a rollicking melody, the tragic betrayal or separation of lovers.

Among both Cajuns and Creoles, the house dance and dance hall traditions were the same, even if the French words that described these social events were different: Cajuns held a *bal de maison* in the same fashion that Creoles held *un diverti*, from the French *divertissement*, or entertainment, or a *la-la au soir* [evening fun]. Younger people sometimes called on older neighbors to host the *la-la*, at which point all the furniture had to be moved out of the house to create a dance floor (Creole cottages were typically single-storey, three-room houses with high gabled roofs). In the evening, men congregated on the front porch or in the yard, waiting their turns to dance in the cramped quarters of the cottage. Creole accordionist Herbert Sam recalled a dance his parents hosted in their rented farmhouse where there were so many people that the floor collapsed, and for the next week, neighbors returned from working the fields every day to jack it back up.[20] Sturdier old Creole cottages were converted into permanent dance halls and moved to a more central location in the community that was easily accessible by foot or horse-and-buggy,[21] providing opportunities for accordion and fiddle-playing Creole farmers to find regular weekend pay as musicians.

Dance halls had become just as common in Creole as in Cajun culture by the late 1930s,[22] with Cajun *bals de maison* moving sooner from homestead to public halls, often into converted barns or warehouses consisting of a wide-open room with high rafters, a sawdust-covered wooden floor, a side room that functioned as a nursery for young children (the *"parc aux petits"*), and a card game room. The *fais do do* as a building was far less impressive than the *"fais do do"* as a social and cultural institution.[23] Cajun dances were loud, lively events that customarily ended at midnight, at which point any Creole musicians hired to play would return home to play Creole house dances, which were often all-night affairs.[24] Cajun musicians routinely played at Creole house parties, according to Creole fiddler Canray Fontenot, who grew up in a family of musicians in L'Anse aux Vaches: "In the early 1900's, black musicians played at white house parties to supplement their meager incomes and white musicians often joined their black friends to play for Creole *'fais do dos'*".[25]

A generation of French Louisiana musicians interviewed by folklorists and music collectors confirmed Fontenot's characterization of the collaborative and dynamic social character of music culture in Southwest Louisiana. Nicholas Spitzer explains that, on the prairies of Louisiana, where there was a lesser degree of social separation between blacks and whites than in the plantation areas in the eastern part of the state, Cajun and Creole musicians appeared to have played together reasonably often, leading to "a good deal of overlap in style" in the performance of a common repertoire.[26] Creole fiddler Bébé Carrière performed at many Cajun house dances during the 1920s and 1930s[27] and Creole accordionist Amédé Ardoin, whose virtuosity and style were profoundly influential on Cajun music in the early twentieth century, spent the 1920s and 1930s playing both on his own and as part of a duet with Cajun fiddler Dennis McGee.

McGee, born in 1893, and Ardoin, born in 1898, met as sharecroppers working the same parcel of land, and became the most cherished performers in Southwest Louisiana. "We played for the whites or the blacks, it

didn't make any difference," McGee said. "They all paid us the same ....
Amédé was a good accordion player for the blacks and he was good for the
whites."[28] Creole farmers would venture into Cajun dance halls just to
hear Ardoin play,[29] and McGee was a protective and affectionate partner
when the two played house dances and small dance halls, where the vola-
tile mix of rousing music, heavy drinking, and close spaces intensified the
racial tensions that always existed right alongside the intraracial tensions
that flared up between Cajun families from rival towns as well as between
Creole families from different communities.

In the only existing photograph of Ardoin, he is handsomely dressed in
a dark suit jacket, fashionably cut trousers and a high-collared white shirt,
his hat tilted to one side, looking much like the New Orleans jazz musicians of his day. He and McGee, with his Irish ancestry, white bowtie and
tailored vest, and beautiful rosewood fiddle, must have been a striking
duo. Many of the tunes that came to represent the French Louisiana repertoire are derived from the 1929 Vocalion recordings McGee and Ardoin
made together in New Orleans.[30]

Ardoin also performed with McGee's brother-in-law, Cajun fiddler
Sady Courville, who played second fiddle to Ardoin's melodies, for both
black and white audiences. "[Amédé] started playing for white people,
private dances, and holidays like New Year's and Mardi Gras. I enjoyed
and learned a lot of music from Amédé," Courville recalled.[31] Cajun music
was popular among the black tenant farmers in Chataignier, ten miles
south of Mamou, and on the Prairie Faiquitaique near the town of Eunice,
and Courville said that he and Ardoin were welcomed in both Cajun and
Creole venues: "Everybody, black and white, was nice to us and I was
respected among the blacks and Amédé was respected among the whites."[32]

In both the provenance of the songs, some derived from medieval
French ballads, and in the melodies and instrumentation, French Louisiana
music constituted a shared tradition of borrowed tunes, revised melodies,
and improvised lyrical adaptations passed back and forth between the two
French-speaking populations of Southwest Louisiana. Amédé Ardoin,
having learned the melodies of two-steps and waltzes from Cajun musicians, played them in a slightly different rhythmic style, improvising and
adapting.[33] And just as Ardoin played Cajun musical forms, McGee played
"*Ma chère bébé créole*" and "*Pa Janvier*," a song he learned from an elderly
Creole woman who sang it at weddings, as well as "*Adieu, Rosa, demain
c'est dimanche*," about a Creole who would stay out dancing all night; the
song's rhythmic structure is derived from the Creole *juré* tradition,[34] *juré*

being the a capella singing of religious testimony punctuated by yells of "*juré*" [I swear] to the percussive accompaniment of hand clapping and the clacking of a mule jaw or the striking and strumming of a washboard, and perhaps an element of a call-and-response structure deriving from contact between Creoles and African-American Baptists.[35]

McGee learned the *juré* form from black musicians. "You're supposed to yell "*Juré*, my lord!" every now and then to excite the dancers," he said. A capella *juré* singers had provided music during Lent or mourning periods when instrumental music was forbidden in the Creole community, but the boundaries between sacred and secular practices blurred in the state that had converted the prelude to Lent into raucous Mardi Gras festivities, so *juré* music was also played at social gatherings when musicians couldn't be found or couldn't be paid. The word *juré* may be linguistically connected to a word used on the West African coast to describe music and dancing.[36] Cajun fiddler Joe Falcon recalled hearing, as a young boy in the early 1900s, white musicians sing the Creole song, "Colinda," a West African song popular in Haiti, Trinidad and New Orleans.[37] One of Falcon's signature songs, "*Hip et taïaut*," was a Creole folksong Falcon learned from Creole accordionist Sidney Babineaux.[38] There were no circumscribed artistic boundaries to transgress in a culture in which the music had been collectively developed and communally owned. In the Cajun song "*La valse du Bambocheur*," the singer laments that as a man scorned by his beloved and left to wander, he will be pointed at and called a good-for-nothing bum ["*le grand vaurien*"] by black and white neighbors alike ["*Blancs et noirs, ça me pointe du doigt*"],[39] underlining both the proximity in which Cajuns and Creoles lived and the ways in which their mutually felt and communally witnessed experience was converted into narrative and set to a melody to be performed, danced to, and passed on to the next generation.

Just as Cajun music was shaped by the strong influences of the black Creole tradition, including *juré*, the lyrics and forms of Creole tunes are indebted to the Cajun tradition. "Extreme prudence" is necessary for any historian of music trying to account for the melodies and lyrics of the songs by looking only at Cajun or only at Creole culture, since they come from "mixed French Acadian Afro Caribbean origins."[40] Indeed, many of the songs have so many lyrical versions and so many different titles that to cordon off any particular song as predominantly the cultural product of a singular population, time period, or style is impossible. In "*Ma chère bébé créole*," one of the signature tunes of Dennis McGee, the term "Creole" may have derived its original meaning from a quite different New Orleanian use of that word, referring to a Louisianan of European or mixed European and African ancestry, but in Southwest Louisiana, the word Creole took on the connotations it had in the Acadian parishes, describing, to Ardoin and McGee's audiences, a black Creole woman. Likewise, the term "*mon nèg*" appears over and over again in Cajun music as a term of endearment meaning "baby" or "darling" when addressed to a woman and "friend" and "buddy" when used by one Cajun man to another, even though the term was obviously borrowed from Creole culture and from the history of black/white interaction in Southwest Louisiana, the term "*nèg*" having derived from the French *nègre*, linguistic analogue to the word Negro, and appearing in both Creole and Cajun music. Nicholas Spitzer explains that the term, so perplexing and objectionable to outsiders, was common among both black and white speakers in Southwest Louisiana, and expressed a degree of affection more intense than "*chère*."[41]

In 1934, Amadie, Ophy and Clifford Breaux recorded "*Fais do do nègre*" for Vocalion. The lyrics urge a child at a Cajun *fais do do* dance hall party to drift off to sleep while the adults carouse: "*Fais do do mon nègre/ Dans les bras de ta chère vieille maman*" [Go to sleep, dear boy/In the arms of your dear old mom]. In Cajun accordionist Angelas LeJeune's 1929 "Bayou Pom Pom One Step," recorded for Brunswick in 1929, the singer laments the fact that he keeps running into his ex with her new love: "*Tout partout où je peux aller/Il semble qu'il faudrait/Que je t'vois avec ton nèg*" [Anywhere I go/Everywhere, it seems/I see you with your beau]. Likewise, in "Waltz of the Mulberry Limb" in 1953 for T.N.T., Iry LeJeune, addressing his beloved, refers to himself as *ton vieux nèg'* as he implores the woman to listen to his pleas: "*Tu devrais bien écouter/Ton vieux nèg' une fois/Quand moi je te dis quelque chose*" [You should pay attention/To your old sweetheart for once/When I tell you something].

Drinking songs and playful dance songs were also handed from one community to the next ("*Chanson de limonade*" originated with New Orleans Creoles,[42] then passed into the Southwest Louisiana repertoire), and the place names of towns on the prairies and bayous figure prominently in the shared musical tradition: "*Valse de la Pointe d'Église*," "Lafayette Two-Step," "Crowley Two-Step," and "*Valse de Bayou Teche*." Kinship is a central theme in tales of courtship thwarted by disapproving family members, and of resignation to loneliness, heartbreak and separation. In "*La valse à Austin Ardoin*," the story of a man rejected by his beloved is concluded with the words: "*Il faut que je prends mes misères*

comme ça vient"[43]—I have to take my miseries as they come—a sentiment
with which both sharecropping Creole farmers and subsistence farming
Cajuns could identify.

Both populations also took their leisure and their pleasures where they
could, as evidenced by the many songs that were invitations to celebrate
and drink. Cajun accordionist Moise Robin recalled summer nights in the
yard behind the dance hall, when, after having worked in the sugarcane
fields all day, the tired and the worn out arrived in buggies, on horseback,
on foot, in wagons, and in cars, and got their second wind: "Instead of
staying in the dance hall, we'd stay outside … when the moonlight was
shining and we waited for our chance. Back then, the people brought their
bottles of moonshine to the dances and hid their bottles everywhere."[44]
Public dances were socially acceptable venues for courtship, and mothers
and fathers vigilantly guarded their daughters against unwanted suitors,
especially those who congregated outside, drinking moonshine. A potential suitor needed the approval of a woman's entire extended family,
including cousins, and a brief and heavily monitored courtship period was
usually followed very quickly by a wedding. Unmarried men entering a
dance hall were corralled into *la cage aux chiens*, a bullpen behind a gate
strung with chicken wire. In a social environment in which blacks and
whites mixed more freely than they did anywhere else in the South, the
social segregation of women and men was taken for granted and was rig-
idly enforced. Men and women sat in different sections of the dance hall,
coming together only on the dance floor, after which women retreated to
tend to children; men, to play cards. Hundreds of families packed into
dance halls, and communities defended themselves aggressively against
out-of-town interlopers, with violence sometimes breaking out among
young Cajun men from different towns. Local newspapers, all through the
post-Civil War era through the Great Depression, documented dance hall
conflicts of "mayhem and bloodshed" instigated by men from rival towns
who had done their drinking first, and then their dancing, and finally went
on to fighting.[45]

Creole fiddler Canray Fontenot described Creole dance halls as vigorously monitored social spaces in which community matriarchs regu-
lated social interaction and insisted on the observance of traditional
customs and forms: "And them old ladies there! It was dancing, but
you had to leave a gap. Oh! That's how come they didn't want no
blues, because they would dance too close to one another."[46] Blues
music was considered raunchy saloon entertainment: "Oh, *lawd*, don't

talk about the blues. In my time that was something nasty," Fontenot explained.[47] Rather, Creole dancers did the two-step and danced waltzes just as their Cajun neighbors did.

Rules governing interaction between men and women were equally strict in Creole and Cajun dance hall culture, subject to the intense scrutiny of the public gaze. In Creole communities, a woman was expected to sit on the bench until approached respectfully by a man who, attired in the mandatory dress shirt in summer or dress coat in winter, extended his handkerchief to invite her to dance. The man then wrapped his hand in the handkerchief so as not to soil the woman's dress with his work-worn hands. The handkerchief was key in Cajun dancing as well, wrapped around the man's hand so that the position of his hand on his partner's back was clearly displayed and there remained another layer of fabric between them. This was meant to lessen the provocation of a stranger dancing with a man's brother or sister. A Creole man was expected to serve his dance partner wine or a plate of gumbo at the conclusion of the dance,[48] in a reversal of the woman-as-cook-and-server custom of the home, and in the Cajun dance hall, the signature dish, a mix of Cajun and Creole culinary traditions, was served communally after a long evening of beer, lemonade, and black coffee.[49]

The rousing music of the dance hall, which had migrated from the home to the community social center, returned to the home again as records and radio brought the dance hall sound into living rooms. In a region where Cajuns and Creoles had lived in close proximity for a century and a half, record albums and radio served to reinforce a shared cultural legacy. Sales of records crashed in the early 1920s as the number of household radios reached three million,[50] and the recording industry fought to recapture some of its market by bringing French Louisiana music into Southwest Louisiana homes. Dance hall music was a belated addition to the region's radio programming, which first featured classical and popular music. The steady stream of unfamiliar sounds and voices of broadcast radio threatened to make the phonograph obsolete in a region in which listeners were accustomed to live, uninterrupted old-time musical entertainment; radio seemed the next best thing to the dance hall, even if the broadcast tunes seemed alien. The "louder, cleaner and richer sound" of broadcast music, with its live announcers, converted the listening experience into an eternal present-tense moment with which the brief playing of a two-song record couldn't compete.

Columbia was the first record label to try anyway, simply by selling Southwest Louisianans what they already had: French Louisiana music. In 1926, looking to expand into new enclaves, Columbia acquired the Okeh label and its catalog of German, Polish and Yiddish music recorded for the immigrant market. Okeh had been founded by Otto Heinemann, a Berlin record label executive who, having traveled to New York in 1914 to investigate the manufacturing side of the American recording industry, was stranded by the outbreak of World War I. Heinemann took the opportunity to set up a recording studio and production plant and sent scouts to do field recordings in North Carolina, Texas, Ohio, and Kansas City, trying to capture the sounds of ethnic America. The recording industry's trade magazine *Talking Machine World* took note of Okeh's French Louisiana recordings in a 1925 editorial: "As portraits of bayou life they are real poetry … telling stories of … the uneventful life of the fisherfolk."[51] The 1920s marked the heyday of foreign-language and minority-population music recording in the United States. This explosion of foreign-language recording is coherent with the boom years for other domestically produced ethnic media, from foreign-language films to specialized press publications that catered to the news and entertainment needs of immigrants, linguistic minority populations, and African-Americans.

Even as the Immigration Act of 1924 newly restricted entry to the United States of foreign nationals from Southern and Eastern Europe, the foreign film industry boomed in American cities. New York City theaters screened German and Italian films during the "dark time" between matinee and evening shows. Foreign-language theaters in Philadelphia and Baltimore drew in immigrants and curious intellectuals. Theater owners from Boston to Washington learned that it was profitable to show Italian language films and to dub Hollywood movies into foreign languages; Polish movie houses and Yiddish language theaters opened in Chicago and New York, while Russian, German and Swedish films flickered on screens from San Francisco to Milwaukee. Spanish-language films filled the theaters in Dallas, Los Angeles, and Denver as French films opened in theaters across New York. The film industry's love affair with the ethnic American didn't last long, however. Once movie-going became an entrenched cultural habit for middle-class Americans, movie houses that had eagerly catered to immigrant markets abandoned foreign-language films in favor of the Hollywood fare preferred by middle-class patrons, who proved to be a more stable source of revenue. But ethnic films remained a key source of movie theater revenue until World War II-era Hollywood Westerns and war movies took over the screens.[52]

The ethnic press underwent a similarly rapid rise and decline. From the early 1900s to World War II, foreign-language newspapers were a newsstand staple in every American city. Publications such as The French New York daily *Le Courrier des États-Unis* presented news about European politics alongside information about local events and practical advice about exchanging foreign currency. Kansas City's Swedish newspaper featured an editorial proclaiming the virtues of George Washington as a way of educating new Americans about the nation's founding. Foreign-language newspapers provided retailers with a way to advertise consumer goods to newly arrived Slavic, Welsh, Scandinavian, and French immigrants overwhelmed by the American department and grocery store. Advertising in the ethnic press cost less than one-twentieth of the cost of advertising in the mainstream English-language press, promising marketers new and loyal markets at small cost.[53] In 1927, there were more than 1100 foreign newspapers in thirty-six languages in the United States, a phenomenon that baffled some of the "very American Americans" who fretted that political publications were radicalizing rather than assimilating immigrants; the same statistic reassured others that the newly arrived foreigners, drawn to news about the old country, were being assimilated into the culture by reading recipes for American dishes, articles on American childrearing practices, and the biographies of "interesting and great Americans" featured in the ethnic press. "The newcomer wants a job ... he wants a home," wrote one zealous defender of the immigrant press: "If he can squeeze in a phonograph, he will do it."[54]

The recording industry, like the film and newspaper industries, was eager to serve its newly arrived, never-assimilated, or simply nostalgic customers. The first and second-generation Polish and Italian immigrants that crowded the working class tenements of Chicago reported that buying a phonograph helped them keep their native culture alive as they danced to the music of the old country at large social gatherings. Chicago became the center of a significant foreign-language record market, and even Chicago's relatively small Mexican community had a shop that sold records of Mexican music.[55]

Like the newsstands and the movie houses, record labels became keen on capitalizing on narratives of immigrant life and the struggles of assimilation. Columbia, inspired by Okeh's success selling traditional old-time music in ethnic and regional markets, began experimenting with recordings of banjo and guitar duets and string bands in the hopes of increasing sales in ethnic rural Southern markets where music played a fundamental role in community life.[56] It would have been difficult for Columbia to find a region in which music played a bigger role than it did in Southwest Louisiana. Creole accordionist Amédé Ardoin was popular with the same listeners who flocked to hear Cajun accordionist Joe Falcon and his wife, guitarist Cleoma Breaux, perform as a duet in packed dance halls throughout Southwest Louisiana. Frank Buckley Walker, the talent scout for Columbia's Country Music Division, traveled to Lafayette from the company's New Orleans recording studio to look for amateur talent and was "astounded at the interest that there was in [the Cajuns'] little Saturday night dances," with a single singer and "a little concertina-type instrument and a one-string fiddle and a triangle ... and of course they sang in Cajun. And to me it had a funny sound." Walker recorded Falcon and Breaux "just to have something different," then was surprised by how well the record sold not only in Louisiana but also across the border into Texas, where many Cajuns had migrated to work in the oil fields.[57]

Sound engineers in Columbia's studio, used to recording jazz artists backed by large orchestras, had looked scornfully at Falcon and Breaux's fiddle and guitar and tried to cancel the session, saying, "That's not enough music."[58] But once the Columbia representatives heard the playback of "*Allons à Lafayette*," which told the story of a man imploring a woman to elope with him if she couldn't get her parents' permission to marry him, and "*La valse qui m'a porter à ma fosse*" [The Waltz that Carried Me to My Grave], they agreed that, despite the incomprehensibility of the Cajun French lyrics, the melodies were compelling and the songs had market potential.[59]

Over the next several years, Falcon and Breaux recorded for Decca in New York and Columbia in Atlanta, as a number of other labels sought to capture the French Louisiana sound. Vocalion brought Creole fiddler Douglas Bellard and Creole accordionist Kirby Riley to New Orleans in 1929 to record four songs, including "*La valse de la prison*" [Prison Waltz] and "*Mon canon, la cause que je suis condamné*" [I Was Convicted Because of My Gun]. McGee and Courville got their start as regional recording stars after having played on the radio in Shreveport.

The term "folk" was not historically capacious enough to encompass performers like these who were busy, locally popular, working musicians, who aspired to have their music broadcast and recorded, and who traveled to the centers of music production and consumption in order to get work in the industry. But whether they were stumbled upon by field workers doing research, or invited to record by commercial talent scouts, these French Louisiana musicians were considered, by their patrons, folk artists.

While Joe Falcon and Cleoma Breaux were able to make a living from music, for most French Louisiana musicians, music had to remain an avocation. Sady Courville put his fiddle away for long periods of time to farm, and McGee divided his time between playing the fiddle, farming, and working as a barber, even after he and Ardoin went from playing together as sharecroppers to recording for Okeh and Brunswick. Leo Soileau, born in 1904, and Mayeuse LaFleur, born in 1906, played violin and accordion for Victor. French Louisiana music made its journey from the prairies and bayous where it was born to distant recording studios, only to be packed up and sent, like prodigal offspring, back into bayou homes.

Record label marketing executives disagreed about how to name and categorize this regional sound. Victor and Atlanta used the phrase "Cajun dialect" on the label, while Columbia used "Arcadian-French" for Ardoin-McGee duets, and Vocalion used "Creole" for McGee's duets with Sady Courville. Douglas Bellard and Kirby Riley's songs were labeled "Creole." Questions about genre and labeling would continue to be part and parcel of academic and commercial discussions of French Louisiana music during the second recording wave in the post-World War II era, and the third wave "revival" era of the 1960s and 1970s.

The modest but steady marketability of ethnic market folk records sustained Columbia in the golden age of radio until the repeal of Prohibition in 1933, which brought music lovers into bars to listen to record-playing jukeboxes, first introduced in 1927.[60] Speakeasy culture became obsolete, and taverns could again send the sounds of dance floor music blaring into the night. Recording companies, which had forbidden the playing of recorded music on the radio, citing copyright claims, abandoned that restriction in the early 1930s,[61] and Joe and Cleoma Breaux Falcon's "*Allons à Lafayette*" was played on the radio, in local clubs, and in private homes throughout Southwest Louisiana. Falcon quit working on his father's sugarcane farm and became a full-time musician: "What I had to do was I had to collect my money, so I'd just sit down and scratch 'em off," Falcon said.[62] He performed in clubs from Southwest Louisiana to Texas, where old-time Louisiana French music was popular with Cajuns and Creoles who had left the state to work in the oil fields across the border.

Those lonely exiles from Acadiana soon had many more choices when they wanted to play the old-time music of their native parishes. Six months after "*Allons à Lafayette*" was recorded, Columbia's archrival label Victor brought Ville Platte fiddler Leo Soileau and accordionist Mayeuse LaFleur to Atlanta, Georgia to record "*Mama, Where You At?*" about a man who wishes to see his mother's face one last time before he dies, and "*Ton père m'a mis dehors*" [Your Father Kicked Me Out]. "*Mama, Where You At?*" became poignantly successful when LaFleur was killed in a speakeasy brawl in Basile mere days after recording the song.[63] Soileau and LaFleur had been introduced to a Victor talent scout by an Opelousas jewelry store owner who sold record players and albums in his store, and who, like other phonograph retailers, knew that local music could sell the equipment it was played on. Record labels usually agreed to record "almost anyone the phonograph retailer suggested."[64] Customers would sometimes buy multiple copies of the fragile records, which quickly wore out under the wear of the heavy needle in the groove, or purchase albums even if they didn't own a record player, in the hopes of playing the music at a neighbor's house.[65] These late 1920s and early 1930s recordings became the golden classics of French Louisiana old-time music. In April 1929, Cleoma Breaux's accordionist brother, Amédée, recorded "*Ma blonde est partie*" for the Old-Timey label, and other labels followed suit in the rush to record Cajun and Creole tunes, with Old-Timey and Okeh recording Amédé Ardoin as a soloist in 1929 and Brunswick recording Ardoin and Dennis McGee in 1930. In October 1929, Creole musicians Douglas Bellard and Kirby Riley recorded for Vocalion.[66] By the early 1930s, Bluebird, Decca, Paramount and Vocalion had added French Louisiana recordings to their catalogs, while Cajun and Creole children, fashioning fiddles out of peach tree branches, sewing thread, cigar boxes, and the thin metal string of screen doors,[67] listened to the recordings and learned to imitate, and improvise upon, the music they heard.

Not every Creole and Cajun musician had been willing to record, however. Those who did constituted a fraction of the population of musicians in a region dense with talented fiddle players and accomplished accordionists, just as only a very small cohort of Southern folk musicians in other states, playing other genres, had ever recorded. They were the musicians who had gotten up the nerve to attend auditions held by Northern recording company scouts, or who had formed bands and "tried to get their fellow men and women, people just like them, to pay attention to them ... people who, if only for a moment, looked past the farms and mines to which they were almost certainly chained. The stories they would later tell of journeying to New York to record are almost all the same .... They arrived in New York City [and New Orleans and Atlanta] like tourists from some foreign land."[68]

Both Creole and Cajun populations shared a set of superstitions about recording, and some didn't want their music to be heard after they were dead.[69] When Mayeuse LaFleur was murdered, the Eunice newspaper ran a story with the headline "Voice of Dead Man Heard by Eunice People," in which the writer, after noting that some were happy to hear again "a folk song of their nationality which had never been written but handed down from generation to generation," explained that others were haunted by LaFleur's music and the sound of his voice: "The tone of his voice seemed to carry with it a certain sadness, betraying his melancholy attitude … for the time of his death and even before when the record was made by the Victor phonograph company domestic difficulties has cast a shadow around this man who was only a youth," the death notice said.

LaFleur's recording sold out quickly, the paper noted, "Before the grim reaper of time summoned LaFleur from this world" (LaFleur was 23).[70]

Amédé Ardoin also suffered a tragic fate by all accounts, and the accounts differ. Dennis McGee claimed that Ardoin was poisoned by a jealous Creole fiddle player,[71] while Creole fiddler Canray Fontenot heard that Ardoin was severely beaten leaving a Cajun dance hall because he had wiped his brow with a handkerchief offered by a white woman. Fontenot sometimes played a song called "*Le pauv' nègre mort d'amour*" about just such relationship and its violent end. Because Ardoin would weave details of provocative or scandalous local stories into his songs, including stories of men feuding with their wives, it has also been suggested that he may have "named the wrong people in his songs"[72] and been violently assaulted. These varied accounts weave together stories of Ardoin's musical ingenuity and revered community status with depictions of racially mixed social spaces and racial violence, and as such they are collectively coherent as a portrait of a time and place, even if the particular details are lost to history. Uncontested is the fact that Ardoin died in 1942 in the psychiatric ward at the Central Louisiana Hospital in Pineville and was buried in an unmarked grave. Folklorists and record label marketers brought Ardoin back into the discussion of Cajun and Creole music for decades to come, citing him as either the forefather of zydeco music, or as the most important innovator in the Cajun tradition.

Cajun and Creole musicians were powerfully influenced by the legacy of Ardoin's music, even as French Louisiana music became, in the late 1960s and 1970s, more focused on the real and imagined exile experiences of the descendants of Acadia rather than on the Cajun and Creole community experiences of home, romantic love, and ritual celebration. Creole musicians, likewise, began to dramatize and privilege the connections between Creole culture and the larger African-American world.

Eventually, the music played by Cajuns and Creoles took separate paths, with Cajun musicians not only preserving old-time music, but writing new songs that provoked (white) listeners with a romanticized version of their unique ancestral past, while Creole accordionists developed a faster style that crossed over into, and was shaped by, the music of urban African-American society. The younger Cajun and Creole population of Southwest Louisiana would grow up in a culture in which the old bonds of the French language and shared cultural traditions were weakened under the pressure of the racial and ethnic politics of the mid-twentieth century, leaving the image of Dennis McGee and Amédé Ardoin's foundational musical partnership nearly obscured in the mists of history.

The oldest recorded songs in the French Louisiana music canon dwell on the act of looking, and of seeking out another's gaze. In Dennis McGee and Ernest Fruge's *"L'Anse de Belair,"* [Belair Cove] recorded for Brunswick in 1930, a desperately disappointed suitor sits at his kitchen window just to see the woman he loves walk down the road, and he wants nothing to obscure the sight of her: *"J'ai coupé la branche de mon mûrier, chère, pour te voir passer, chère, quand toi tu es partie"* [I cut off the branch of my mulberry tree, darling, to see you go by, dear, when you went away]. The singer continually appeals to the woman's knowledge of his suffering, repeatedly using phrases that implicate her understanding of their history, and of his plight: *"Rappelle-toi"* is an imperative plea urging her to remember him. *"Tu connais"* and *"gardez donc"* indict her for being the cause of his suffering. Even when he is asleep, he beholds her in his dreams: *"Malheureuse, chaque fois, chère, tu m'as fait rêvé à toi/Déjà, j'le prends dur de t'voir, jolie coeur"* [Unhappy darling, every time you make me dream about you/But it's already hard enough to see you, lovely sweetheart]. This dwelling on the beholder's gaze is the leitmotif of French Louisiana music, often interwoven with scolding, lamentation, or a warning: *"Tu connais le bon Dieu va t'punir pour tout ça ... Tu m'as tourné l'dos"* [You know that God is going to punish you for that ... You turned your back on me]. "Turned your back" refers not only to an emotional and social fact, but also to a physical act that is the most final form of rejection, as the thwarted suitor can no longer see her face, nor can she know that he is still gazing at her. In *"Assis dans la fenêtre de ma chambre,"* recorded by Blind Uncle Gaspard and Delma Lachney in 1929 for Vocalion, the man swears that he can see the woman's face even when he closes his eyes, since her features are imprinted so vividly on his mind.

Spurned suitors torment themselves with the idea of seeing their beloved even momentarily, like the man in Amédé Ardoin's *"Two Step de*

Eunice," who imagines going to the dance hall on Saturday night just to catch a glimpse of the beautiful woman he knows will end up marrying another man: "*Tous les samedis soir, catin/Oh, je serais curieux d'être là/ Pour voir où t'es, jolie mignonne*" [Every Saturday night, babe, I'd love to be there to see you, pretty little darling]. He wants to look at the face of the woman who has hurt him so profoundly, as if the solitude of the unreciprocated gaze will consummate his broken-heartedness.

Tragic love songs have primary importance in social culture because they perform the function of effectuating personal catharsis while broadcasting messages about community systems, values, and mores. They are descriptive, providing a forum in which men take stock of the damage their passions have done to their state of mind, as in Angelas LaJeune's "*Bayou Pom Pom One Step*," recorded in 1929 for Brunswick: "*C'est malheureux de te voir à présent me quitter ... Oh, c'est malheureux de me voir, comme je suis là, aujourd'hui, tout le temps dans la misère.* [It's terrible to have to see you now that you've left me ... It's terrible to see myself this way, miserable all the time]. They are also prescriptive, warning women about the hard consequences of being perceived as sexually unconstrained. The word "*catin*" often appears in these ballads, and although in the French Louisiana music repertoire, the term is used as an endearment meaning "darling" or "babe," in its origins in standard French, it refers to a woman whose sexual promiscuity is well known. The ballad singers position themselves as the aggrieved party expelled from the intimacy of a woman's affections and forced to see her cavorting in public with another man: "*Oh, tout partout où je peux aller, mais ça me ressemble, il faudrait que je te vois avec ton nèg*" [Everywhere I go, it seems, I have to see you with your man]. In Dennis McGee's "*Valse d'amour*," the woman is chastised for her casual flirtations: "*Tu cours trop les hommes, ma petite fille qui a autant*" [You chase men too much, my darling, and too many]. In Moise Robin and Leo Soileau's "*Ma mauvaise fille*" [My Naughty Little Darling] recorded in 1928 for Paramount, a man protests the fact that even though he avoided the pitfalls of falling in love with an older or a younger woman, the woman he pursued turned out to be just as much trouble and heartache, shutting the door in his face. And in "*Le blues du petit chien*," recorded by the Breaux Brothers for Vocalion in 1929, a man takes a good look at a woman's disheveled appearance in the morning and asks her: "*Où t'as resté hier au soir ?/T'as des cheveux tous mêlés/Et ton linge te fait pas bien*" [Where did you sleep last night? Your hair is all messed up, and your clothes look a wreck].

The songs reinforce social mores and the value of proper social behavior by telling stories about tragic or transgressive relationships, focusing on the singer's assessment of whether or not the passion, behavior, and outcomes were warranted. The lovesick man in Dennis McGee's 1929 "*Ma chère bébé créole*" [My Sweet Creole Mama; the Vocalion label erroneously uses the possessive "*mon*," as if the object of the singer's affection is masculine], calls on the unattainable object of his affections to look at the emotional state he has been left in: "*Regardez donc.../Tu m'abandonnes pour toujours.../Je suis de près m'en aller pour mourir*" [Look at me/You left me for good/I'm going off to die].

The songs constantly deploy the verb *regardez* [look] in the context of an outcry to the departing lover to "Just look what you've done," and this appeal is extended to the community: look what she did to me. Rarely do the men take the blame as the singer does in "*Aimer et perdre*" [Loving and Losing], recorded by Joe Falcon and Cleoma Breaux for Columbia in 1929: "*Je t'ai perdu par roulailler les grands chemins*" [I lost you by wandering the highways], the singer confesses, "*Regarde donc voir quoi j'ai fait avec moi-même*" [Look what I've done to myself].

Such jilted lovers and spurned suitors often take to wandering. "*La valse des chantiers pétrolifères*," recorded by Ardoin in 1934, is the story of a man who is leaving to go work in the oil fields, having been scorned by a woman: "*Toi, tu me fais, toi, ouais, catin/Moi, je suis tout seul, et je m'en vais au puits/Je vais jamais encore revenir*" [You, this is all your doing, babe/That I'm all alone, heading off to the oil fields/I'm never coming back]. With the earnings from his new job, the man will be able to go to the dance hall and look at all the pretty women, compensating, he says, in some very small measure, for his mistreatment at the hands of the woman he loves and will never see again. In "*Ma blonde est partie*," recorded by Cleoma Breaux and her brothers for Okeh in 1929, the singer tells the woman who abandoned him that he'll quickly find another blonde:

Jolie blonde, tu croyais qu'il y avait juste toi,
Il y a pas juste toi dans le pays pour m'aimer.
Je peux trouver juste une autre jolie blonde,
Bon Dieu sait, moi, j'en ai un tas.

[Pretty blonde, you thought you were the only one
That you were the only one I could ever love
I can find another pretty blonde
The good Lord knows, I've got plenty.]

Being forever shut out from the sight of a loved one is the primary theme of much early French Louisiana music, with variations on the idea of what precipitated the painful separation. In Amédé Ardoin and Dennis McGee's "*La valse à Abe*" [Abe's Waltz], recorded for Columbia in 1929, the singer tells his beloved that she will never see him again, nor will her father, or his own parents: "*Je pense que je vais faire en sorte que jamais vous autres vous me reverrez*" [I think I'll make it so that none of you ever has to see me again]. The singer announces that he will take to the road as a wanderer, then that he will be locked up in prison: "*Non, je sais pas si je vais revenir/ce sera pour voir mes parents, ouais, et ma femme*" [I don't know if I'm ever coming back again, but if I do, it'll be to see my parents and my woman]. Love affairs in French Louisiana music often lead either to aimless wandering or to a feeling of being imprisoned in a state of psychological torment, and in some songs, the imprisonment is not merely figurative but literal, as in "*La valse de la prison*" by Douglas Bellard and Kirby Riley, recorded in New Orleans in 1929. The convict's mother covers her face with her hands, crying, as her son enters through the prison doors: "*J'ai fini de te voir, maman,/j'ai fini de te voir sur la terre du bon dieu*" [I've seen you for the last time, Mama. I'll never see you again on the good Lord's earth].

In Moise Robin and Leo Soileau's "*La valse pénitentiaire*," recorded in 1929 for Victor, the singer is off to Angola Prison, a vast prison complex built on the site of a plantation on the Mississippi River. The singer, addressing his mother, recounts the stinging gaze of the townsfolk as he was ushered off to a life of hard labor in the penitentiary: "*Hier matin, tout l'monde était près à m'observer m'en aller pour toujours*" [Yesterday morning, everyone was there to watch me go away forever]. As his movements were being tracked by the eyes of the community members who assembled to see him for the last time, he could only look at his weeping mother's face: "*Et quand moi, je suis parti, tu t'es mise à pleurer*" [At the moment I left, you started weeping]. Looking is the most vital, intimate, consequential act in early French Louisiana music. In Mayeuse LaFleur and Leo Soileau's "*Chère maman*," titled "Mama, Where You At?" by Victor in 1928, a man longs to see his mother's face: "*Chère maman, comment ça se fait/Que jamais je ne te reverrai...*" [Dear mother, why is it that I no longer see you?]. Singers in this genre tell tales of being figuratively orphaned by having become estranged from parents who disapproved of a love affair, but in this case, LaFleur grieves the fact that his mother apparently didn't wish to raise him, and left him with other caretakers. She was never heard from again, and her loss remains profound: "*Je voudrais te voir quand même/Une fois avant de mourir*" [I'd like to see you once before I die].

Disapproving relatives often sentence a couple to a lifetime of broken-hearted separation. Some men defer to the opinion of the woman's parents on the suitability of the match, as in Ardoin's "*Blues de Basile*": "*Se tes parents veulent pas, je te demanderai pas*" [If your parents don't want me to, I won't ask you].

This is also the stance of the suitor in Columbus Fruge's "*La valse de Bayou Teche,*" recorded in 1929 for Victor in Memphis: "*Ta famille est tout contre moi/Je ne peux pas te voir, chère*" [Your family is completely against me/So I can't see you, dear]. These are grievance recitations, but in a spirit of resignation to the family's will. The intense gaze of an admirer or lover is directed furtively at the desired woman, who is trapped in a social world in which families and neighbors constantly watch, look, assess, and judge. In Ardoin's "*Two-Step D'Elton,*" the singer gets to the heart of the blame: "*Tes parents, ils ne veulent pas de moi … C'est la faute à ta maman*" [But your parents don't want me … It's your mother's fault] and in "*Valse à Alcee Poullard,*" the singer protests that the couple will never find a place to meet out of her parents' watch: "*Je connais tes parents, ils ne veulent pas, catin*" [I know your parents don't approve, darling]. In "*La valse de Madame Sosten*" [Madame Sosten's Waltz] recorded by Joe Falcon for Decca in 1934, the disappointed suitor implicates the woman's mother, pleading with her to let him be with the young woman he has been in love with for years: "*Tu verras par toi-même ce que tu as fait de moi*" [You'll see for yourself what you've done to me].

Though the male narrators of these ballads may challenge the authority of the woman's family and implore her not to heed their warnings, most of the time, all that's left is a moment of retrospect and regret, as when the woman in "*Valse des Opelousas*" is told "*P'tite fille, si tu m'aimais, comme t'as voulu me dire/Si tu n'écoutais pas les histoires qu'ils racontent*" [If only you'd loved me like you said that you wanted/If you hadn't listened to all the things they told you]. The man's family is the obstacle in "*La valse d'amitié*": "*Mes parents ne veulent pas que je sois avec toi*" [My parents don't want me to stay with you]. Faced with opposition to the courtship, men urge women to be defiant, as in In "My Sweetheart Run Away," recorded by The Segura Brothers in 1928 for Okeh: "*Dis bye bye à ton papa, ta maman, chère/Pour t'en venir dans mes bras, dans ma chambre/ Dans ma chambre, dans mon lit pour la vie*" [Say goodbye to your papa and your mama, darling, and come into my arms, into my room. Into my room, into my bed forever].

Women very rarely got their say in early commercial French Louisiana music, since Cleoma Breaux was the only woman to record, but in "*C'est triste sans lui*" [It is so Blue Without Him] recorded in 1929 for Atlanta, Breaux testifies that the hurt runs just as deep when the woman is on the losing side of love: "*Quand il a quitté la maison/Il m'a dit de l'observer/Pour que je ne puisse jamais l'oublier*" [When he left the house/He told me to take a good look at him/So that I'd never be able to forget]. The man has gone off with someone else, and tells the broken-hearted woman he leaves behind to mourn him: "*Il m'a dit d'attacher du crêpe noir sur la porte/Parce que lui, il ne reviendrait jamais*" [He told me to hang black crepe on the door/Because him, he wasn't ever coming back]. In a cogent distillation of the pathos and regret of a failed love affair, the departing lover tells the woman to "take a good look at him" so that she'll never be able to forget him, what she has done to precipitate his leaving, and his departure. The brief act of looking at the loved one for the last time instantiates the sorrow of parting and an indefinite temporal experience of remembering.

The cutting line is the man's prediction that she will continue to suffer:

"*Il m'a dit que ce que j'avais fait, il ne pouvait jamais oublier*" [He said he did it so that I'd never be able to forget].

These earliest recorded French Louisiana songs document over and over again stories of separation from loved ones—either socially enforced separation because of a family's disapproval of a relationship, or geographic separation—and the concomitant conditions of physical and emotional impoverishment. In Joe Falcon's "*Quand je suis parti pour le Texas*," recorded in 1929 for Okeh, and featuring Cleoma and Ophy Breaux, the singer describes his departure from home when he left for Texas, as so many Louisianans did, often to work in the oil fields. His mother breaks down, weeping, and begs him not to go: "*Ne fais pas ça, ça va peiner deux vieux*" [Don't do this, you're going to break your old parents' hearts.] A year later, Dennis McGee and Ernest Fruge recorded "*Les blues du Texas*" for Brunswick. The narrator recounts his lonely troubles on the road begging for help from strangers. He gives the price of bread in French francs, pointing to the song's provenance as a beggar's ballad from France: "*J'ai parti*

pour aller dans le Texas/J'ai passé à Eunice, m'acheter un pain de cinq sous"
[I left and set out for Texas/I passed through Eunice and bought a loaf of
bread for five francs]. This wayfarer, now thirty-eight, has haunted the
roads since he was fifteen: "*J'ai plus rien de père et de mere/J'ai traîné les
chemins*" [I've had nothing, neither father nor mother/I've walked every
road]. The solitude and misery of being orphaned, either literally or meta-
phorically, through estrangement, is one of the enduring themes of the
French Louisiana ballad tradition; starting in the 1960s, separation from
French Canada becomes the grievance.

Dennis McGee told the woman he was estranged from in "*La valse
d'amour*," "*T'es la seule dans la Louisiane moi je peux aimer*" [You're the
only one in Louisiana I can love], but in the songs written by Southwest
Louisianans who've left for Texas, the line could just as well have been:
Louisiana, you're the only one I can love. Women are sweetheart, babe,
and pretty little darling, but the songs call out the specific places where the
love affair happened, or the place where the song was learned: Church
Point, Mamou, Lafayette, Bayou Chene, Crowley, Pointe Noire, Grande
Prairie. Traditional songs are often titled after place names. This is one of
the reasons French Louisiana had such a loyal constituency of listeners—
the songs were a paean to the landscapes and communities of Southwest
Louisiana.

Notes

1. Inscription: "11-20-46 Fred purchased Tate's Bar, now known as Famous
   "Fred's Lounge," Mamou, L.A. In 1950 Courir de Mardi Gras was revived
   at Fred's Lounge. June, 1962 the late Revon Reed began remote radio
   program at Fred's Lounge which is still alive today (KVPI 1050 AM)
   Radio station. French Renaissance (Cajun Music, Language and Culture)
   after WWII originated at Fred's Lounge."
2. Mark Mattern, "Cajun Music, Cultural Revival: Theorizing Political
   Action in Popular Music," *Popular Music and Society* 22.2 (1998): 31.
3. Brasseaux, *Cajun Breakdown*, 76.
4. Mattern, "Cajun Music, Cultural Revival": 31.
5. Paul C. Tate to Joan Baez, Mamou, LA, January 27, 1965.
6. David E. Whisnant, *All That is Native and Fine, The Politics of Culture in
   an American Region* (Chapel Hill: The University of North Carolina
   Press, 1983), 260.
7. Sara Le Menestrel, *Negotiating Difference in French Louisiana Music,
   Categories, Stereotypes, and Identifications* (Jackson: University Press of
   Mississippi, 2015), 35–61.

8. Revon Reed, *Lâche Pas La Patate: Portrait des Acadiens de la Louisiane* (Montreal: Éditions Parti pris, 1976), 86. Reed was the first to publish a book in Cajun French.
9. Jeff Katz, "Cajun French Fever Rages Early for Tribute: For 50 years, Fred's Lounge is where le bons temps roulet. Governor, priest mark day," *Los Angeles Times*, November 26, 1996.
10. Falcon and Soileau, in an interview with Ralph Rinzler, October 1965, University of Louisiana at Lafayette, Center for Louisiana Studies, The Archives of Cajun and Creole Folklore, RI1.011, audio recording.
11. Sara Le Menestrel, "The Color of Music, Social Boundaries and Stereotypes in Southwest Louisiana French Music," *Southern Cultures* 13.3 (2007): 87.
12. Ned Sublette, *The World That Made New Orleans, From Spanish Silver to Congo Square* (Chicago: Lawrence Hill Books, 2008), 64–80.
13. Sublette, *The World That Made New Orleans*, 275.
14. Matt Sakakeeny, "New Orleans Music as a Circulatory System," *Black Music Research Journal* Vol. 31, No. 2 (Fall 2011), pp. 295–325. Sakakeeny points out, for example, that early jazz cornetist Buddy Bolden was born four decades after the Congo Square gatherings were ended.
15. Henry Cogswell Knight, *Letters from the South and West* (Boston: Richardson and Lord, 1824), 122–127.
16. Samuel Charters, *A Trumpet Around the Corner, The Story of New Orleans Jazz* (Jackson: University of Mississippi Press, 2008), 6.
17. Wallace Fowlie, *The Kenyon Review* 6.4, (1944): 578–579.
18. Carl Van Vechten, "*Au Bal Musette*," *The Merry-Go-Round* (New York: A.A. Knopf, 1918), 137–140.
19. Van Vechten, "*Au Bal Musette*," 144.
20. Michael Tisserand, *The Kingdom of Zydeco* (New York: Avon Books, 1998), 44.
21. Tisserand, *Kingdom of Zydeco*, 46.
22. Malcolm L. Comeaux, "The Cajun Dance Hall," *Material Culture* 32.1 (2000): 52.
23. Lauren C. Post, *Cajun Sketches: From the Prairies of Southwest Louisiana* (Baton Rouge: Louisiana State University Press, 1962), 156.
24. Ann Allen Savoy, *Cajun Music: A Reflection of a People, Vol. 1* (Eunice: Bluebird Press, 1984), 327.
25. Savoy, *Cajun Music*, 327. See also John Broven, *South to Louisiana, The Music of the Cajun Bayous* (Gretna: Pelican Publishing Company, 1983).
26. Nicholas Spitzer, "Zydeco and Creole Mardi Gras: Creole Identity and Performance Genres in Rural French Louisiana" (dissertation, University of Texas at Austin, 1986), 317.
27. Savoy, *Cajun Music*, 342.

28. Raymond E. François, *Yé Yaille, Chère!* (Ville Platte: Swallow Publications, 1990), 65.
29. Tisserand, *Kingdom of Zydeco*, 72–74.
30. Charles J. Stivale, *Disenchanting Les Bon Temps, Identity and Authenticity in Cajun Music and Dance* (Durham: Duke University Press, 2003), 146.
31. François, *Yé Yaille*, 65.
32. Savoy, *Cajun Music*, 40.
33. Savoy, *Cajun Music*, 46.
34. Savoy, *Cajun Music*, 59–61.
35. Nicholas Spitzer, "Zydeco and Mardi Gras," 330.
36. Barry Jean Ancelet, "Zydeco/Zarico: Beans, Blues and Beyond," in *Roots Music*, Mark F. DeWitt, ed. (Burlington: Ashgate Publishing Company, 2011), 141.
37. Shane K. Bernard, *Swamp Pop, Cajun and Creole Rhythm and Blues* (Jackson: University Press of Mississippi, 1996), 93.
38. Lauren C. Post, "Joseph C. Falcon, Accordion Player and Singer: A Biographical Sketch," *Louisiana History: The Journal of the Louisiana Historical Association* Vol. 11.1 (1970): 69.
39. Savoy, *Cajun Music*, 251.
40. Stivale, *Disenchanting Les Bon Temps*, 136.
41. Nicholas Spitzer, "Zydeco and Mardi Gras: Creole Identity and Performance Genres in Rural French Louisiana" (dissertation, The University of Texas at Austin, 1986), 297.
42. François, *Yé Yaille*, 201.
43. Savoy, *Cajun Music*, 78.
44. François, *Yé Yaille*, 30.
45. Brasseaux, *Cajun Breakdown*, 40–46.
46. Tisserand, *Kingdom of Zydeco*, 43.
47. Savoy, *Cajun Music*, 328.
48. Tisserand, *Kingdom of Zydeco*, 41–42.
49. Comeaux, "The Cajun Dance Hall," 41.
50. Sean Wilentz, *360 Sound, The Columbia Records Story* (San Francisco: Chronicle Books, 2012), 56.
51. Murphy, *Cowboys and Indies, The Epic History of the Record Industry*, 51.
52. Douglas Gomery, *Shared Pleasures: A History of Movie Presentation in the United States*, (Madison: University of Wisconsin Press), 172–180.
53. Berkley Hudson and Karen Boyajy, "The Rise and Fall of an Ethnic Advocate and American Huckster, Louis N. Hammerling and the Immigrant Press," *Media History*, 2009, Vol. 15(3): 291–293.
54. Marshall Beuick, "The Declining Immigrant Press," *Social Forces*, Vol. 6, No 2 (Dec., 1927): 257–258.

55. Lizabeth Cohen, "Encountering Mass Culture at the Grassroots: The Experience of Chicago Workers in the 1920s," *American Quarterly*, Volume 41, Issue 1 (Mar., 1989): 9.
56. Wilentz, *360 Sound*, 61.
57. Frank Buckley Walker. "The Seeger-Walker Interview, June 19, 1962." http://www.stateoffranklin.net/johnsons/oldtime/frankwalker_interview1.pdf
58. Post, "Joe Falcon," 66.
59. John Broven, *South to Louisiana, The Music of the Cajun Bayous* (Gretna: Pelican Publishing Company, 1983), 17.
60. Wilentz, *360 Sound*, 76.
61. Wilentz, *360 Sound*, 58.
62. Falcon and Soileau, in an interview with Ralph Rinzler, October 1965, University of Louisiana at Lafayette, Center for Louisiana Studies, The Archives of Cajun and Creole Folklore, RI1.011, audio recording.
63. Broven, *South to Louisiana*, 20.
64. Brasseaux, *Cajun Breakdown*, 56.
65. Broven, *South to Louisiana*, 17.
66. Brasseaux, *Cajun Breakdown*, 56.
67. Savoy, *Cajun Music*, 328.
68. Greil Marcus, "That Old, Weird America," in booklet accompanying reissue of *Anthology of American Folk Music*, ed. Harry Smith, Smithsonian Folkways, 1997, compact disc, liner notes, 23.
69. Dewey Balfa, in an interview with Barry Ancelet, 1981, AN1.193, The Archives of Cajun and Creole Folklore, University of Louisiana at Lafayette, Lafayette, Louisiana.
70. Savoy, *Cajun Music*, 136.
71. Savoy, *Cajun Music*, 52.
72. Tisserand, *Kingdom of Zydeco*, 74.

BIBLIOGRAPHY

Ancelet, Barry Jean. "Zydeco/Zarico: Beans, Blues and Beyond." In *Roots Music*, ed. Mark F. DeWitt. Burlington: Ashgate Publishing Company, 2011.

Balfa, Dewey. Interview with Barry Ancelet, 1981, AN1.193, The Archives of Cajun and Creole Folklore, University of Louisiana at Lafayette, Lafayette, Louisiana.

Beuick, Marshall. "The Declining Immigrant Press," *Social Forces*, Vol. 6, No 2 (Dec., 1927): 257–263.

Bernard, Shane K. *Swamp Pop, Cajun and Creole Rhythm and Blues*. Jackson: University Press of Mississippi, 1996.

Brasseaux, Ryan André. *Cajun Breakdown, The Emergence of an American-Made Music.* New York: Oxford University Press, 2009.

Broven, John. *South to Louisiana, The Music of the Cajun Bayous.* Gretna: Pelican Publishing Company, 1983.

Charters, Samuel. *A Trumpet Around the Corner, The Story of New Orleans Jazz.* Jackson: University Press of Mississippi, 2008.

Cohen, Lizabeth. "Encountering Mass Culture at the Grassroots: The Experience of Chicago Workers in the 1920s." *American Quarterly,* Volume 4.1 (March 1989): 6–33.

Comeaux, Malcolm L. "The Cajun Dance Hall." *Material Culture* 32, no. 1 (Spring 2000): 37–56.

Falcon, Joe. Interview with Ralph Rinzler, October 1965, University of Louisiana at Lafayette, Center for Louisiana Studies, The Archives of Cajun and Creole Folklore, RI1.011, audio recording.

Fowlie, Wallace. "Memory of France: April 1944." *The Kenyon Review* 6.4 (1944): 570–582.

François, Raymond E. *Yé Yaille, Chère!* Ville Platte: Swallow Publications, 1990.

Gomery, Douglas. *Shared Pleasures: A History of Movie Presentation in the United States.* Madison: University of Wisconsin Press, 1992.

Hudson, Berkley and Karen Boyajy. "The Rise and Fall of an Ethnic Advocate and American Huckster, Louis N. Hammerling and the Immigrant Press." *Media History,* 2009, Vol. 15(3): 291–293.

Katz, Jeff. "Cajun French Fever Rages Early for Tribute: For 50 years, Fred's Lounge is where le bons temps roulet. Governor, priest mark day." *Los Angeles Times,* November 26, 1996, http://articles.latimes.com/1996-11-26/news/mn-3039_1_fred-tate.

Knight, Henry Cogswell. *Letters from the South and West.* Boston: Richardson and Lord, 1824.

Le Menestrel, Sara. "The Color of Music, Social Boundaries and Stereotypes in Southwest Louisiana French Music." *Southern Cultures* 13.3 (2007): 87–105.

———. *Negotiating Difference in French Louisiana Music, Categories, Stereotypes, and Identifications.* Jackson: University Press of Mississippi, 2015.

Marcus, Greil. "That Old, Weird America," in booklet accompanying reissue of *Anthology of American Folk Music,* ed. Harry Smith, Smithsonian Folkways, 1997, compact disc, liner notes.

Mattern, Mark. "Cajun Music, Cultural Revival: Theorizing Political Action in Popular Music." *Popular Music and Society* 22.2 (1998): 31–48.

Murphy, Gareth. *Cowboys and Indies, The Epic History of the Record Industry.* New York: Thomas Dunne Books, 2014.

Post, Lauren C. "Joseph C. Falcon, Accordion Player and Singer: A Biographical Sketch." *Louisiana History: The Journal of the Louisiana Historical Association* Vol. 11.1 (1970): 63–79.

Reed, Revon. *Lâche Pas La Patate: Portrait des Acadiens de la Louisiane.* Montreal: Éditions Parti pris, 1976.

Sakakeeny, Matt. "New Orleans Music as a Circulatory System." *Black Music Research Journal* Vol. 31, No. 2 (Fall 2011): 291–325.

Savoy, Ann Allen. *Cajun Music: A Reflection of a People, Vol. 1.* Eunice: Bluebird Press, 1984.

Soileau, Leo. Interview with Ralph Rinzler, October 1965, University of Louisiana at Lafayette, Center for Louisiana Studies, The Archives of Cajun and Creole Folklore, RI1.011, audio recording.

Spitzer, Nicholas R. "Zydeco and Mardi Gras: Creole Identity and Performance Genres in Rural French Louisiana." PhD diss., The University of Texas at Austin, 1986, ProQuest (8700283).

Stivale, Charles J. *Disenchanting Les Bon Temps, Identity and Authenticity in Cajun Music and Dance.* Durham: Duke University Press, 2003.

Sublette, Ned. *The World That Made New Orleans, From Spanish Silver to Congo Square.* Chicago: Lawrence Hill Books, 2008.

Tate, Paul C. Paul C. Tate to Joan Baez, January 27, 1965.

Tisserand, Michael. *The Kingdom of Zydeco.* New York: Avon Books, 1998.

Van Vechten, Carl. *The Merry-Go-Round.* New York: A.A. Knopf, 1918.

Walker, Frank Buckley. "The Seeger-Walker Interview, June 19, 1962." April, 2018. http://www.stateoffranklin.net/johnsons/oldtime/frankwalker_interview1.pdf

Whisnant, David E. *All That Is Native and Fine, The Politics of Culture in an American Region.* Chapel Hill: The University of North Carolina Press, 1983.

Wilentz, Sean. *360 Sound, The Columbia Records Story.* San Francisco: Chronicle Books, 2012.

CHAPTER 3

From the War on French to the War in France: World War II and Cultural Identity

World War II transformed the music culture of French Louisiana by exposing Southwest Louisianans to a national pop and country music soundtrack that was, both on the home front and on military bases, the aural backdrop of a bombastic American nationalism. Country music, heralded by Nashville promoters as the language of patriotism, blared over radios on American military bases. Kate Smith proclaimed in the 1942 "My Great, Great Grandfather" that her Revolutionary War ancestor had migrated to the United States because "in America, a man is free," and in "This is My Country," Fred Waring asked "What difference if I hail from North or South/Or from the East or West?" The World War II years heightened Southwest Louisianans' awareness of the outsider status of French Louisiana language, music, and heritage as they joined other Americans in rallying around symbols of national culture. A war on French had been raging in Southwest Louisiana for decades, with French banned from schools, government offices, and public life, and many of the Louisiana Thibodeauxs, Landrys and Delfours, who had learned to confine the speaking of French to the home, felt a stinging sense of cultural inferiority as soon as they arrived in boot camp. The French language had been steadily losing in Louisiana, with more and more young people unable to converse with their monolingual Francophone grandparents. But for a cohort of Southwest Louisianans who were deployed to France and asked to serve as military interpreters, providing vital assistance in intelligence work in occupied territory, the experience of wartime service in a French-

© The Author(s) 2019
P. Peknik, *French Louisiana Music and Its Patrons*,
https://doi.org/10.1007/978-3-319-97424-8_3

speaking country prompted a positive reevaluation of the French language and Francophone cultural practices. Southwest Louisianans far from home kept being confronted with reminders of their regional language and native music, and after the war, as returning soldiers sought out the signature music of their pre-war, teenaged years, Louisiana record companies produced the second recording era of the French Louisiana sound.

All across Louisiana, the aspirations and initiatives of a generation of returning World War II soldiers reshaped the self-identify of people of French descent in New Orleans, of black Louisianans across the state, and of French-speaking Cajuns in the Acadian parishes. Wartime industries had brought a flood of Anglophone Texans across the border, bringing country music and a nationalist sensibility into a region in which many still identified with the history, culture, and customs of colonial France. Thus the revitalized interest in disappearing French dialects and music was both associational—the result of a wartime affiliation with France—and oppositional—a reaction against the Texas incursion.

World War II was a watershed in the history of the entire American South, with over one and a half million Southerners joining the rural-to-urban migration from their ancestral homeland to other parts of the country,[1] especially to the northern cities of Chicago and Detroit, even as industrialization and urbanization were transforming the South. Meanwhile, many of the thirteen million Americans who served in the wartime military, including northern white ethnics who had never ventured beyond their city neighborhoods, were brought together on military bases in the South, where nine of the country's largest army training camps were located, from Camp Claiborne in Alexandria, Louisiana, and Camp Shelby near Hattiesburg, Mississippi, to Fort Knox south of Louisville, Kentucky.[2] Southern blacks pledged their support to the war effort, with over 1,154,000 blacks nationwide joining the US military between 1941 and 1946.[3] Many southern blacks discovered, through conversations carried out in their shared segregation with northern blacks, that they had lived a different history than people of African descent in other parts of the country. Proud of their service as Americans and increasingly distraught at their status as second-class citizens, many black southerners would return after the war with an intensified determination to challenge southern race relations, founding local chapters of the National Association for the Advancement of Colored People (NAACP) and launching voter registration drives. The bus boycott movement began not in Alabama or Mississippi but in Baton Rouge, Louisiana in 1953,[4] as the racial consciousness shaped by the war generated a set of expectations and actions that would drive the Civil Rights movement.

And it was not only black southerners who were changed by the war. More young men returned with a sense of purpose—political, social and reformist—than from any other American war: returning GIs participated in campaigns to reform local politics, overthrow entrenched political machines, and boost the economic status of the South as a region.[5] Southern GIs, encountering northerners for the first time in boot camp and in military exercises, had become painfully aware of the South's image as a region still burdened by a history of racial injustice and violence, rampant and casual political corruption, backwardness and illiteracy.[6] Southwest Louisiana native DeLesseps S. Morrison, a reform-minded liberal whose family was from Pointe Coupée Parish, won the mayoral election of New Orleans in 1946 after being discharged from the army and immediately launched a program to promote the "New South" as a place of racial moderation, political reform, and urban progressivism.[7]

The statement that French-speaking Louisiana was less racially intolerant than the rest of the Deep South is no great claim on behalf of political, social, and economic justice, but in some parishes, blacks had been voting long before the 1965 passage of the Voting Rights Act.[8] Some of Morrison's political enemies, alarmed by Southwest Louisianans' more relaxed ideas toward race, issued a poster condemning Morrison as a traitor: "Morrison Betrays White Race! Mayor of N.O. Gives Negroes Equal Political and Social Rights. It is even reported that King Zulu will take Rex's place at the next Mardi Gras."[9] Black working-class men in New Orleans had, since early in the century, performed a satire on the white Mardi Gras celebrations of King Rex, the crowned monarch of carnival, by assembling the Zulu Krewe, black men in blackface, decked out in grass skirts and palmetto leaves. The Mayor of New Orleans traditionally presented the key to the city to the newly crowned King Rex. Two years after the anti-Morrison poster appeared, Louis Armstrong returned to his native New Orleans to serve as Zulu King, and was presented with the key to the city by Morrison. Armstrong, disgusted that he had to stay in a Jim Crow hotel, vowed never to return to New Orleans.

Morrison's tenure as mayor was marked by debate over changing race relations and by the rise of New Orleans to the status of gleaming Southern gem. Morrison appointed New York City's celebrated urban planner Robert Moses to oversee a master plan to improve New Orleans's infrastructure and public services, adding parks, playgrounds, and a new public library. During Morrison's fifteen-year tenure, New Orleans became the second-busiest port in the United States,[10] and New Orleanians took renewed pride in their historic city and its French heritage.

Louisianans had a complicated relationship with the French language, with elite bilingual New Orleanians cultivating pride in their French heritage, the legacy of the opera and the costumed masquerade ball, while Southwest Louisianans were dismissed as speakers of an inferior dialect of French. But the historic contributions of France to the American colonists' struggle against Great Britain in the Revolutionary War were a shared theme. Southwest Louisiana's Abbeville newspaper *The Méridional* had explained to nineteenth-century readers that the colonists had won their independence only with the help of France and the Marquis de Lafayette, so it was therefore only proper that French be maintained as the language of commerce and society in the entire country. English was described as incoherent, neither literary nor poetic, the language of the defeated British army rather than the French "saviors" of the colonists. The use of English even interfered in day-to-day commerce in busy shops, the article's author claimed, citing the absurdity that a local resident who ordered bacon was mistakenly sent the works of Bacon. "Let's speak the language of the liberators of the United States," the editorialist argued. "If France hadn't helped the American people to gain their independence, they would still be the horrible slaves of the British. This is why the Americans should hate the British and never open their mouths to say a word in English."[11] The Americans: that is what French speakers in Louisiana went on calling English-speaking Protestants late into the twentieth century.

The most widely read newspaper in Louisiana, New Orleans's *Time-Picayune*, focused its World War II coverage on the consequences of the war in France, describing, in headlines such as "France Shall Live Free," the bravery of the French people despite their physical, material, spiritual and moral trials. Such stories had particular resonance with Louisiana's Francophone population, which was comprised of several hearth populations: the white New Orleans descendants of the first French colonists and the black New Orleans population, sometimes of mixed European and African ancestry; the rural black Creole population descended from free and enslaved people of African descent, including Caribbean immigrants; the French-speaking Houma Indian; and the Cajuns of Southwest Louisiana.[12] Louisiana newspapers documented the pity felt by French Louisianans over the wartime suffering of the French: in New Orleans, traditional Bastille Day celebrations were suspended and a high Mass was held at St. Louis Cathedral in the French Quarter in memory of French soldiers killed in the war—not New Orleanian soldiers, but French soldiers.[13] General DeGaulle was likened to Joan of Arc,[14] and the lyrics of the *Marseillaise* were quoted in articles that proclaimed the valor of the Free French forces and extolled the virtues of the "ideas and institutions" of France.[15] The Old French Quarter Civic Association sponsored a benefit fundraiser called Free France, and the chairman of the American Friends of France told *Times-Picayune* readers, "More than ever, France needs friends to stand by her in this, the most tragic hour of her long and brilliant history."[16] There was anxiety about the safety of Louisianans living in unoccupied France, where there was "no milk, no heating and no coal. In the center of Tours there isn't a single house left standing."[17] And there was melancholy among New Orleanians over the fact that in wartime Paris, there were "no big dances, no large parties, jazz music is forbidden by the French authorities, and only classical music is heard."[18] Assurances were made that France would be restored to its greatness, that Paris would be liberated, that the Resistance fighters would prevail. At war's end came the proclamation that "Frenchmen were never conquered!" and that the French spirit, exemplified by Paris, was unconquerable: "Long live France!"[19]

In Southwest Louisiana, rural *mardi gras* festivities were suspended, and old-time music dance hall culture was transformed, when men went off to Camps Beauregard and Livingston in the Anglo-Protestant north of the state, Camp Claiborne in Rapides Parish, Camp Polk in Vernon Parish and Camp Shelby in Mississippi, or to jobs in wartime industries in Baton Rouge, Shreveport and across the border in Texas. Nearly 25,000 Cajuns served in the US armed forces during World War II, in units with nicknames like "The Bayou Battalion," a US Marine Corps brigade, and the "Swamp Angels."[20] Once at boot camp, soldiers were offered the country and pop fare of the Grand Ole Opry's Camel Caravan, which, starting in 1941, provided musical entertainment to servicemen on military bases. Designed to boost morale among the troops, support the war effort and, of course, sell cigarettes, the Camel Caravan traveled more than 75,000 miles, rolling across thirty-two states in four red buses painted with logo of Nashville's WSM radio station. Country and pop music starts Roy Acuff, Ernest Tubbs, Eddy Arnold, the Golden West Cowboys, Sarah Colley's Minnie Pearl, and Caravan troupes from Nashville, New York, and Hollywood performed in sixty-eight military camps, hospitals, airfields, and bases, bringing the same country music format into the bunkhouse.[21] The station broadcast segments of its country-pop fare on NBC's Sunday afternoon *Army Hour* as well as from an airborne B-24 bomber.[22] Wartime was a boon to the folk music of the white Protestant

South, a music that became identified with patriotism and core American experiences and values. Ernest Tubb's recording of Redd Stewart's "Soldier's Last Letter"—in which a mother receives a letter written from the trenches by a son about to go into the battle that will cost him his life—was a *Billboard* hit for seven weeks in 1944.[23]

In the summer of 1941, the United States War Department staged, across much of the state of Louisiana, the largest war exercises ever held in the United States. WSM's reporters and engineers set up camp at the war games headquarters in Winnfield, famed for being the hometown of former Louisiana governor Huey Long. Generals George Marshall, Dwight Eisenhower, George Patton, and Omar Bradley participated in the mobilization of the Blue Army and the Red Army, and WSM broadcast the sounds of a pontoon bridge being built, the rumbling of tanks, and the boom of artillery fire.[24] WSM, broadcasting from Winnfield alongside national media organizations NBC and CBS, gained prestige from its wartime reporting and did much to introduce American servicemen from Northern cities to country music, but it did just as much to quiet regional music by establishing country music as the popular genre of a nation at war. Southern radio stations, after presenting news of the war, broadcast country and pop music to provide a diversion on the home front. The Opry's "homespun music" may have spoken to many white Southern soldiers and, for some, been "inextricably tied to the vision of hearth and home that inspired the troops,"[25] but for many other troops, including white northerners, ethnic Americans, and African-Americans, it was an alien sound.

With the departure for war and for wartime jobs of a number of the most locally celebrated Southwest Louisiana musicians, including Cajun fiddler Dewey Balfa, who worked in a shipyard in Orange, Texas, and Cajun accordionist Nathan Abshire, who was drafted into the army, and, given the wartime difficulty of obtaining German accordions—it was notoriously difficult to repair old ones, and there were as yet no Louisiana manufacturers—a number of Cajun musicians turned to the new country and swing styles. For some, this was a pragmatic, not necessarily an aesthetic, choice. It had been impossible to import German Sterling, Monarch and Eagle brand accordions during the pre-war and war years, and the war would devastate the German factories that produced them.[26] Even after the war, because the most successful surviving manufacturing interests were located in the Russian sphere of influence, Louisiana craftsmen had to teach themselves how to repair and refurbish the old German accordions and then how to build accordions from scratch.[27] Characterizing the wartime disappearance of traditional music as entirely a function of changing popular tastes in Louisiana ("The accordion fell victim to the newly Americanized Louisiana French population's growing distaste for the old ways")[28] ignores the political dimensions of government sponsorship of country music and the wartime scarcity of one the key instruments of traditional music. In fact, as Ronald Flynn documents in *The Golden Age of the Accordion*, the period of the mid-1930s to the early 1960s was with the exception of the war years, a boom era for the accordion all across the United States, with music stores carrying more accordions than guitars, pianos, wind instruments, violins or percussion instruments. The association between French Louisiana music and the accordion would hardly have been stigmatizing. Accordions were so popular that American soldiers returning from war sometimes brought Italian-made accordions home as souvenirs.[29] Working-class soldiers who had heard the sound of the accordion in the old country fueled the market for the sale of the instrument stateside, and for music lessons.[30] For other musicians, the desire to experiment with new styles, genres, and instrumentation was a natural result of musical curiosity, proficiency, and new opportunities to perform with musicians who were outsiders to French Louisiana music.

Cajuns who left their towns and region for the first time to serve alongside Anglo-Protestant Americans from Virginia, Hawaii, and New York didn't simply abandon and forget their ethnic and regional identities. Rather, for a core group of Cajun soldiers, wartime experiences provided evidence of the vitality and usefulness of their cultural identity, native language, and heritage. According to Shane Bernard, in 1942, French was still the primary language of nearly seventy-five percent of Cajun GIs, and some spoke only French, with eighty percent of older GIs using French as their first language.[31] Since the US military needed French-speaking soldiers to act as interpreters in France, Belgium, North Africa, and Southeast Asia, Cajuns were recruited by the Office of Strategic Services, predecessor to the Central Intelligence Agency, to meet with operators in the French resistance, serving as linguistic liaisons between the American military and French troops. Cajun French, spoken with its anglicizations and irregular grammatical structure in a Franco-Southern accent, wasn't the US military's strategic and diplomatic language of choice for its interpreters, but it turned out that Southwest Louisiana French sounded so much like the dialect of French spoken by farmers in the southwest of France that German linguists didn't suspect that Cajun speakers of French were in fact

American soldiers. As French filmmaker Jean-Pierre Bruneau explains in *Mon Cher Camarade*, Pat Mire's documentary film about Cajun soldiers in World War II France, if the US military had used Québecois speakers of French, expert German code-breakers could have figured out that the Canadians weren't actually French peasants, whereas Cajuns passed for French locals, fooling the Germans.[32]

Cajun soldiers did more than pass for Frenchmen—they identified with, socialized with and depended on French men and women they could imagine as distant, distant ancestors. When retired Brigadier General Robert J. LeBlanc from Abbeville, Louisiana, served as an Office of Strategic Services agent in France in 1944, he found Normandy, Brittany, and the Loire Valley to be "a land of people like we are." LeBlanc felt that his life was "more in French people's hands than it was in American hands," since he counted on French locals to get him back and forth from one side of the German line to the other. The locals acted with generosity and courage in putting themselves at risk, LeBlanc said: "A lot of Americans don't know how many Frenchmen laid down their lives to save American lives during World War II."

The generation of Louisiana soldiers who served in World War II had grown up at a time when French was spoken at home but forbidden in schools, and finding that their French-language skills were now critical to war strategy was a point of great pride. "I don't think there was a day [during my service] that officers didn't get me to speak French," Bernard said.[33] Bernie LeJeune of Church Point, who worked as a translator in Casablanca, was very proud when a Frenchman asked him where he had learned English. Elvin Thibodeaux of Grand Coteau was called on to interpret for a group of Alsatians and Lorrainers who had been trying to tell an American officer that they had been forced into the German army and wanted to fight for the Allies.[34] The war gave Cajun soldiers a new understanding of the global reach of the French language and brought new relevance, meaning, and cachet to their identities as Francophones who were citizens of an Anglophone United States. Revon Reed found that Cajun pride in the French language was revitalized by the war: "After World War II when we came back from overseas in France, North Africa, we saw the value of our second language," Reed said.[35]

As an OSS agent, Robert LeBlanc would communicate with the French Resistance by going to a local café and ordering a certain aperitif, the ordering of which was a coded message to the Resistance. As convincing as LeBlanc was as a Frenchman, he was always careful not to extinguish and toss a half-finished cigarette, since that simple act would have aroused German suspicions: "You better damn well smoke 'em 'til they burnt your fingers or they'd know you were an American. A Frenchman would stick a toothpick in it and smoke it to the bitter end," LeBlanc said. It wasn't until commanders in the field saw that Cajuns could be very effective operators, obtaining valuable intelligence and communicating strategy, that they stopped thinking of Cajuns as "peasants from Louisiana who had been surrounded in the swamp," LeBlanc said, and Cajun speakers became an essential part of the military communications network in France, Indochina, and North Africa.

Cajun soldiers felt more at home in France than any of their fellow American soldiers could have. Felix Mire, who left Pointe Noire to serve in Patton's 3rd Army, 11th Armored Division, told his fellow soldiers while fighting at the Siege of Bastogne in Belgium, "I can get things you can't because I can speak French." Mire, needing medical help when his eyes were burning with the sting of gas, knocked on the door of a local home, where a French-speaking couple gave him water to wash out his eyes. Lee Bernard of Erath, whose three brothers were also in the army, was with the first Americans to liberate the village of Mailly-Champagne, arriving with the 739th Battalion. Bernard befriended a grateful local man, who gave him five cases of wine to carry in his tank.[36] And Creole accordionist Moss Anderson, a native of Maurice, Louisiana whose family had moved to Texas in 1928 when the price of rice dropped precipitously, played his accordion on a street corner in France to an appreciative French public: "Talk about people who can dance all night long," he remembered. Moss was ordered by an officer to get rid of his accordion because the old-time music he played was making the other Louisiana men in his barracks too homesick.[37]

Military life dramatized the outsider culture of Cajuns not only at war but also on military bases in the United States. One recruit from Breaux Bridge, arriving at boot camp, said that he felt as if he had come from a foreign country, and was treated as such. Cajun soldiers were referred to as "A Foreign Legion" or nicknamed "Frenchies" in military training camps across the country.[38] These soldiers spoke French among themselves, cooked traditional Southwest Louisiana crawfish bisque and oyster gumbo together, and sang French Louisiana songs together in camp. Their wartime immersion in "Anglo-American society" was, Bernard says, "a bewildering experience."[39]

French-speaking Creole soldiers must have felt the same outsider status encamped with African-American soldiers under the US military's strict segregationist policies, which were enforced in training programs, recreational and barracking facilities, and the assigning of military duties. Black soldiers were restricted for the most part to non-combat military assignments, as one southern black war veteran explained: "They never did decide we was equal … It was just a mirror of our civilian life, that's all. The way of life that we've been living all them many years."[40] The national media, as evidenced in NBC Blue's August 1941 broadcast program "America's Negro Soldiers," sponsored by the War Department, portrayed only one kind of black soldier—the English-speaking soldier who liked tap dancing.[41]

After years of separation from the traditions, food, and music of their home region, soldiers returning to Southwest Louisiana sought out the social events, cuisine, and culture of the pre-war years. They returned to the dance halls and requested old-time two-steps, waltzes and ballads like *"Jolie blonde," "J'ai passé devant ta porte"* and "Eunice Two Step," each of which told stories about men who had been betrayed and heartbroken in love, as those soldiers had also been who had come home to find their girlfriends had not waited for them faithfully.

Another post-war favorite was *"Jole blon,"* one of the first commercially recorded Cajun songs. The song is likely descended from one of many medieval French folk songs about lovely blondes, the most famous of which is *"Auprès de ma blonde."* A 1946 version of the song, sung by a Texan, popularized far beyond Acadiana the story of a man's heartbreak and rebound. With the release of *"Jole Blon,"* the Texas label Gold Star Records became the first independent record label to produce a national hit, with Harry Choates's rendition becoming Hit #4 on the *Billboard* charts for "Most Played Juke Box Folk Records."

Gold Star founder Bill Quinn was the son of Irish immigrants in the heavily French-Canadian mill town of Amesbury, Massachusetts, and had moved to Texas just before World War II. By trade a sound engineer, Quinn became intrigued by the mechanics and technology of recording and taught himself how to record phonograph records, a complicated production process that was a jealously guarded industry secret of the commercial labels. From a record pressing shop in the back room of his radio repair store, Quinn set out to capture his little share of the independent recording industry in Texas, opening his studio in 1941 and founding his own label, Gold Star Records.[42] Quinn began experimenting with record production at a time when the major labels were suffering under both an American Federation of Musicians recording ban and a War Production Board order that severely limited new recordings by rationing the supply of shellac, a key material in record production. Musicians' union president James Petrillo, worried that union musicians were losing live gigs to album sales, imposed a ban on all new recordings beginning in August 1942 and lasting until November 1944. Petrillo believed that if Americans could buy recorded music, they wouldn't pay to hear live bands in nightclubs, and musicians would find it hard to make a living as performers. His assumption was that the experience of listening to recorded music at home was so analogous to the experience of listening to music socially in taverns and clubs that consumers would opt for the least expensive option of a one-time purchase of an album over the continued expense of going out to hear live bands.[43] Petrillo's scheme was also designed to pressure record companies to pay royalties into a union trust fund to support musicians.[44]

In 1942, the War Production Board ordered a seventy-nine percent reduction in the non-military use of shellac, freezing new album production.[45] Record labels zealously scouted clubs and house parties so that as soon as the recording industry could return to pre-war production levels, the talent would be lined up and waiting in the wings. Quinn's strategy was to make the kinds of records that might be stocked in jukeboxes. He bought all the old 78s he could find at second-hand shops and pulverized them in a coffee bean grinder, then melted them down to extract the shellac and press new albums, which would be recorded direct from microphone to disc in the back room of his shop, Gold Star Studios, and then mastered. Quinn was entirely self-taught, a pioneer of independent record production, and because his goal was to put regional talent in record stores and in jukeboxes, he recorded everything that would appeal to the regional demographic, from gospel to blues and country to French Louisiana music, with lyrics in French or in English.[46] Quinn's studio recorded both black and white musicians years before Sam Phillips founded his more famous Sun Records label in Memphis in the early 1950s, the label that became renowned for recording both blues musicians and the white rockabilly singer Elvis Presley.

With an ear for the musical preferences of older Louisianans who had migrated across the Texas border during the early twentieth-century oil boom, and younger Louisianans who had moved to Texas in search of wartime jobs, in 1946 Quinn recorded Vermilion Parish native Harry Choates singing *"Jole blon."* Choates worked at the shipyards of Texas

Consolidated Steel in Sabine, Texas, where he played for workers as they came off shift, and this is one of many stories in which Southwest Louisiana musicians heard their regional music interpreted by outsider musicians far from home. At Consolidated, Choates, who, during the Depression had moved to the heavily Cajun town of Port Arthur, ninety miles east of Houston, met a fellow Southwest Louisiana native, fiddler Dewey Balfa, who had moved to Texas for wartime work. Choates sang the mournful ballads of the French Louisiana tradition with a "plaintive enthusiasm,"[47] bringing an energy and excitement to his performance that inspired Balfa's longing for the music of Mamou, Louisiana. Throughout the 1930s and 1940s, Choates played at clubs and dance halls in east Texas and Southwest Louisiana, and his decision to audition "*Jole blon*" for Quinn's Gold Star label was inspired by the popularity of the song among the soldiers who frequented the Lake Charles, Louisiana club where he played on Saturday nights.[48]

The song was so popular that Choates recorded a series of Southwest Louisiana traditional songs, including "*Allons à Lafayette*" and "*Basile Waltz*," for Gold Star and other labels. "*Jole blon*" turned out to be Choates's only hit record, but Quinn's interest in French-language music was not an exception. A number of entrepreneurs in Louisiana launched labels in the post-war years to record and promote regional music, although the music they were promoting under the label "old-time tradi-tional French-language music" was more often a hybrid of traditional French-language music and the newly popular string band, country and hillbilly styles. Music retailers, by necessity more opportunistic than nos-talgic, knew that French lyrics were a key selling point in Southwest Louisiana. Crowley's J.D. Miller founded the *Fais Do Do* label to meet the demand for French-language music at a time when the old recordings were no longer available. Major labels like Columbia and Decca solved the problem of the shortage of French-language music by having "hillbilly songs" translated into French, and country swing bands like the Rayne Bo Ramblers wrote French lyrics for country music songs,[49] capitalizing on the rage for French: "They called for [French], man," said the group's fiddle player. "We're selling that from here to Houston."[50]

Old-time music, still played in homes and in dance halls, existed in a social world parallel to the commercial world of recorded country-Cajun music, which was not looked upon favorably by purists of the old-time tradition. Arhoolie Records founder Chris Strachwitz, who in the 1960s became a passionate advocate of old-time French Louisiana music, called the popular singer Happy Fats "one of the oldest and worst exponents of that brand of pseudo-Cajun music which is really more Country-and-Western than Cajun." Reviewing a 1968 reissue of one of Fats's albums, Strachwitz referred disparagingly to the singer's television appearance, his large following, especially among non-Cajuns, and the fact that there was no accordion in his band: "His commercial, sweet, phony style represents the worst outgrowth of the Cajun tradition."[51] To old-time music purists like Strachwitz, that outgrowth included all recordings that featured Western-hillbilly instrumentation, the string band sound, amplification, and any slickness in production values or self-consciousness in performance. Country music, like other commercial pop music, put the focus on the performers by dressing them in flashier clothing and elevating them on the stage at one end of a performance venue, whereas in old-time French Louisiana music culture, the musicians were dressed in their everyday attire and played in the middle of the venue, and all eyes were on the dancers and not on the band. Many small label owners listened to country and swing radio programs and concluded that the market for country music was more sustainable than the market for old-time music, phasing out their French Louisiana repertoire in order to record and promote country songs. Yet there was a disconnect between the assumptions and ambitions of many entrepreneurial independent label owners and the realities of public demand. Local investors new to the recording business erred on the side of the novel and popular "hillbilly" and swing sounds, taking their cues from radio stations in Nashville, Shreveport, and Houston and from conversations with recording studio owners in New Orleans; meanwhile, from the late 1940s and all throughout the decade that followed, Cajun accordionists played traditional French songs night after night in dance halls packed with patrons from ages fifteen to seventy-five.

Eddie Shuler, who founded Folk Star Records in 1949 in Lake Charles, described the post-war years as a boom era for French-language music, popular on military bases and with listeners of Shuler's popular radio show. Shuler was the first to record French Louisiana music's second-wave recording hero, the Pointe Noire accordionist Iry LeJeune, who had learned to play by listening to Ardoin's recordings and is considered the purest, most traditional of second-wave French Louisiana recording stars, and second only to Ardoin himself. Once LeJeune's "high-pitched hurting vocals" were broadcast on Shuler's KPLC radio show, the station wound up broadcasting eight hours a day of French Louisiana music.[52] So even while radio shows like Shreveport's "Louisiana Hayride" promoted the country music sound, and string bands became increasingly popular among younger music enthusiasts, Southwest Louisiana business owners understood that what attracted French-speaking listeners in rural Acadiana was an older brand of French Louisiana music, and they used their advertising dollars to support radio shows that played it. Although LeJeune's music was described in later years as having been a throwback to an earlier time, old-time music had been very much alive then anyway, Cajun fiddler Dewey Balfa remembered. Balfa was playing traditional music six days a week in nightclubs, lounges and at weddings.[53] Record companies simply hadn't been recording old-time music in the later years of the Depression and the war. While country music influences, both lyrical and instrumental, and the jaunty, amplified rhythms of popular banjo and steel guitar music were becoming embedded in commercial French Louisiana music, and popularized among younger listeners (who are notorious for their attraction to the novel in music), traditional French Louisiana music continued to be performed at house parties and in dance halls by musicians who, with very few exceptions, had always had day jobs in farming or industry. LeJeune, an exception, was forced to try to earn a living as a musician because he was nearly blind and couldn't work on his father's farm. In 1948, fiddler Floyd LeBlanc and LeJeune traveled to Houston to record "*La valse du Pont D'Amour*" ("Lovebridge Waltz") and "Evangeline Special" for the Opera label, and these recordings, featuring LeJeune's wailing vocals, modeled on Ardoin's emotional performance style, lifted old-time music above the clamor of country and swing, and the songs became big regional hits.

These were the very same rich, complex songs the World War II generation had grown up with, and LeJeune's impassioned style and melancholy lyrics spoke to Southwest Louisiana listeners in a way that the happy-go-lucky melodies of popular country songs could not. The French Louisiana sound was upbeat, but in a way that was defiant of circumstance, mournful as well as celebratory, more down-on-the-luck than lucky, and LeJeune's music embodied the enduring mood and themes of the French Louisiana tradition. In "*J'ai eté au bal*" [I Went to the Dance], LeJeune recounts his experience at the dance hall looking at all the pretty girls: "*Personne qui veut m'aimer/Gardons voir si ça c'est pas/Mais misérable pour moi*"[54] [No one wants to love me/Let's see if that's anything but miserable for me]. But, the singer says, he's going back to the dance hall that night if he can afford to. "Duraldo Waltz" was another favorite. Duraldo is a small community near Mamou. The singer, addressing the woman who has left him to return to her family, tells her: "*Tu vois pour toi-même, bébé/Tous nos chagrins qu'on après se passer/Ça fait pas de bien.*" [You'll see for yourself, baby/That all the troubles we've been through/Didn't help us after all.]

At a time when string and country bands had "charming, scrubbed band-leader personas and kept smooth, gliding beats to please the dancers,"[55] LeJeune, who carried his accordion in a pillowcase and had to hitch a ride from the prairie to the nearest town to play a gig at a dance hall, had a deeply moving presence. Rather than fronting a polished, freshly rehearsed band, with instruments in conversation with each other, LeJeune seemed to make the music about himself as the performer, as Ardoin had done, backed by musicians who played for each other and for themselves. LeJeune delivered the message, in a modern commerce-driven urbanizing world, that "a man could be himself … he could wear his own clothes, he could speak his own French and he could let out his deepest emotions …. He could, in fact, be a Cajun…"[56] Like Ardoin and LaFleur, LeJeune died tragically, hit by a car while changing a flat tire on US highway 190 on the way home from a performance in Eunice. He was 26.

LeJeune is credited with "reviving" the French Louisiana accordion-based musical tradition, but in order to call the post-war era a revival era, the music must have first disappeared. But the timeframe for its disappearance, if we take at face value the testimony of traditional musicians, is confoundingly narrow. Accordionist Shirley Bergeron remembers that his father, Alphee Bergeron, "got rid of his accordion" in the forties, "and then after the war, when everyone was coming home they wanted to hear their own music again and the Cajun accordion music got popular once more … A bunch of war veterans had started a band and people started asking for the accordion in the dance hall, so they asked daddy to join the band."[57] Thus Alphee Bergon, who had performed over many years with Amédé Ardoin, Nathan Abshire, Joe Falcon, and Mayeuse LaFleur, merely stopped playing accordion from the pre-war to the post-war years, at which time the band he joined, the Veteran Playboys, began broadcasting over radio stations all over the region, in Crowley, Opelousas, Eunice, Ville Platte.[58] Likewise, Abshire is said to have switched to fiddle in the early forties "when the Texas oil people 'invaded' South Louisiana," at which time the accordion, "had died down in popularity," but "a few years later, [Abshire] went back to his favorite instrument,"[59] again making the silencing of the accordion, and traditional French Louisiana music, a very short "few years."

Certainly it was the case that commercial music, meaning country, swing and pop, was broadcast throughout Southwest Louisiana, and that entrepreneurial record labels, musicians, and radio stations capitalized on every opportunity to profit from the new mass culture trends. The English-speaking, Protestant "Anglo-Americans" who moved into Louisiana to work in the oil industry formed a lucrative market for pop music, and new styles of French-language music developed under the influence of country and swing. But this doesn't mean that old-time traditional music wasn't still being played in the homes of Cajun and Creole families, or at neighborhood events or community gatherings. It is impossible to label as "traditional" only that music played by self-taught musicians for friends and family and at local dance halls, and then claim that such music disappeared, using as evidence the fact that country and swing music were being performed by professional bands, and commercially recorded and broadcast.

There was no single music aesthetic either locally, regionally or nationally. French Louisiana music was the signature sound of Southwest Louisiana, but not the sole sound. Folklorists' anxiety about old-time French Louisiana music's demise or corruption by new stylistic influences was reflective of a larger anxiety about modern technological "intrusions" into traditional rural cultures, and about the compromises that had to be made between the values and practices of regional culture and the practical demands of living in a mass-media nation in which the music of eight-piece swing bands, with their polished orchestral sound, was nationally popular. Old-time French Louisiana music was declared the loser in the post-World War II war era by critics who saw performance of country or swing music by Southwest Louisiana-born musicians as evidence of the failure of traditional music to endure in a mass-media age of national markets, and it was declared the winner by those who saw the influence of French Louisiana music on swing and country as evidence that Southwest Louisiana musicians "Cajunized" other genres by introducing swing and country bands to new songs and styles.[60] Evidence for this "Cajunization" argument is that Buddy Holly produced, for the Brunswick label, Waylon Jennings's cover of "*Jolie Blonde*," and Hank Williams Jr.'s "Jambalaya" was based on the French Louisiana "Pine Grove Blues.[61]" It is natural that such debates about boundaries took place in a region in which cohabitation and territorialism always existed in dynamic tension. One of the symbolic functions of the Mardi Gras *courir*, a costumed run characterized by rowdy pageantry, was to demarcate "the perceived geographical and social boundaries" of each neighborhood and then "socially integrate" particular neighborhoods by inviting the more dispersed members of the community to participate in a communal dinner at day's end.[62] Musicians, too, made incursions into the territory of other genres, borrowing and imitating where they could. But there is also a demographic force at work beneath discussions of musical taste. When music historians described the drum kits, steel guitars, and electric guitars of country music as becoming more common in Louisiana, they could just as easily have been describing what the "French" population of Louisiana felt about the Texans migrating across the border for jobs: "The hillbilly element was becoming more intrusive."[63]

That "hillbilly element" dominated the commercial airwaves in much of Louisiana. And some traditional Southwest Louisiana musicians did experiment with the hillbilly sound to challenge themselves technically and to develop their musicianship, just as listeners turned to new genres to develop and challenge their appreciation of music. The diversity and vitality of the post-war music scene in Southwest Louisiana is evidence of a sensibility of experimentation, curiosity, and collaboration that always marks the richest musical traditions. Most importantly, though, while some Southwest Louisiana musicians formed string bands and played swing and country music in nightclubs, the rural Cajuns who danced to traditional French-language music at a neighbor's house party were not the same people who danced to the music of country and string band sounds in Acadiana's growing cities. In the first decades of the twentieth century, following the discovery of oil in Acadiana in 1901, hundreds of oil companies were extracting oil and gas from fields in Evangeline, Hell Hole Bayou and Anse La Butte, bringing Anglo-Protestant workers from Texas to Southwest Louisiana and creating new urban centers that were transformed by the migrating population. Lafayette, a farming town of 19,200 in 1940, became a city of 33,500 by 1950, with subdivision after subdivision built to house the petroleum industry laborers. A Lafayette newspaper noted in 1949 that "the buggies and leisurely pace of an earlier Cajun day have given way to all the furor and speed of modern wealth and initiative."[64]

Savvy dance hall owners in newly urban Lafayette catered to these 15,000 new residents by hiring Texas-style country and string bands to play in the dance halls. This doesn't demonstrate that the musical taste or habits of long-time residents of what had been "a sleepy Cajun town" in 1940 had completely changed by 1950, only that a population boom created by Texans brought Texas music into Acadiana. Likewise, petrochemical companies built factories and transplanted workers from Texas to Lake Charles, where Leroy "Happy Fats" LeBlanc appeared at the Silver Star

Club. A new population brought new music: Texans and other Anglo-Protestant migrants found Texas country and swing appealing, and this new music then coexisted with old-time French Louisiana music, which was still a cherished traditional activity in the lives of French-speaking Catholic Southwest Louisianans. Country and swing bands may have appealed as well to younger listeners, but old-time music was still the only music for adults, Creole fiddler Canray Fontenot testified: "Most of the old people, whether they was white or black, they didn't care too much about string music. They wanted to hear an accordion and a fiddle."[65]

The migration of Texans to Southwest Louisiana throughout the first decades of the twentieth century alternated with the movement of Cajuns and Creoles to East Texas. French Louisiana music took root in Texas Gulf towns with Nathan Abshire's 1949 recording of "Texas Waltz." Abshire taught himself to play accordion when he was eight, and by the time he was a teenager, was asked by Amédé Ardoin to play during Amédé s breaks at house parties.[66] Like LeJeune, Abshire had made somewhat of a living from his music, although getting to dance halls, which were sometimes fifty miles apart, could mean walking twenty miles to play for three dollars.[67] Abshire had switched to playing violin during the wartime years when accordions weren't available. "*Aussi, le monde aimait mieux le son du violon,*" Abshire said, "*particulièrement les Texans.*"[68] [And everyone liked the sound of the violin better, especially Texans.] When Abshire took up the accordion again after the war, his emotional personality and dramatic playing style quickly popularized the Creole song "Pine Grove Blues," and he developed such a loyal following that a year later, he was playing to a packed house at Basile's Avalon Club seven nights a week.[69]

Eh, négresse! (Quoi tu veux, nèg?")
Où toi, t'as été hier au soir, ma négresse?
Tu as 'rive a c'matin
Soleil 'tais après s'lever
Ça m'fait d'la peine pour toi![70]

[Hey, darling! (What is it, dear?)
Where were you last night, my darling?
You came home this morning when the sun was coming up.
I feel so bad for you!]

Sung by Ardoin, "négresse" would have had a racial connotation, but like the term "*nég,*" it was a common term of endearment in many

Cajun songs. Another popular Abshire tune was "Service Blues," in which a soldier going off to World War II breaks into tears when he hears the train whistle blowing, knowing he has to leave behind all that he loves:

> *Quand j'ai parti pour aller dans l'armée,*
> *J'ai quitté tout ça moi, j'aimais*
> *Moi, j'ai pris le grand chemin de fer*
> *Avec le coeur aussi cassé.*

> [When I left to go into the army
> I left everything that I loved
> And I look the train
> With a broken heart.]

Abshire performed for fifty-six years and recorded on many labels, including Swallow Records, Old Timey, and La Louisiane, yet hoped his music would die with him: "When I die, I'd like all my records to be broken, so that they'd never be played again. I don't think it's right for radio stations and everyone to keep playing the music of a musician after he's gone. When I die ... I'd like to be remembered the way I was ... and that my music would be buried with me in my grave."[71]

Abshire's belief in music as belonging to an individual in a particular historical time and place, an art that should disappear along with its maker lest it haunt the future, is, like the desire to recapture a lost historical or autobiographical past, inherently romantic. Abshire saw his music as so particular an expression of his own life experiences and circumstances that he could not conceive of it as having a universality that would appeal to people who hadn't endured a life of field labor and poverty, and who had never experienced the urgent and joyful obsession with music, dancing, and drinking that he saw all around him in the dance halls. Both poverty and the musician's life took a toll on Abshire, and at the end of his career, he wrote in colorful letters on the side of his accordion case: "The good times are killing me."[72] In *"La vie d'un musicien,"* Abshire warned musicians against ever getting married.

During this second commercial recording wave, many old-time French Louisiana songs were reinterpreted and recorded for major labels as Southwest Louisiana musicians paired new lyrics with old melodies and incorporated steel and electric guitars, telling the same stories of outcast suitors, wandering orphans, and the obstructions of family and community in love affairs. But because many women worked in wartime industries or spent the war years running the farm without boyfriends, husbands, and fathers at home, the post-war courtship dynamic put more emphasis on women's autonomy. In "*La valse de Cajun*" [Cajun Waltz], recorded by Iry LeJeune for Goldband in 1955, a man tells the woman he is courting, "*Jongle voir quand ton papa/T'as déjà aussi maltraitée*" [Look at how how much your papa/Has already mistreated you], and urges her to go back to being her old self with him: "*Je veux que toi tu sois/Comme toi, chère, t'es après faire*" [I want you to be/Just like you used to be, darling]. That same year in national music culture, in Nate King Cole's *Billboard* hit "A Blossom Fell," the song's narrator tells his girlfriend, "I saw you kissing someone new beneath the moon," and Eddy Arnold, in "Lonesome," called his beloved heartless. Popular music culture was in conversation about whether the post-war woman would be more like the sought-after heroine of Ernest Tubb's "Give Me a Little Old Fashioned Love," modest, loyal and without "worldly ways," or like the woman in Hank Williams Jr.'s "*Your Cheatin' Heart*." French Louisiana music, however, had always been more focused on failed love affairs, alienation, and betrayal. In Adam Hebert's "*Cette-la j'aime*," a woman is compared to a little bird flying from one branch to another, and in the Balfa Brothers' "*Chère bassette*," a wife leaves her husband and her home to run off with another man. In Nathan Abshire's songs, women stayed out all night, and in the end, got told "*Je veux pas de toi ... C'est trop dur*" [I don't want you anymore. ... It's too tough].

In LeJeune's "Lacassine Special," recorded for Folk Star Records in 1950, a husband tells his wife that she can be the one to hit to road: "*Mais garde toi tu peux voir/Le chemin et t'en aller*" [Take a look at the road that leads away from here/You can take it and go]. In LeJeune's "I Made a Big Mistake," recorded for Goldband in 1955, a man shoulders the blame for driving his ex away, tearfully realizing that once he walked out on her, she went on with her life without him. He runs into her walking down the street with another man: "*Dans la clarté du soleil/Et la lumiere de la lune/Moi j'ai vu personne qu'est si heurese*" [In the brightness of the sun/And the light of the moon/I'd never seen anyone so happy.]

Recording industry marketing executives had the same trouble labeling this French Louisiana music in the 1940s and 1950s as they had had during the 1920s and 1930s, settling on the term "French" or "Cajun French, "French vocal," or "French accordion." Southwest Louisiana place names again insinuated themselves into every story, with songs whose titles included Iota, Riceville, Calcasieu, Choupique, Duraldo, and Mamou, but, with the mobilization of World War II and the experiences of Southwest Louisianans at boot camp and factories far afield, so did place names in Texas. Moise Robin tells the story, in *"Touche pas ça tu vois,"* [Look, But Don't Touch] of a man who is seduced and robbed by a blonde woman in Port Arthur, Texas, the title likely the singer's advice to himself about pretty women in strange towns.[73] In Nathan Abshire's "Texas Waltz," recorded for Khoury's in 1954, a man mourns the fact that his girlfriend has run off to Texas and will probably never return to Louisiana.

The popularity of Abshire and LeJeune's recordings of French Louisiana classics convinced Fred Tate, Paul Tate, whose law office was at the corner of Sixth and Chestnut, next door to Fred's Lounge, and Revon Reed, a teacher from Mamou High School, that the French language, music, and culture of Southwest Louisiana could be successfully fostered in a mass-media age. Their cultural preservation work intersected with a historical moment in America in which the old documentary and regionalist sentiments of the 1920s and 1930s were bubbling up to the surface in other places as well, manifesting as a "nationalist regionalism" in which Western frontier states could claim to be the most rustically authentic, storied terrain in the country, and New England staked its claim to being the most distinctive historic region on a map of America by opening a series of recreated colonial villages, including Old Sturbridge Village and the Plimoth Plantation in Massachusetts, Strawbery Banke in Portsmouth, New Hampshire, and the Shelburne Museum in Vermont.[74] Each region wanted its chapter in the national story. The markers and artifacts of regional identity in New England were visual: stone walls marking a property line, massive red barns guarding the land behind white clapboard houses, Revolutionary War battlefields, and statues and monuments to illustrious Protestants. It was going to be harder to make the argument that the aural markers of Southwest Louisiana distinguished it as a sort of region-within-a-state—the foot stomping, fast dancing and loud accordion sounds of a prairie dance hall—and made it just as important in the long national narrative of the country. Yet as if crafted from the words of the region's old ballads, the refrain coming out of French Louisiana, addressed to Anglo-Protestant, urban America, seemed to be: your elders told you to ignore me, but all I want to do is catch your eye, and if you won't look this way just once, I'm telling you, you might be sorry.

The local patrons of French Louisiana music must have felt encouraged not only by the popularity of LeJeune's and Abshire's French-lyric songs but by the fact that during the prosperous, booming post-war years, American consumers were having a love affair with continental French cultural products, from music to fashion to film. In 1950, Louis Armstrong covered Edith Piaf's "*La Vie en Rose*"; Eartha Kitt's version of the popular French song "*C'est Si Bon*," which Kitt sang entirely in French, was a 1953 *Billboard* hit. French-language music was, for a brief moment, on national radio, as Hank Williams Jr.'s "Jambalaya (On the Bayou)" about a Southwest Louisiana sweetheart hit the country charts.

Notes

1. Morton Sosna, "Introduction" to *Remaking Dixie, The Impact of World War II on the American South*, ed. Neil R. McMillen (Jackson: University Press of Mississippi, 1997), xv.
2. Sosna in *Remaking Dixie*, ed. Neil McMillen, xvi.
3. Harvard Sitkoff, "African American Militancy in the World War II South," in *Remaking Dixie*, ed. McMillen, 73.
4. Neil McMillen, "Fighting for What We Don't Have: How Mississippi's Black Veterans Remember World War II," in *Remaking Dixie*, ed. McMillen, 94–95.
5. Cobb, "World War II" in *Remaking Dixie*, ed. McMillen, 5–6.
6. Sosna in *Remaking Dixie*, ed. Neil McMillen, xviii.
7. Michael L. Kurtz, "deLesseps S. Morrison: Political Reformer," *Louisiana History: The Journal of the Louisiana Historical Association*, 1 January 1976, Vol. 17 (1): 20.
8. J. Heppen and D. Mesyanzihnov, "Political Geography and Regionalism in Louisiana: The Impact of the French Influence in the post-World War II Era, *Political Geography*, 2003, Vol. 22(5): 521.
9. Kurtz, "deLesseps Morrison," *Louisiana History*, 29.
10. Kurtz, "deLesseps Morrison," *Louisiana History*, 36–37.
11. C.A. Mouisset, *The Méridional* (Abbeville) October 8, 1881.
12. Adapted from Cécyle Trépanier, "The Cajunization of French Louisiana: forging a regional identity," *The Geographical Journal*, Vol. 157, No. 2. (July 1991): 161.
13. *Times-Picayune*, July 14, 1942.
14. *Times-Picayune*, May 19, 1942.
15. *Times-Picayune*, July 15, 1942.
16. *Times-Picayune*, June 21, 1940.
17. *Times-Picayune*, January 14, 1941.
18. *Times-Picayune*, April 2, 1941.
19. *Times-Picayune*, September 18, 1944.
20. Shane K. Bernard, *The Cajuns, Americanization of a People* (Jackson: University Press of Mississippi, 2003), 14.

21. Craig Havighurst, *Air Castle of the South: WSM and the Making of Music City* (Urbana: University of Illinois Press, 2007), 118.
22. Havighurst, *Air Castle*, 199.
23. William H. Young and Nancy K. Young, *Music of the World War II Era* (Santa Barbara: Greenwood Publishing, 2007), 157.
24. Havighurst, *Air Castle*, 114.
25. Colin Escott, *The Grand Ole Opry: The Making of an American Icon* (New York: Center Street, 2006), 85.
26. Barry Jean Ancelet, *Cajun and Creole Music Makers* (Jackson: University of Mississippi Press, 1999), 25.
27. Malcolm L. Comeaux, "The Cajun Accordion," *Louisiana Review* 7 (1978): 117–128.
28. Barry Jean Ancelet, *Cajun and Creole Music Makers* (Jackson, University of Mississippi, 1999), 25.
29. Ronald Flynn, Edwin Davison, and Edward Chavez, *The Golden Age of the Accordion* (Schertz, Flynn Publications, 1984), xviii.
30. "A History of the Accordion in Americana Music," Accordion Americana, https://accordionamericana.com/2017/09/01/a-history-of-the-accordion-in-americana-music/
31. Bernard, *The Cajuns*, 6–7.
32. Pat Mire, dir., "*Mon Cher Camarade.*" DVD. Pat Mire Films, 2008.
33. Pat Mire, "*Mon Cher Camarade.*"
34. Robin Meche Kube, "Cajun Soldiers During WWII: Reflections on Louisiana's French Language and People," *Louisiana History, The Journal of the Louisiana Historical Association,*" Vol. 35, No. 3. (Summer 1994): 345–349.
35. Alan Lomax, dir., "American Patchwork: Cajun Country." DVD. 2006.
36. Pat Mire, "*Mon Cher Camarade.*"
37. Michael Tisserand, *The Kingdom of Zydeco* (New York: Avon, 1998), 94.
38. Bernard, *The Cajuns*, 11.
39. Bernard, *The Cajuns*, 7.
40. Twelve-year military veteran Henry Murphy, quoted in *Remaking Dixie, The Impact of World War II on the American South*, ed. Neil R. McMillen (Jackson: University Press of Mississippi, 1997), 101.
41. Donald Meckiffe and Matthew Murray, "Radio and the black soldier during World War II," *Critical Studies in Mass Communication* 15:4: 341–343.
42. Andy Bradley and Roger Wood, *The House of Hits, The Story of Houston's Gold Star/Sugarhill Recording Studios* (Austin: University of Texas Press, 2010), 12.
43. Robert Gordon, *Can't Be Satisfied: The Life and Times of Muddy Waters* (New York: Back Bay Books, 2002), 70.

44. Gareth Murphy, *Cowboys and Indies, The Epic History of the Record Industry* (New York: Thomas Dunne Books, 2014), 75.
45. Young, *Music of the World War II Era*, 90.
46. Bradley and Wood, *The House of Hits*, 17–18.
47. Bradley and Wood, *House of Hits*, 21.
48. Broven, *South to Louisiana*, 31.
49. Broven, *South to Louisiana*, 37–40.
50. R. Brasseaux, *Cajun Breakdown*, 141.
51. Chris Strachwitz, "Cajun Music on LP – A Survey," The American Folk Music Occasional (New York: Oak Publications, 1970), 27.
52. Broven, South to Louisiana, 52.
53. Dewey Balfa, Interview with Barry Jean Ancelet in Basile, 1981, AN.193, Archives of Cajun and Creole Folklore, University of Louisiana at Lafayette.
54. Francois, *Yé Yaille*, 169–170.
55. Savoy, Ann. Liner notes for "Iry Lejeune, The Definitive Collection," Ace Records UK, CDCHD 428, 5.
56. Savoy, *Cajun Music*, 4.
57. Shirley Bergeron, "French Rocking Boogie," Ace Records UK, CDCHD 353, 1993, compact disc, liner notes.
58. Bergeron, "French Rocking Boogie," liner notes.
59. Revon Reed, liner notes, "Nathan Abshire, The Great Cajun Accordionist," Ace Records UK, CDCHD 401, 1992, compact disc, liner notes by Revon Reed, 1973, 4.
60. Chris Strachwitz, *"J'ai Été Au Bal*, The Cajun and Zydeco Music of Louisiana," Vol. 2, Arhoolie Records, CD 332, 1993, compact disc, 11.
61. R. Brasseaux, *Cajun Breakdown*, 170; 179–180.
62. Sexton, Rocky L. "Cajun Mardi Gras: Cultural Objectification and Symbolic Appropriation in a French Tradition," *Ethnology* Vo. 38, No. 4 (Autumn, 1999): 300.
63. Broven, *South to Louisiana*, 30.
64. Bernard, *The Cajuns*, 37.
65. Savoy, *Cajun Music*, 330.
66. Nathan Abshire, "French Blues," liner notes.
67. TVTV, "The Good Times Are Killing Me," 1975, DVD.
68. Reed, *Lâche pas*, 76.
69. R. Brasseux, *Cajun Breakdown*, 179.
70. Francois, *Yé Yaille*, 445.
71. Ancelet, *Cajun and Creole Music Makers*, 103–105.
72. "Nathan Abshire, The Great Cajun Accordionist," liner notes.
73. Francois, *Yé Yaille*, 474.
74. Joseph A. Conforti, *Imagining New England, Explorations of Regional Identity from the Pilgrims to the Mid-Twentieth Century* (Chapel Hill: The University of North Carolina Press, 2001), 310.

BIBLIOGRAPHY

Abshire, Nathan. "Nathan Abshire and His Pine Grove Boys, French Blues," Arhoolie, 373, compact disc. Liner notes.

———. "The Good Times are Killing Me." 1975, TVTV. DVD.

Ancelet, Barry Jean. *Cajun and Creole Music Makers.* Jackson: University Press of Mississippi, 1999.

Balfa, Dewey. Interview with Barry Jean Ancelet, Basile, LA., 1981. AN.193, Archives of Cajun and Creole Folklore, University of Louisiana at Lafayette.

Bergeron, Shirley. "French Rockin' Boogie," Ace Records UK, CDCHD 353, 1993, compact disc. Liner notes.

Bernard, Shane K. *The Cajuns, Americanization of a People.* Jackson: University Press of Mississippi, 2003.

Bradley, Andy and Roger Wood, *The House of Hits, The Story of Houston's Gold Star/Sugarhill Recording Studios.* Austin: University of Texas Press, 2010.

Brasseaux, Ryan André. *Cajun Breakdown, The Emergence of an American-Made Music.* New York: Oxford University Press, 2009.

Broven, John. *South to Louisiana, The Music of the Cajun Bayous.* Gretna: Pelican Publishing Company, 1983.

Cobb, James C. "World War II and the Mind of the Modern South" in *Remaking Dixie: The Impact of World War II on the American South,* edited by Neil McMillen. Jackson: University of Mississippi Press, 1997, 3–20.

Comeaux, Malcolm L. "The Cajun Accordion." *Louisiana Review* 7 (1978): 117–128.

Conforti, Joseph A. *Imagining New England, Explorations of Regional Identity from the Pilgrims to the Mid-Twentieth Century.* Chapel Hill: The University of North Carolina Press, 2001.

Escott, Colin. *The Grand Ole Opry: The Making of an American Icon.* New York: Center Street, 2006.

Flynn, Ronald, Edwin Davison, and Edward Chavez. *The Golden Age of the Accordion.* Schertz: Flynn Publications, 1984.

François, Raymond E. *Yé Yaille, Chère!* Ville Platte: Swallow Publications, 1990.

Gordon, Robert. *Can't Be Satisfied: The Life and Times of Muddy Waters.* New York: Back Bay Books, 2002.

Havighurst, Craig. *Air Castle of the South: WSM and the Making of Music City.* Urbana: University of Illinois Press, 2007.

Heppen, J. and D. Mesyanzihnov, "Political Geography and Regionalism in Louisiana: The Impact of the French Influence in the post-World War II Era." *Political Geography,* Vol. 22.5 (2003): 519–533.

Kurtz, Michael L. "deLesseps S. Morrison: Political Reformer." *Louisiana History: The Journal of the Louisiana Historical Association* Vol. 17.1 (Winter, 1976): 19–39.

Lomax, Alan, director. "American Patchwork: Cajun Country." Originally aired on PBS in 1991. DVD. 2006.

McMillen, Neil. "Fighting for What We Don't Have: How Mississippi's Black Veterans Remember World War II" in McMillen, 93–110.

Meche Kube, Robin. "Cajun Soldiers During WWII: Reflections on Louisiana's French Language and People." *Louisiana History, The Journal of the Louisiana Historical Association* 35.3 (Summer 1994): 345–349.

Meckiffe, Donald and Matthew Murray, "Radio and the black soldier during World War II." *Critical Studies in Mass Communication* 15.4 (1998): 337–356.

Mire, Pat, director. *"Mon Cher Camarade."* Directed by Pat Mire. Lafayette, Louisiana: Pat Mire Films, 2009. DVD.

Murphy, Gareth. *Cowboys and Indies, The Epic History of the Record Industry.* New York: Thomas Dunne Books, 2014.

Reed, Revon. *Lâche Pas La Patate: Portrait des Acadiens de la Louisiane.* Montreal: Éditions Parti pris, 1976.

———. "Nathan Abshire: The Great Cajun Accordionist." CDCHD 401 Ace Records, 1992, compact disc. Originally released in 1973. Liner notes.

Savoy, Ann Allen. *Cajun Music: A Reflection of a People.* Vol. 1. Eunice: Bluebird Press, 1984.

———."Iry LeJeune, The Definitive Collection." Ace Records CDCHD 428, 1994, compact disc. Liner notes.

Sexton, Rocky L. "Cajun Mardi Gras: Cultural Objectification and Symbolic Appropriation in a French Tradition." *Ethnology* Vo. 38, No. 4 (Autumn, 1999): 297–313.

Sitkoff, Howard. "African American Militancy in the World War II South" in McMillen, 70–92.

Sosna, Morton. "Introduction" in McMillen, xiii–xix.

Strachwitz, Chris. "Cajun Music on LP – A Survey." In *The American Folk Music Occasional,* ed. Chris Strachwitz and Paul Welding. New York: Oak Publications 1970.

———. *"J'ai Été Au Bal,* The Cajun and Zydeco Music of Louisiana," Vol. 2, Arhoolie Records, CD 332, 1993, compact disc. Liner notes.

The *Méridonial* (Abbeville), October 8, 1881.

Times-Picayune (New Orleans), January 1941–September 1944.

Tisserand, Michael. *The Kingdom of Zydeco.* New York: Avon Books, 1998.

Trépanier, Cécyle. "The Cajunization of French Louisiana: forging a regional identity." *The Geographical Journal* 157.2. (July 1991): 161–171.

Young, William H., and Nancy K. Young, *Music of the World War II Era.* Santa Barbara: Greenwood Publishing, 2007.

CHAPTER 4

"It's All French Music": Patrons on the Trail

The work being done at Fred's Lounge to preserve and promote the French-language music of Southwest Louisiana came at a time when academic and governmental interests were focused on discovering, preserving, and promoting the art and music of regional cultures. The work of intellectuals and the interests of community culture boosters came together in an ongoing conversation over three decades in which federal folklorists like Alan Lomax and Ralph Rinzler were collecting music to serve the culture interests of the nation, while academic music collectors like Harry Oster and commercial collectors like Chris Strachwitz went over the same ground in the interests of the state, the university, and the record label. Government musicologists, record label executives, and folklore academics had very different ideas about the relationship between folk music, identity, and the larger culture. Musicologist Charles Seeger, who described folk music as "a defensive weapon on the [wartime] home front" because of its status as pure Americana[1] believed that folk music, with its narratives about the lives of ordinary impoverished Americans, could inspire economic and social reform. Academic folklorist Harry Oster, one in a long line of college literature professors-turned-collectors, was part of a

---

Creole musician Danny Poullard, quoted in *Acadiana: Louisiana's Historic Cajun Country*, Carl A. Brasseaux (Baton Rouge: Louisiana State University Press, 2011), 161. Poullard was often asked about the differences between Cajun and Creole music. This was his (exasperated) response.

© The Author(s) 2019
P. Peknik, *French Louisiana Music and Its Patrons*,
https://doi.org/10.1007/978-3-319-97424-8_4

generation of scholars keen on professionalizing folklore studies. Universities had been building their folklore programs throughout the 1920s and 1930s, offering folklore courses in their music, literature, anthropology, and sociology departments. Independent record label owner Chris Strachwitz wanted to record and market to northeastern and west coast urban consumers music that he thought of as the last authentic old-time Southern music. But local activists did not, of course, conceive of their work as the preservation of folklore, nor did they conceive of musicians as folk or the French language as an exotic cultural artifact. They returned from World War II believing, as the federal government would declare three decades later in the American Folklife Preservation Act, that they simply had a right, as did all Americans, to preserve the distinctive "ways" of their family, ethnic group and region,[2] the good time ways of French Louisiana culture.

In Evangeline Parish, those ways had always meant music, dancing, cooking and Mardi Gras. In Mamou, as in other rural communities, the war had taken some of that away, but as soldiers returned, married, and started families, the population of Mamou doubled, from 1379 in 1943 to 2254 by 1953, and once again young couples went out to dance halls like Piersall's Cocktail Parlor, bringing their young children with them. Mamou, with its lucrative rice and cotton farming, was a fairly prosperous community by Evangeline Parish standards; Mayor J. Classie Duplechin told a New Orleans *Times-Picayune* journalist that the number of pick-up trucks lining 6th Street, the main thoroughfare, was evidence of prosperity in a parish in which horse and buggy remained a common mode of transportation.

Wednesday night was the big night out for older couples at Vidrine's, where the most requested song was a new version of the French Louisiana waltz "Big Mamou." Doxie Manual, an old-time fiddler in Mamou, recalled at mid-century having heard the old-time version of the song as far back as 1895, and having played it at many *fais do dos* as a "sad, very sad waltz with no words."[3] In the two main variations in the lyrical storyline, someone, either a two-timed boyfriend or a disloyal girlfriend, is coming or going to Mamou, either setting out to live there in a state of brokenheartedness or getting left behind there. The song had been "sung, hummed and fiddled" in Mamou dance halls, on farms, and in homes for decades before country pop versions were recorded. In 1953, Link Davis recorded a new version of the song, and according to a June 1953 *Times-Picayune* story about Mamou, every week, local dancers in one of the community's seven bars dropped 6500 nickels in one of the town's eleven jukeboxes to hear it. Revon Reed described Mamou as "a town that had been hit hard by a hit song."[4]

Reed returned to his native Mamou in 1946 after serving as a stevedore officer in World War II. Long before the war, he had left Mamou for Lafayette, where he taught at a Catholic school after receiving a graduate degree from Boston University, but while stationed in Okinawa with fellow Mamou native Pascal Fuselier, he decided he would move back to Mamou, where the bonds between extended family members—the Fontenots, the Landreneaus, the Soileaus, the Ardoins, the Deshotels—were strengthened by wartime service, and by the combat deaths and grief of many Southwest Louisiana families from Ville Platte to Eunice and Breaux Bridge. The names Ardoin, Fontenot, LeJeune, and Breaux filled the rosters of the war dead.

Reed worked as a part-time insurance salesman to supplement his teaching salary, but gave up that job to devote himself, as head of the local Rotary club's "Big Mamou" committee, to promoting Mamou as a great place to live.

Reed and Paul Tate, on the other hand, weren't joining the cultural mood of nationalism but rather participating in a small-town civic boosterism that looked back to their home region's very different origins. The latter had served as an Army Tech Sergeant in the war, and explained what his motivations for boosting the region had been in a February 1, 1974 letter to the Tourist Development Commission in Baton Rouge: "My efforts in the field of Acadian Music have not been and are not now primarily concerned with tourism (nor music for that matter)." Tate was focused on the preservation and development of Southwest Louisiana cultural traditions, and on resisting "the attitude of early Anglo-Saxon intruders (principally roughnecks from Texas and Oklahoma) towards our people, our culture, and our music." Traditional music was important because "the reality of Acadian culture is reflected most obviously by its sounds, of which music is primary and the spoken word is secondary," he wrote, and "the technical skill of the individual musician is of far less importance than the authenticity of the music he plays."[5]

Veterans took a leadership role in the post-war Mamou community: Jack Tate became the elementary school principal, Calvin Landreneau became mayor, and Matthew Guillory returned home and opened the town's first movie theater, the Joy Theater.[6] And Fred Tate, who had purchased "Tate's Bar" on Sixth Street with his twin brother Alphan and a friend named Dudley Rozas, bought out his partners, renamed the bar Fred's Lounge, and decided, along with Paul Tate and Revon Reed, to make Mamou the center of French heritage folkways in Evangeline Parish. That heritage meant not only old-time music but the Mardi Gras *courir* and *tournoi* that had been centuries-old festival practices among Cajuns and Creoles, traditions that had disappeared during the war.

Each year, to mark the arrival of Lent, farmers, sharecroppers, oil indus-try workers and shop owners had gathered in the town center to mask and costume themselves as peasants, clowns, and women for the annual *courir de Mardi Gras*, or run. Men ages eighteen to seventy-five would gather at seven o'clock in the morning and ride on horseback or in covered wagons a thirty to forty mile course around the prairie of Mamou, stopping at farm houses so the uncostumed "captain" of the *courir*—a role assigned to a highly respected townsman (in Mamou, Paul Tate served as captain)— could ask for ingredients for the communal gumbo that would be made that evening: "*Une petit poule maigre, un sac de riz, un ou deux pieds de saucisses, or quelque cinq-sous.*"[7] ["A skinny little chicken, a bag of rice, the heel end or two of a piece of a sausage, or five sous."] Begging quests— *faire courir carnaval*—had been part of rural tradition in parts of nineteenth-century France,[8] and riders expected entrance into the house-hold. In the Cajun version, *courir* participants, linking arms as they approached the house, would congregate in the front yard and sing a Mardi Gras song in their ragged and outrageous clothing, grotesque masks, and pointed *capuchon* hats with bells and streamers. Donations were expected in exchange for the singing, dancing and comedic carry-ings-on of the assembled *courir* troupe, and intoxicated and rowdy revel-ers were likely to enforce that expectation. Likewise, a seventeenth-century description of a begging quest in France documents the way that "over-zealous" celebrants made their requests in a manner that bordered on extortion. The ritual of begging and donating made a social event out of the harsh necessities of economic interdependence. The *courir* was thus a theatrical expression of communal interrelationships in a culture in which subsistence "lived and died by reciprocity."[9]

There was much beer drinking and eating of "*boudin chaud*" (blood sausage, a Cajun speciality) along the route, and at day's end, the *courir* arrived in procession on the main street of Mamou, followed by a street dance, the singing of Mardi Gras songs, and the cooking of the gumbo in large iron pots. A masked ball at a dance hall followed, and then midnight Mass was held in the town church to usher in the first day of Lent. The *courir* was common to both Cajun and Creole traditions, and in both cases, participants used the event as a way to anonymously settle old scores or grievances or to remind social outliers about the consequences of defying social mores. In the Creole *courir*, the riders might playfully "rough up" or scare "community miscreants" or "perpetual drunks" encountered along the route, while in the Cajun *courir*, the whip-wielding captain would eject from the festivities any participant who violated the expectations for cooperation and comportment.[10] The structure and style of the Cajun and Creole *courir* were fundamentally similar, and in both, the event was a rite of passage for aspiring musicians, who would play fiddle and accordion for the householders in an attempt to demonstrate that they were preparing for the time when they would be recognized as competent performers in the community.[11]

Mamou, like most rural towns, had suspended Cajun Mardi Gras first during the Civil War, then during World War I, and again during World War II because there weren't enough men left in town to carry on the tradition. No military parade for returning veterans could have felt as much like a homecoming for Southwest Louisiana soldiers as the *courir*: all across the landscape, on the vast prairie where the horizon receded far beyond the sugarcane fields, men in homemade costumes rode past the massive oak trees draped with Spanish moss, down narrow dirt roads that cut through rice fields, drinking and reveling under the late winter Louisiana sun.

Creole Mardi Gras *courir* ran in an uninterrupted fashion from the time of settlement in the eighteenth century, and was not suspended during wartime because the US military quota for the number of black Americans who could serve in the armed forces kept Creole men back home in their rural communities. Creole revelers, unlike their Cajun counterparts, had also never found their festival traditions scrutinized under the 1926 Louisiana law that banned the wearing of masks outside of religious or cultural events "in any open place in view," a law aimed specifically at members of the Ku Klux Klan. The Creole participants in L'Anse de Prien Noir, a rural community founded in the mid-eighteenth century by Cyprien Ceazer, a free man of color of Spanish, French, Native American and African descent, dressed as clowns, devils, beggars and women, wearing the same pointed hats, decorated with the diamond pattern of medieval French harlequins, as the Cajun revelers wore, although many more participants were on foot because fewer could afford to own horses.

The fact that both Cajun and Creole communities celebrated Mardi Gras and valued traditional French Louisiana cultural practices is not to say that such celebrations were co-equivalent in meaning across communities or that categories of racial identification and tension disappeared into the pageantry. Scholars continue to debate the racial dynamics and symbolism of mid-twentieth-century rural Mardi Gras, with some folklore scholarship positing mutual respect and commonalities between Cajun and Creole revelers, and other more recent work by anthropologists and ethnographers pointing out the ways in which Mardi Gras provided a theatrical staging area for the performance of race. Inviting particular scrutiny is the fact that among the clowns and comical masked figures of Cajun Mardi Gras, characters in blackface called *le nègre* and *la négresse* emerged in the post-war Mardi Gras of Tee Mamou on lower Mamou Prairie. Scholars studying the history of Mardi Gras masking and disguise traditions in Southwest Louisiana and New Orleans Mardi Gras confront a wealth of imagery, from Cajun carnival goers running *courir* in blackface on Mamou Prairie and Creole carnival runners wearing clownish white face paint or Ku Klux Klan outfits, to black New Orleanians elaborately costumed as Mardi Gras Indians. In his famous homecoming to the New Orleans Mardi Gras in 1949, Louis Armstrong donned blackface as the Zulu King on the Zulu Social Aid and Pleasure Club float. Racial politics and the history and psychology of group identity formation are complex, contested topics in French Louisiana. According to Nicholas Spitzer, Mardi Gras run is "used by rural Creoles to address cultural and social similarities and differences with Cajuns" and to emphasize Creole "aesthetics, identities, values, behaviors" and social networks. He quotes one reveler's description of the freedom and agency experienced through masking: "Mardi Gras is *libre*. Nobody can tell you shit for Mardi Gras, white, black, nothing....That's a free day you got." Spitzer's description of the sociopolitical significance of the festival illustrates the high stakes and analytical difficulties in any discussion of masking traditions: "If Creole Mardi Gras is a time of relative integration (e.g. visits to Cajun homes, Cajuns and other whites following the band, and attending the supper and dance), it is also a time of segregation, with the history of the social barriers heightened in the minds of some (e.g. separate bands...)."[12]

The objective of the discussion at hand is to point out that Mardi Gras was a cultural practice common to both Cajun and Creoles and to emphasize that although the Cajun and Creole Mardi Gras runs were separate events, the bands would sometimes visit the same households, and Creole bands made a point of visiting the homes of "crucial Cajun figures" in their mixed communities, including store owners and priests. Cajuns would be invited to the Creole gumbo dinner at day's end, and ideally, the *courir* heightened "a sense of inclusion in the Cajun/Creole community"[13] whose traditions descended from a shared Francophone heritage.

It was this Francophone cultural heritage that Fred Tate, Paul Tate and Revon Reed wanted to reassert after the war, and thus the plaque attached to the brick front of Fred's Lounge also reads "In 1950 *Courir de Mardi Gras* was revived at Fred's Lounge." Wanting the community to focus on the pageantry and symbolism of Mardi Gras, Paul Tate and Revon Reed put rules and checks in place to prevent the Mamou Mardi Gras run from becoming too rowdy and hedonistic. These rules served as models for other local communities that were inspired to revive the traditional *courir*,[14] including Church Point, Ville Platte, and Eunice, where participants gathered in front of the National Guard Armory in 1946 to depart for the ride. The *courir* may also have seemed, for returning soldiers, like a paramilitary exercise, with "troops" massing in front of the captain and the entire crew riding into neighboring towns in a posture of rivalry and triumph, returning home to share the spoils with the assembled community.

The *tournoi*, a Mardi Gras version of a medieval French jousting tournament designed to train men for cavalry combat, reappeared in the postwar era as well, reestablished in Ville Platte by members of the American Legion and Veterans of Foreign War posts. Said to have been introduced to Southwest Louisiana by Marcellin Garand, an officer in Napoleon's army and the founder of Ville Platte, the *tournoi* had been played in Ville Platte by the eighteenth-century settlers of the town, and had been the predominant source of entertainment until the arrival of baseball and horseracing. Nineteenth-century participants had dressed as knights and masked their faces; twentieth-century competitors rode a quarter-mile track trying to lance rings suspended from posts along the route. The town of Sète in the south of France is still renowned for its annual *tournoi*, a ritualized display of combat reminiscent of the running of the bulls.

Veterans held the first revival *tournoi* on July 4, 1948, and in anticipation of the first tournament of the twentieth century, the *Times-Picayune* in New Orleans ran a story with the headline "Ville Platte Revives the Sport of Knights," featuring a photo of 74-year-old Jules Tate on horseback passing a lance through an iron ring hanging from a post. Tate, born in the 1870s in Evangeline, had won his first tournament at 19. Most of the contestants were World War II veterans, and rather than wielding lances and charging either other as French medieval riders had done, the veterans battled the seven deadly enemies of the cotton crop by attempting to capture a series of seven rings that represented the environmental foes of cotton—flood, drought, the boll weevil and the bollworm—and the market enemies of cotton in the industrial age: silk, rayon and nylon.

Some veterans, perhaps nostalgic for the drama and action of war, may have embraced the *tournoi* as a war game, and *courir* planning was customarily done at a local bar, giving veterans another reason, and location, to assemble.[15] Other revivalists, like J.D. Buller, whose son Sergeant Wilton Bernie Buller, First Gunner, was killed in action in World War II,[16] may have conceived of the Cajun *tournoi* as reminiscent of an earlier historical moment before combine harvesters filled the rice fields and Anglo-Protestants moved into Southwest Louisiana to work in agribusiness and oil. Veterans founded the Ville Platte Cotton Festival in 1953 to provide a venue and occasion for an annual grand *tournoi*, which, like the *courir*, combined the spirits of revelry and rivalry. *Courir* and *tournoi* events were, in the period between 1946 and 1961, reestablished in a number of Acadian parish towns, and returning veterans took up the cause on the airwaves, bringing French-language talk radio and news programming to the parishes. Bertrand DeBlanc, returning to Lafayette after three years in the US Army Signal Corps, used his training in military communications networks to begin broadcasting a daily French-language news program over KVOL in 1948. Dudley Bernard, who had served as a French interpreter in North Africa and southern France, returned to Louisiana after five years to work as a French announcer and disc jockey on KLFT in Golden Meadow. The host of Jennings's KJEF "*Allons Danser*" show, Jerry Dugas, reported an exasperating number of requests demanding "that the same French recordings be played time and time again."[17] Lee Lavergne of Lanor Records in Church Point remembered that it was French-language music that dominated local radio in the post-war years: "People started getting radios. You'd hear some country music, there wasn't all that much. And then after a while there started being some Cajun bands that started broadcasting. I'm talking about somewhere around 1947 .... And they started promoting local talent, like Nathan Abshire was coming in."[18] Cajun fiddler Dewey Balfa was playing dances every night of the week and broadcasting over KSLO Opelousas. Soldiers were returning to Acadiana with money, and they wanted to hear old-time music.[19]

It was the enduring popularity of traditional French-language music, and the reemergence of French cultural traditions, that attracted the attention of folklorist Harry Oster when he began teaching in the English Department at Louisiana State University in Baton Rouge in 1955. Oster, the son of Russian-Polish parents who had immigrated to Cambridge, Massachusetts, gave a well-appreciated lecture and concert at Louisiana State on the work of the nineteenth-century folk music collector Francis James Child, an early and influential collector of English and Scottish ballads. Child, a Shakespearean scholar whose home base was Harvard, had collected, analyzed and published every ballad and known variant of every Anglo-Scotch ballad he could find, and his meticulously compiled *The English and Scottish Popular Ballads* became the foundational text in music folklore scholarship. Oster's presentation on Child's work prompted the state of Louisiana to sponsor fieldwork, to be conducted by Oster, in which the folk music of Louisiana would be documented and recorded.

On this music hunting trip, Oster found "a profusion of unusual material" that constituted "an abundance of riches—ancient French ballads, some of them sung by blacks; Cajun dance music as well as a Mass over dead (empty) bottles, Afro-Cajun blues; Afro-French spirituals; a survival of a West African shout ceremony." Oster was especially drawn to what he called "the Negro French *cantique*," a song form analogous to the Protestant "Negro spiritual," probably taught by Catholic priests to Creole parishioners. He was fascinated by the parallels between nineteenth-century religious songs collected in France and the twentieth-century songs he heard sung in Louisiana.[20] Oster's interests ran from the sacred to the vernacular and the historical, and he sought to document each song's provenance and antiquity, collecting songs that were popular "in the Paris of the Revolution and in the Empire," songs known in French-speaking Canada, and songs brought to Louisiana by enslaved people from the Antilles and Santo Domingo.[21]

In 1958, Oster produced "Folksongs of the Louisiana Acadians," featuring music recorded in Mamou. With no real understanding of the production process, Oster undertook a project of "record production as a kind of folk craft," using an eighteenth-century lithograph process in which a stone was hand-cranked onto paper to produce the album jacket art. The design on the lithograph stone melted in the Louisiana heat and humidity. In his liner notes for the album, Oster describes a prairie culture in which the nineteenth-century construction of roads, along with twentieth-century television's "mass-produced, homogenous entertainment" had exposed a French-speaking population to modernized Anglo-Protestant systems and values, and threatened, he insisted, the "old folk dances and songs."

Oster stated, with no elaboration, that the return of World War II soldiers after years living elsewhere was "upsetting the ancient ways," as if the now-worldly soldiers were transmitters of modern international culture, and lamented that the disappearance of French Louisiana music constituted a case study in "the modification of a minority culture." Despite this conclusion, Oster quickly thereafter attested to the enduring and vital role of the *fais do do* dances featuring accordion and fiddle music, and on the "hilarity and exuberance" of the family-attended gatherings in which all danced to traditional fiddle and accordion music, including "*La Dance de Mardi Gras*" and "*Contredanse Française*." Oster's descriptions of the musicians he recorded reveal much about his conception of the "Cajun folk." He describes Cyprien Landreneau as a big man full of *joie de vivre*, "father of a typically large Louisiana French family of eleven children" and the head of a household in which "almost every weekend there is a family party … enlivened by an ephemeral case of whiskey. The whole family joins in the furiously spirited dancing." The jovial Arcemus Dupre "spontaneously bursts into song"—songs sung by "lively carousers," in which "love, liquor and food are given strong emphasis" because, Oster wrote, "the typical Cajun has no inclination to sing about the supernatural": "When a Cajun's woman has run off with someone else and the bottle is empty, he sings of his sadness… [tunes that have been] "sung, hummed and fiddled in dance halls, on farms and in homes for as long as anyone around Mamou can remember," Oster explains in the liner notes. Cajun women are, like the guitarist Mrs. Rodney Fruge, built "of matronly proportions" and the men have physiques "like a bull." "Of course," Oster wrote, "no collection representative of Mamou would be complete without a drinking song." Oster returned to Mamou many times over the next two decades, riding in the Mardi Gras celebration beside Paul Tate and accompanying Ralph Rinzler on some of this field recordings. Oster made the observation that it was only the monolingual French-speaking older generation who "still sing songs of early France," songs that had been handed down from grandparents and parents, and that only the older musicians still played in a "pure folk style characteristic of the country fiddling of the nineteenth century and earlier,"[22] yet in his descriptions of dance hall culture, as well as in his depiction of Mardi Gras, it is clear that he understands both as cross-generational social celebrations in which teenagers participated as a rite of passage.

Oster's key interest was the survival of French folk music in the New World, and in May 1958, he received a grant from Louisiana State University to study French folk songs in Quebec and Ottawa. Although Oster's mission was to trace the songs of Acadiana back to the Canadian provinces, later folklorists found that Canadian and Louisianan folk music had little in common beyond the language of the lyrics because of the strong contribution made by Creole musicians to "Cajun" music: "The percussive improvisational African influence especially sets Cajun music stylistically so far apart from its Acadian and Quebecois counterparts that comparisons have not been tempting."[23]

Oster didn't understand, or didn't wish to highlight, this "improvisational African influence," and in his liner notes to the album, he ignores the Creole-Cajun collaborations that drove the development of French Louisiana music. Importantly, although the Oster recordings include the Afro-Caribbean "Colinda," along with a song called "*Tu peux cogner mais tu peux pas rentrer*" [You Can Keep on Knockin' But You Can't Come In],[24] a song that most likely had its origins in the red light district of early New Orleans, as well as "*La danse de Mardi Gras*," which is sung with minor variations by both Cajuns and Creoles, Oster titles this collection "Folksongs of the Louisiana Acadians," and not, as the musicians themselves called it, "*musique française*," French music, or even "Cajun-Creole Songs" or "Creole-Cajun Music." Ignoring the way the musicians themselves conceived of the music, Oster insisted on the category "Cajun folksong." Genre existed in the eye of the beholder: Irene Whitfield Holmes's 1939 study of Cajun-Creole folk music was titled *Louisiana French Folk Songs*, while Irene Petitjean's 1930 Columbia University graduate thesis had been titled "Cajun Folk Songs of Southwestern Louisiana," imputing proprietorship to white, not black, musicians. Folklorist Alan Lomax titled his 1934–1937 recordings from Southwest Louisiana "Cajun and Creole Music."

Traveling in the Lake Charles and Jennings area during the Depression, Lomax had made the first recordings of Creole *juré* music (which Lomax called "ring shouts"). Although some of the songs Lomax recorded in Acadia in the 1930s were old enough that they could have originated in medieval France and then made their way to Nova Scotia in the sixteenth century, and then to Louisiana in the eighteenth, most of the French-language songs sung by Cajun and Creole musicians on the Lomax recordings have a complex and mixed provenance, some written in continental France long after the Acadians arrived in Louisiana[25]—evidence that musicians in Southwest Louisiana constantly absorbed and adapted newly introduced French-language songs rather than simply working from a repertoire that was inherited, memorized, transmitted whole cloth, frozen in time. Thus the fact that the songs are sung in French by musicians living in Southwest Louisiana is what constitutes them as a genre, whether those songs were written by or adapted by Creole or Cajun musicians.

For Lomax, the crucial designator was the word "folk": he was drawn to the self-taught, or family-taught, musicians who were known only in their own immediate communities, or who traveled the same ground to play in small venues. The distinction between professional, commercial musicians and amateur folk musicians mattered more to Lomax than racially determined genre categories like "Cajun" and Creole"; in a letter to his father, he refers to the "remarkable Negro Cajun songs" he'd heard sung by Joseph Johns and Cleveland Benoit in Jennings.[26]

Lomax's field work in Louisiana captured the attention of the *Times-Picayune* in New Orleans, which featured a story headlined "Music of Cajuns Termed Untapped State Resource": "To date, [Louisiana] has failed to either develop or conserve one of the richest heritages of her glamorous past—the unplumbed mine of folk music and culture in her Cajun country. This is the opinion of Alan Lomax, assistant in the Library of Congress' music division..."[27]

Lomax was after the non-commercial "home music"—the older, unaccompanied, unamplified sound that had not attracted the attention of record labels and that Lomax feared was "being smothered by the urbanized, orchestrated sound" blasting from radios.[28] He went to dramatic lengths to record musicians in their own time and place, preferring to sacrifice sound quality for the "authenticity" of on-the-spot recording, which, for Lomax, did not preclude a stage-managed authenticity: after Cajun ballad singers Lennis Vincent and Sidney Richard stopped off at a bar while riding a borrowed horse to church, Lomax persuaded them to record in a loading chute at one of the local rice mills.[29]

Volume 1 of the Lomax recordings includes "Cajun Waltz" and "Creole Blues," and these pairings might have been instructive to Harry Oster, for the fact that songs in the French Louisiana traditions are variously titled "Blues" or "Waltz" is evidence of a shared tradition: Creole musician Alphonse "Bois Sec" Ardoin's "*Valse de Opelousas*"/Opelousas Waltz; Cajun musician Nathan Abshire's rendition of "Pine Grove Blues"; Creole fiddler Canray

Fontenot's "*La valse de mom et pop*" and Douglas Bellard's "*La valse de la prison*"; Cajun musician Amedee Breaux's "Tiger Rag Blues." But in his liner notes to "Folksongs of the Louisiana Acadians," Oster never mentions Creole musicians or the shared music tradition that created the folksongs he wished to preserve.

A year earlier, Oster had produced "A Sampler of Louisiana Folksongs: Negro, Negro French, Cajun, Old French, and Anglo-Saxon," on which he had established his categories: "Negro French" music included religious songs inspired by the Catholic hymn tradition, whereas "Cajun" songs were danceable polkas and two-steps about Mardi Gras. In 1959, Oster produced "Louisiana Folksong Jambalaya," singing traditional French Louisiana songs himself. Oster believed that collecting was "both an art and an addiction," and that it was important for folklorists to build an intense rapport with informants by themselves performing, and sustaining an atmosphere in which the musician would "play and sing naturally and enthusiastically."[30] Oster had located the musicians through his friendship with Sarah Gertrude Knott, who had organized the Louisiana Folk Festival in 1955 in southwestern Louisiana. Knott introduced Oster to Paul Tate and Revon Reed, who explained that they were eager to perpetuate the French traditions of their town, urging Oster to record in Mamou. Oster returned to Mamou many weekends, often, he said, just letting the tape recorder run while he danced with the locals at *fais do dos*.

Following Lomax's trail, Oster went on to record prison work songs at Angola, a project for which he became esteemed as a popularizer of the blues. He had worried that work songs were being eliminated by the grinding metal noise and deafening motors of industrial machinery like cotton pickers and cane cutters. Largely as a result of the success of Angola Prison Blues (1959) and Angola Prison Spirituals (1958), his recordings of New Orleans jazz and what he called "bayou bluegrass," in 1960 Oster received a Guggenheim fellowship.

In 1970, Chris Strachwitz of the one-man record label Arhoolie in Berkeley, California, bought all of Oster's field recordings. Strachwitz became a passionate commercial recorder and promoter of traditional, regional, and ethnic music. Thus Oster's collection, second only to Lomax's, became one of the founding compilations of French Louisiana music. Oster had enacted a perfect model of categorization and exclusion over the course of his three albums: first, he established the category "Acadian folksong" as a separate tradition from both "Old French" music in the New World, and from "Negro French" music; then, rather than further recording local musicians, Oster became the performer of the music, not acknowledging in his notes that the music had innovators, writers, and performers from both European and African traditions. But the old-time Southwest Louisiana music Oster collected was exactly like the "Jambalaya" in the title of his third album: although parts could be traced back to Europe, Africa, and the Americas, the whole could never be called simply African-derived or European-influenced. Likewise, although the spicy Louisiana rice and meat dish "jambalaya" has been variously described as developing primarily from a Catalan, Provençal, Congolese, Dominican, Native American or African cuisine, it becomes apparent through a study of New Orleans cookbooks, books on the plants of West tropical Africa, the immigration history of the French Huguenots to the Carolinas, the Occitan language, and the nineteenth-century poetry of southern France, that while both Cajuns and Creoles have a long-held belief that "jambalaya is their dish," it belongs collectively to all the groups whose ingredients and culinary styles contributed to its creation—meaning French, Spanish, African, American and American Indian: "Depending on where any individual learned the recipe, they would have different folk stories to support their ideas of its origins ... Many would have no particular name for it at all, simply referring to it as the dish mama always made.... [Africans] would point to the long history of rice cultivation on the West African coast ... Cajuns might then tell you with equal assurance that they invented it to use the rice they found when they arrived in their *Nouvelle Acadie*."[31]

Beyond the work of academic folklorist Oster, talented Creole musicians went unrecorded in the war and post-war years. "Race record" labels like Queen and Apollo recorded gospel and rhythm and blues, and in 1942, *Billboard* introduced the first chart of black music, Harlem Hit Parade, but there was no national African-American audience for French-language Creole music. The fact that labels weren't soliciting records by Creole musicians didn't reflect local attitudes about race, as Creole accordionist "Bois Sec" Ardoin continued to be a revered figure in old-time music, performing for black and white audiences alike. There were social boundaries between whites from different communities and between blacks from different communities, Ardoin recalled, just as there were boundaries between blacks and whites, but a common musical tradition and a common mother tongue softened the edges, if not entirely, Ardoin explained: "Back then, you stayed in your own neighborhood ... If young people from around here went to Mamou to court girls, there was always trouble. You just couldn't do that." Ardoin described the initial tension between the "lighter-skinned" residents of one neighboring community and the inhabitants of the town where he lived, a tension that could be diffused through the experience of music: "They didn't want to mix with us. They were mulattoes. We couldn't go to their dances … it was just like trying to go to a white dance in those days. Then, once they started going out of their own community to other dances, they saw that they didn't know how to dance. So in order to have a good time, by and by they started going out with us. Then, later, once we really started to have a good time together, we all became brothers and sisters."[32]

Ardoin, Amédé Ardoin's cousin, recalled the many talented Creole musicians who never recorded and who died without ever being known. Accordionist Adam Fontenot, a cotton and corn farmer in l'Anse des Rougeaux near Mamou, had played with Amédé Ardoin, and Fontenot's music was so appreciated that "any person in the black race or the white race, they heard of him," his son, fiddler Canray Fontenot said.[33] But Adam Fontenot, like Nathan Abshire, didn't want to be remembered through his recorded music: "You see, black and white alike would come home all the time to meet my late father …. People came several times to get my father to record. 'No,' he would say, 'when a person is dead, he is supposed to be gone. You're not supposed to hear him on records. When I die, I want to be finished.' And he never did make a record. But he sure could play."[34]

Although in the post-war years talented Creole fiddlers and accordionists were either ignored by labels or didn't aspire to being recording artists, Nathan Abshire and Iry LeJeune, by reintroducing the accordion into traditional French-language music, paved the way for a contemporary accordion-based music, zydeco, to develop among Creole Louisianans who had migrated to the industrial towns of Houston, Galveston and Port Arthur, Texas. Younger Creole musicians began experimenting with rhythm and blues and rock music using the accordion, imitating the highly amplified blues sound they heard on records and on the radio, and this new urban sound would come to eclipse the popularity, among the younger generation, of the waltz and ballad-based old-time Creole repertoire. Bill Quinn's Gold Star Records again played a key role in the story. In the wake of his success with Harry Choates's recording of "*Jole Blon*," in 1949 Quinn began recording blues guitarist Sam "Lightnin'" Hopkins, who lived in the Third Ward neighborhood of Houston near Quinn's studio. Hopkins's

"Zolo Go," which he played on the organ in an attempt to imitate the sound of the accordion music popular among the French-speaking Creoles who lived in his neighborhood, was soon featured on Houston jukeboxes,[35] along with Louisiana guitarist Clarence Garlow's hit song "Bon Ton Roula" on the Macy's label. (Since Cajun French and Creole French were not written languages, many variations in spelling appear when even common phrases like "*laissez les bons temps rouler*" are transcribed; for example, the Bon Ton Roulet was a popular dance hall in World War II-era Lafayette.) Quinn, unaware of the music of the local subculture of Southwest Louisiana immigrants in Houston's French Town neighborhood,[36] wasn't even aware that the term "Zolo Go" was Hopkins's version of a term, zydeco, that had been used for decades by Southwest Louisiana Creoles to describe a fast-tempo accordion-based dance music and the dance hall parties at which it was played.

Hopkins's and Garlow's hit songs, by showcasing French-language music, lyrics and instrumentation, introduced accordion-based Louisiana music to a wider audience unfamiliar with French Louisiana music traditions. "Zydeco" was a word that had long been used by Creoles to describe a dance hall party and the old-time accordion music played there, and John and Alan Lomax had encountered the word on their fieldwork tour in 1934. The Lomaxes traveled some 32,000 miles in nine southern states and recorded about 600 songs, including, in Port Arthur, a song by the Creole singer Jimmy Peters. Peters performed in *juré* style a song whose lyrics date back to an old Acadian folksong. But Peters included the lyric "*O mam, mais donnez-moi les haricots. O yé yaie, les haricots sont pas salés.*" [Oh, mama, give me the snap beans/Oh (high-pitched cry), the snap beans aren't salty.] The interjection "*Oh yé yaie*" (or *Yé yaille!*) appears commonly in the lyrics of Cajun dance hall music, just as the lyric about snap beans without salt became the signature phrase of zydeco music. Cajun fiddler Dewey Balfa, in response to a question about the characteristic yell in Cajun singing, recalled a time when someone had asked singer Jimmy Newman the same question: "'Well,' he says, 'back in Louisiana, in the bayous, among the bayous and the woods, whenever you hear a yell like that,' he said, 'somebody yell back.' And he say, 'You can be sure that he's lost, too.' ...When you yell like that, you're just letting your heart out," Balfa explained.[37] Crying out loudly that the snap beans aren't salty is the zydeco musician's way of letting his heart out, serving as a catch-phrase for all sorts of lamentation and protest, including financial or romantic. The grievance phrase also appears in the lyric of a song sung by

Wilfred Charles in New Iberia: "*Pas mis de la viande, pas mis à rien/Juste des haricots dans la chaudière*"[38] ["There's no meat, there's no nothing/ just beans there in the pot."]

To Creole fiddler Canray Fontenot, the word "zydeco" was an old word for an old kind of music: "That's just a word.... The black people used to call a party "*un diverti.*" And the white people would call that "*une amusette.*" Then, when we was coming out in our prime, they started callin' that a "zydeco," because they had an old guy there that had a big house and a lot of children. And we'd go around there and he'd say, "We're gonna' have a zydeco at the house." We knew it was a dance. Then the blacks learned about it, zydeco here and zydeco there. And the whites had *fais do dos.*"[39]

Opelousas, Louisiana native Clifton Chenier, who grew up cutting sugarcane, began playing accordion in 1947, accompanied by his brother Cleveland on washboard, and because the older generation called a dance party a "zydeco," Chenier labeled his syncopated dance music zydeco. But in regards to his own style of urban rhythm-and-blues influenced music, Chenier used the word "zydeco" simply to mean music sung by Creoles in a band that included an accordion, even if there were few French words in the lyrics and the accordion was one of several amplified instruments rather than one of two or three unamplified instruments, as in the old Creole music of his childhood. That old French Louisiana music, as it was played by Creole musicians, with just an accordion, a fiddle, and a washboard, was remembered by Creole accordionist Sidney Babineaux as being older than even his nineteenth-century childhood. "That's been here since before I was born," Babineaux told Chris Strachwitz.[40] That old-time sound was exactly what Strachwitz was after.

The son of German immigrants, Strachwitz began a love affair with American music when he first listened to swing bands on Armed Forces Radio as a teenager living in the British zone of West Central Germany. His family had been removed from Silesia under the terms of the Potsdam Conference in August 1945, under which the Allies agreed that Silesia would be resettled with Poles in a territory to be administered by the Russians. This experience of a "massive evacuation," "one of the great social upheavals of recorded history," may account for Strachwitz's deeply felt sympathies with the Acadian "*Grand Dérangement*" that brought French-speaking Catholics to Louisiana after the French and Indian War and his particularly strong sympathy for people of African descent whose ancestors had been brought against their will to the New World.

When Strachwitz's family moved to the United States in 1947, to Nevada and then California, he tuned into Los Angeles stations playing New Orleans jazz and blues, Baptist church gospel music, and Bill Quinn's recordings of Lightnin' Hopkins. Radio, Strachwitz said, was "such a democratic system. As long as you had a dial, you had access to everything. There was nothing like the late 1940s and early 1950s for that."[41] Like Quinn, Strachwitz developed an interest in recording technology, and began playing around with rudimentary equipment, recording a blues musician working a shoeshine stand on the University of California at Berkeley campus where Strachwitz was a talented and restless student who majored in engineering, then physics, then political science, before being drafted into the US Army in 1954. Like the Cajun soldiers whose native language had gotten them stationed in France, the German-speaking Strachwitz was stationed in Austria and then Germany, and when he returned to Berkeley in 1956 and finished his education on the G.I. Bill, he got a job teaching high school German. Strachwitz spent evenings at the V.F.W. Post listening to jazz bands and going to nightclubs to hear rhythm and blues. On a summer road trip to Albuquerque, New Mexico in 1959, he took a detour to Houston in the hopes of meeting with Lightnin' Hopkins at Quinn's Gold Star studio. Inspired by Quinn's achievements with his one-man label, and by the heritage recording work of Moe Asch, Strachwitz bought new recording equipment with money he had made selling some of the thousands of vintage albums he had collected in the 1950s (he had once driven to Georgia and hauled back 4000 old jazz albums in a laundry truck) and set up his own label, Arhoolie Records, developing, over the decades that followed, a rich, extensive, varied catalog of Louisiana music. Quinn's studio would, over the long course of the two men's friendship, host a number of recording sessions for Strachwitz's label, including many with Clifton Chenier, who was Hopkins's cousin by marriage. Arhoolie would become one of the primary recorders of French Louisiana music and the primary re-issuers of the music of classic old-time musicians, including Améde Ardoin.

Strachwitz was fascinated and confounded the first time he listened to Ardoin's recordings. Hearing the accordion played by a French-speaking Southwest Louisiana musician, he assumed that Ardoin was "a white Acadian." "I never would have guessed that he was a Negro, and since he often was recorded in company with the white Acadian fiddler, Dennis McGee, I had assumed he was a white Acadian as well. It was not until Clifton Chenier told me that Ardoin 'was the first colored man to play the accordion' (on record, at least) that I was made aware of the true situation," Strachwitz explained in a 1970 article "Zydeco Music—i.e., French Blues" in *The American Folk Music Occasional*. Strachwitz realized that to understand what was being called "zydeco" music or "Negro-French" or "Negro Cajun" music, he would have to look "primarily at the evolution and development of Acadian (of 'Cajun') music in general."[42]

The fact that Strachwitz thought he had to find a way to distinguish music played by Cajuns from music played by Creoles, then had an epiphany about the deep connectedness of the music of black and white Louisiana musicians, would have brought a triumphant smile to the face of another old-time music collector, the eccentric and brilliant Harry Smith, whose "Anthology of American Folk Music," released in 1952, first introduced Strachwitz and a whole generation of folklorists and folk musicians to the music of Southwest Louisiana. It had been Smith's goal for listeners like Strachwitz to hear the songs of the French Louisiana music tradition as a pure expression of the spirit and legacy of a diverse democracy, and to hear all American folk music as neither black nor white, but as a communal artistic folk expression steeped in the strange, particular history of the American South. The folk-lyric form, as Greil Marcus explained in the liner notes to Smithsonian Folkways' 1997 reissue of Smith's compilation, came together in the South where there were "enough fragments, passing back and forth between Blacks and Whites as common coin, to generate more fragments, to sustain within the matrix of a single musical language an almost infinite repertory of performances, to sustain the sense that out of the anonymity of the tradition a singer was presenting a distinct and separate account of a unique life."[43]

The folk revival of the late 1950s and early 1960s, including the introduction of French Louisiana music to a national audience, is, fundamentally, the legacy of Smith, a record collector, experimental filmmaker, erudite visual artist and itinerant bum who believed that the true narrative of American national life could only really be told through the warped and scratched-up albums recorded in the down-and-out American past of the Southern poor. An anthropologist by training, Smith took a social scientist's approach to folk song as artifact, collecting, analyzing and arranging the most important old-time songs in American recording history into an anthology he hoped would compel listeners to reexamine their understanding of democracy, race, and art, and cause them to see that, despite the strange and alien-seeming voices of regional music and the unfamiliar ways of regional culture, Gunnar Myrdal had got it right in his 1944 *An American Dilemma: The Negro Problem and American Democracy*. Myrdal had argued that despite being a vast democracy of great cultural disparities, America had preserved its exceptional emphasis on the "essential dignity of the individual human being." Smith believed that folk song was a powerful expression of that dignity, and that while the "cacophony" of American life hadn't exactly become a "melody" inspired by the common national belief in liberal humanistic ideals, as Myrdal had put it,[44] the cacophony had at least become, in his view, a discordant, captivating, dissonant and intensely beautiful series of songs that had the power to inspire a new national narrative of a less divided and alienated American life.

Notes

1. Charles Seeger, quoted in Bendix, *In Search of Authenticity*, 151.
2. The American Folklife Preservation Act S.1591, March 20, 1969.
3. *Times-Picayune*, June 14, 1953, 37.
4. *Times-Picayune*, June 14, 1953.
5. Paul Tate, Letter to Gus Cranow, February 1, 1974. Ralph Rinzler Papers Fieldwork Box 4 Louisiana, Correspondence 1–3, Smithsonian Center for Folklife and Cultural Heritage, Washington, DC.
6. Richard Deshotels, personal correspondence with author.
7. Reed, *Lâche Pas*, 111.
8. Harry Oster, "*Une 'Tite Poule Grasse ou la Fille Ainée* (A Little Fat Chicken or The Eldest Daughter): A Comparative Analysis of Cajun and Creole Mardi Gras Songs," *Journal of American Folklore*, Volume 114, Number 452, Spring 2001, 205–206.
9. R. Brasseaux, *Cajun Breakdown*, 43.
10. Sexton, "Ritualized Inebriation," 31–32.
11. Nicholas Spitzer, "Zydeco and French Mardi Gras: Creole Identity and Performance Genres in Rural French Louisiana" (PhD diss., The University of Texas at Austin, 1986): 431.
12. Nicholas R. Spitzer, "Mardi Gras in L'Anse de 'Prien Noir: A Creole Community Performance in Rural French Louisiana" in *Creoles of Color, The Gulf South*, ed. James H. Dorman (Knoxville: University of Tennessee, 1996), 87–125.
13. Spitzer, "French Mardi Gras," 432.
14. Barry Jean Ancelet, "Mardi Gras and the Media: Who's Fooling Whom?" in *Mardi Gras, Gumbo, and Zydeco: Readings in Louisiana Culture*, ed. Marcia G. Gaudet et al (Jackson: University Press of Mississippi, 2003), 4.
15. "Folksongs of the Louisiana Acadians," liner notes, 16.
16. World War II Honor List, Louisiana, 1946, National Archives 305293.
17. R. Brasseaux, *Cajun Breakdown*, 190–191.

18. Broven, *South to Louisiana*, 267.
19. Cheryl Brauner, "A Study of the Newport Folk Festival and the Newport Folk Foundation" (M.A. thesis, Memorial University of Newfoundland, 1986): 270.
20. Harry Oster, "Negro French Spirituals of Louisiana," *Journal of the International Folk Music Council*, Vol. 4 (1962): 166.
21. "Folksongs of the Louisiana Acadians," liner notes, 2.
22. "Folksongs of the Louisiana Acadians," liner notes.
23. Barry Jean Ancelet, "Lomax in Louisiana: Trials and Triumph," *Folklife in Louisiana*, http://www.louisianafolklife.org/.
24. Most famously covered by Little Richard in 1957.
25. Joshua Clegg Caffery's *Traditional Music in Coastal Louisiana: The 1934 Lomax Recordings* (Baton Rouge: Louisiana State University Press, 2013) provides a comprehensive and learned account of the Lomax's Louisiana recordings, including Alsatian ballads sung by the Hoffpauirs, whose ancestors were from the border of northeastern France and Germany, and a number of songs that also existed in the French-Canadian Maritime provinces. See also Joshua Caffery, Folklife Lecture on Louisiana Music, Library of Congress, Washington, DC, December 11, 2013.
26. Cohen, Alan Lomax, *Assistant in Charge*, 253.
27. *Times-Picayune*, April 17, 1938, 32.
28. Ancelet, "Lomax in Louisiana," *Folklife in Louisiana*, March 8, 2018.
29. Caffery, *Traditional Music in Coastal Louisiana*, 264.
30. Harry Oster, "Evolution of Folk-Lyric Records," *JEMF Quarterly*, Volume XIV No. 49 (Spring 1978): 148–149.
31. Sigal, "Jambalaya," 115–116.
32. Ancelet, *Cajun and Creole Music Makers*, 85.
33. Savoy, *Cajun Music*, 326.
34. Ancelet, *Creole and Cajun Music Makers*, 79.
35. Tisserand, *Kingdom of Zydeco*, 17.
36. Chris Strachwitz, *Folk Music Occasional*, 23.
37. Brauner, "Newport Folk Festival," 140.
38. Tisserand, *Kingdom of Zydeco*, 12.
39. Savoy, *Cajun Music*, 350.
40. Broven, *South to Louisiana*, 119.
41. Chris Strachwitz, interview with author.
42. Chris Strachwitz, "Zydeco Music—i.e., French Blues," *The American Folk Music Occasional* (New York: Oak Publications, 1970): 22–23.
43. Marcus, *Anthology* liner notes, 18.
44. Gunnar Myrdal, "Selection from *An American Dilemma* (1944)," in *The American Intellectual Tradition, Volume II: 1865 to the Present*, sixth edition, ed. David A. Hollinger and Charles Capper (New York: Oxford University Press, 2011), 277.

BIBLIOGRAPHY

Ancelet, Barry Jean. *Cajun and Creole Music Makers*. Jackson: University Press of Mississippi, 1999.

———. "Lomax in Louisiana: Trials and Triumph." On *Folklife in Louisiana*, and originally published in *Louisiana Folklore Miscellany*, 2009. http://www.louisianafolklife.org/.

———. "Mardi Gras and the Media: Who's Fooling Whom?" In *Mardi Gras, Gumbo, and Zydeco: Readings in Louisiana Culture*, ed. Marcia G. Gaudet et al, 3–15. Jackson: University Press of Mississippi, 2003.

Brauner, Cheryl Anne. "A Study of the Newport Folk Festival and the Newport Folk Foundation." M.A. thesis, Memorial University of Newfoundland (Canada), 1986, ProQuest (MK68253).

Brasseaux, Carl A. *Acadiana: Louisiana's Historic Cajun Country*. Baton Rouge: Louisiana State University Press, 2011.

Brasseaux, Ryan André. *Cajun Breakdown, The Emergence of an American-Made Music*. New York: Oxford University Press, 2009.

Broven, John. *South to Louisiana, The Music of the Cajun Bayous*. Gretna: Pelican Publishing Company, 1983.

Caffery, Joshua Clegg. Folklife Lecture on Louisiana Music, Library of Congress, Washington, DC, December 11, 2013. http://www.loc.gov/today/cyberlc/transcripts/2013/131211afc1200.txt

Cohen, Ronald D., ed. *Alan Lomax, Assistant in Charge: The Library of Congress Letters, 1935–1945*. Jackson: University Press of Mississippi, 2010.

Marcus, Greil. "Anthology of American Folk Music," edited by Harry Smith. Folkways Records FP 252, 1997, compact disc. Liner notes.

Myrdal, Gunnar, "Selection from *An American Dilemma*," in *The American Intellectual Tradition, Volume II: 1865 to the Present*, sixth edition, ed. David A. Hollinger and Charles Capper (New York: Oxford University Press, 2011), 276–284.

Oster, Harry. "Evolution of Folk-Lyric Records." *JEMF Quarterly* XIV, No. 49 (Spring 1978): 148-149.

———. "Folksongs of the Louisiana Acadians." Arhoolie Records, 1994, compact disc. CD 359. First released by Folk-Lyric in 1959. Liner notes

———. "Negro French Spirituals of Louisiana." *Journal of the International Folk Music Council* 4 (1962): 166–167.

———. "*Une 'Tite Poule Grasse ou la Fille Ainee* [A Little Fat Chicken or The Eldest Daughter]: A Comparative Analysis of Cajun and Creole Mardi Gras Songs." *Journal of American Folklore* 114.452 (Spring 2001): 204–224.

Reed, Revon. *Lâche Pas La Patate: Potrait des Acadiens de la Louisiane*. Montreal: Éditions Parti pris, 1976.

Savoy, Ann Allen. *Cajun Music: A Reflection of a People, Vol. 1.* Eunice: Bluebird Press, 1984.

Seeger, Charles, quoted in *In Search of Authenticity, The Formation of Folklore Studies*, Regina Bendix. Madison: The University of Wisconsin Press, 1997.

Sexton, Rocky L. "Ritualized Inebriation, Violence, and Social Control in Cajun Mardi Gras." *Anthropological Quarterly* 74.1 (January 2001): 28–38.

Sigal, Andrew. "Jambalaya By Any Other Name." PETITS PROPOS CULINAIRE 84 (2007): 101–119.

Spitzer, Nicholas R. "Mardi Gras in L'Anse de'Prien Noir: A Creole Community Performance in Rural French Louisiana." In *Creoles of Color of the Gulf South*, edited by James H. Dormon. Knoxville: The University of Tennessee Press, 1996.

———. "Zydeco and Mardi Gras: Creole Identity and Performance Genres in Rural French Louisiana." PhD diss., The University of Texas at Austin, 1986, ProQuest (8700283).

Strachwitz, Chris. "Zydeco Music – i.e., French Blues." *The American Folk Music Occasional* (New York: Oak Publications, 1970): 22–23.

Tate, Paul. Letter to Gus Cranow, February 1, 1974. Ralph Rinzler Papers Fieldwork Box 4 Louisiana, Correspondence 1–3, Smithsonian Center for Folklife & Cultural Heritage, Washington, D.C.

Times-Picayune (New Orleans), April 17, 1938; June 14, 1953.

Tisserand, Michael. *The Kingdom of Zydeco.* New York: Avon Books, 1998.

CHAPTER 5

Brand New Old-Time Southern Americana: Harry Smith's Anthology Brings French Louisiana Music into the Folk Canon

In the post-World War II years, American folk art and its aesthetic of the modest symmetry of homespun craftwork occupied a prominent place in the hearts of American modernists.[1] John D. Rockefeller's wife Abby's collection of Americana—weathervanes, decoys, doorstops, cigar store figures, lawn ornaments, and watercolor paintings—had been one of the founding collections of the Museum of Modern Art in New York when it opened the week after the stock market crashed in 1929, introducing lovers of avant-garde painting to the handiwork of the anonymous American everyman at the very moment that he was being thrown into a state of financial despair. Sidney Janis's *They Taught Themselves, American Primitive Painters of the 20th Century*, published in 1942, looked back in admiration at the labor and craftwork of previous decades of sign painters, cabinet makers, blacksmiths, and stained-glass workers. The art critics who assessed the paintings featured in Janis's text emphasized the important ways that traditional American virtues of independence, resourcefulness, and spontaneity were manifested in the lives and work of folk artists. The works appealed to a "national sentiment," and there was a coherence between folk art and folk music forms, as if the folk artist was inextricably bound to history, to experience, and to landscape. Writing about the work of "Horace Pippin, Disabled War Veteran (Negro)," Alfred C. Barnes, an early collector of the work of Picasso and Cézanne, describes Pippin's oil painting of a regiment of World War I African-American soldiers capturing enemy German soldiers as "distinctly American" because its "picturesqueness, and accentuated rhythms, have

© The Author(s) 2019   109
P. Peknik, *French Louisiana Music and Its Patrons*,
https://doi.org/10.1007/978-3-319-97424-8_5

their musical counterparts in the spirituals of the American Negro." Janis refers to folk painters as "spiritual innocents," a revealing and fantastical compliment in the aftermath of the horrors and devastation of World War II. Driven more by a "craft sense" than a love of beauty, "each creates in his own world," Janis wrote of the painters. "They are unafraid."[2] He admired the awkwardness and humility of art that could only be discovered by crossing to "the wrong side of the tracks": "Here were poverty, obscurity, and the creative impulse,"[3] Janis wrote, romanticizing the Pittsburgh house painter John Kane as a man who had "felt the Whitmanesque epic of [the city's] industrial growth" as a laborer working on its buildings and bridges.[4]

The encounter with folk art forms inspired some lovers of the avant-garde to find correspondences between "high art" and folk forms, celebrating the primitive topical and stylistic elements in modern art as if the infusion of folk energy could restore art to innocence in the consumer age. The most eccentric avant-garde figure of the time, the visual artist Harry Smith, was also the age's most avid and prolific collector of folk music and folk crafts, obsessively gathering, documenting and arranging—although then losing or abandoning—collections of folk music, carved wooden crafts, tarot cards, and even an assortment of paper airplanes he had found on the streets of New York, which he wanted because they had been "made by white American children, made by black children, made by Puerto Rican children ..."[5] For Smith, folk music, like the paper airplanes, was touching evidence of the ingenuity and resourcefulness of ordinary people, of both their practicality and their whimsicalness, of their aspiration to a momentary transcendence above the quotidian streetscape.

Smith, who in the 1960s became a revered visual artist and experimental filmmaker among a cohort of Greenwich Village artists, started out as a collector of music, and was from the beginning to the very end of his life both a bohemian itinerant and a hoarder. He roamed the United States in the World War II years hunting for American folksong records, begging and borrowing his way through used record stores, the Salvation Army, and the record collections of friends and strangers. Smith believed that American political life could be changed if mainstream America were made to hear out the experiences of the impoverished, the homeless, and minorities, experiences that were captivatingly documented in old-time music.[6] In the merging of his mission and his person, in the intensity of his democratic sensibilities and his artistic appetites, Smith was a Whitmanesque character, one whose sympathetic engagement with all that seemed foreign and outcast in art, music, and social culture drove his work.

Allen Ginsberg remembered Smith, late in his life, as "a high, broke genius"[7] who haunted the corridors of the Chelsea Hotel, working on "Materials for the Study of Religion and Culture in the Lower East Side," which included recordings of "murderers babbling on amphetamines in the streets, jump rope rhymes, bawdy songs."[8] And therefore no Creole accordionist or Cajun fiddler would have believed that Smith was part of the story of their old-time music's journey from the front porches and dance halls of Southwest Louisiana to the concert halls of New York and the festival stages of Newport, Rhode Island, and Washington, DC. And indeed Smith, who cherished mysteries and riddles, would have appreciated that no one believed it.

Smith started collecting as a teenager growing up in South Bellingham, Washington, where in 1940 he bought a Mississippi blues album in a record shop. "[It] had somehow gotten into this town by mistake," Smith concluded, and, his curiosity piqued, he began to seek out folk and roots music albums, rummaging around in the Seattle Salvation Army and discovering Tennessee banjo music, jug bands, bluegrass, southern gospel, and Francis Child's collection of English and Scottish popular ballads. Musing over the Carter Family records he found in a store in Tacoma, Smith concluded that they must have been brought by families who migrated from the southern mountains to the hill country of Washington in the 1890s, and that this was the music that had reminded them of home. He struck gold when record company warehouses had to be cleared out to make way for military supplies, and stockpiles of traditional albums from the 1920s and 1930s were hastily sold by the labels for almost nothing; Smith, whose common appearance was "that of a derelict," was used to paying nothing, or almost nothing.[9] Records were being smashed to pieces to see if they were laminated with shellac, a scarce, important war materiel, and Smith was determined to find and save the most important recordings from suffering the fate of the rare King Oliver record he found broken in half, an artifact of the golden age of American recording.

The 1920s and 1930s had been boom years for commercial recording because labels like Columbia, Victor, and Okeh were determined to find new markets in rural America as city dwellers turned away from the phonograph and tuned into radio. Old-time music, blues, and "hillbilly" were the genres favored by Americans who lived in rural areas without electricity and couldn't listen to radio, so label executives sent talent scouts into the South to ask phonograph retailers where to find marketable talent, knowing that consumers would be more likely to buy phonographs if they could play music indigenous to their region. Record company scouts would hold auditions, recording many musicians only once, in original pressings as small as 500; those whose records sold well were invited to record again. Some who purchased the records didn't even own phonographs on which to play them, but bought them anyway in a curious reversal of the antiquarian's love of vinyl albums: rather than being objects that were interesting because they were constituent pieces of an outdated technology, as they are now, the albums were objects that might someday be useful, if only the possessor could one day buy a phonograph. They were component parts of a future coming-into-being through visions of a better rice crop, a higher price for sweet potatoes. In the act of buying an album, people discovered "the thrill of mechanical reproduction. Something that survived orally for a very long time suddenly turned into something that Sears Roebuck sold," and the same songs that had been played on the neighbor's porch or at a Saturday night dance hall came into the living room, the sound emanating from a box.[10]

Labels distributed their folk and roots albums to the same nationwide retailers that carried big band jazz and swing, contractually requiring a Columbia record retailer in New York City, for example, to take a certain number of blues and country albums.[11] This meant that traditional music recordings were dispersed in shops and warehouses throughout the country. Then, when the federal government needed storage space for military material, the labels dumped their holdings at fire sale prices, selling records as wartime scrap for eighteen to twenty cents a lot.[12] Smith, with his mastery of machinery and technology, made money during the war by mounting guns in the fuselages of airplanes, and with his pay, bought up all the records he could find. Many of the recordings he collected were already rare at the time he acquired them, as the recording companies had either lost or damaged the master recordings.[13] He was inexhaustible in his search, advertising for old records in small rural newspapers in North Carolina,[14] or borrowing for a week, and keeping forever, some rare album he had spotted in an acquaintance's collection.

Smith was meticulous and visionary in curating his collection, developing a definition of "American folk music" that excluded all of Lomax's field recordings, all Library of Congress holdings, and anything "validated only by scholarship or carrying the must of the museum." In collecting obscure commercial records, he was learning about music "to which people really had responded; records put on sale that at least somebody had thought were worth paying for," songs that seemed "exotic" in relation to what people in the war years thought of as "the world culture of high class music."[15] But he was hardly fascinated with the records as sheer music, and collected for "epistemological" as well as "musicological" reasons.[16] He thought of the records as documentary texts of the traumas and injustices of American culture, analyzing the lyrics to see how many times the words "food" and "railroad" were used during the Depression.[17] He saw folk music as the oldest evidence of the human desire, across civilizations and centuries, to relay information, facts and values, to communicate heightened experience and tell stories. The technology of the book was relatively recent in human history, and music remained the most pervasive and accessible art form.

And then, Smith believed that his collection constituted an argument against the homogenizing culture of the war and the post-war years, an era in which the lonely crowd of urban and suburban Americans understood their past through the distorting medium of television and the thin slogans of patriotic rhetoric, a time in which the image of a more diverse, radical and creative America already seemed to be a myth or a fable.

Smith had grown up hearing stories of that fabled America from his parents, and invented plenty more fables on his own: his mother's family, he said, were Romantics who escaped from the industrialization of Sioux City, Iowa in the 1880s to found a school which was supported by the Czarina of Russia; his mother had told him that she was Anastasia, the last of the Romanovs. His parents, he claimed, were devoted to philosophy and the occult, and his father was a cowboy, or perhaps a fisherman, or a British Satanist—for Smith was a masterful storyteller, and so his true upbringing remains "a garden of confusions" and mysteries. His great-grandfather had been Ulysses Grant's aide-de-camp during the Civil War, he claimed, and had been involved in the re-founding of the Knights Templar, a group of medieval monks who were said to have possessed the Holy Grail.[18]

Smith's own Holy Grail, his massive collection of early twentieth-century jazz, blues, folk, and gospel records, consisted of the thousands of albums he had collected while living in Berkeley, California and then in the Fillmore District of San Francisco in the late 1940s. He would bribe, chide and hustle people to turn over their vintage albums to him, promising that they would mean something much more in his collection. Smith was driven by political, aesthetic and sociological interests to recover these forgotten and ignored early folk albums, and to study and understand them as historical texts that opened onto an earlier world. As a high school student immersed in his parents' "fantasies, their poverty and delusions of grandeur," Smith had become infatuated with the music and dancing of Washington's Lummi Indian tribe and had gotten permission from the tribe to record drumming and chanting rituals at their winter festival. This marked the beginning of a lifelong obsession with the unusual, the marginal, and the experimental, an obsession that Smith tried unsuccessfully to channel into the academic study of anthropology at the University of Washington. He was interested in stories tragically untold, collecting Japanese records that had been hastily sold by Japanese residents of Seattle who had been relocated to internment camps. At home among the displaced and the transient, Smith became a lifetime itinerant, drawn to Berkeley and the North Beach San Francisco coffeehouse scene where he could mingle with a changing cast of painters, poets and folk singers talking art and communism.[19]

It was no coincidence that Smith's *Anthology* was issued during the anxious and fearful first years of the Cold War at the height of Senator Joseph McCarthy's anti-communist crusade. In 1952, in a middle-class America fueled by the bombastic patriotic rhetoric of dichotomies and absolutes, Smith "made his own country."[20] Smith's country was that "old, weird America" of fiddle music and acoustic guitar, railroad hobos and coal mine workers, farm hands and John Hardy, and the laborers and cowboys who had animated the American landscape before the fears and anxieties of the post-war era had chilled Americans' sympathetic identification with the other, the stranger, and the outcast. Without permission from Columbia, Paramount, Brunswick and Victor, the copyright holders, Smith compiled an eighty-four song, three-album set (by his reasoning, he was the Robin Hood of folk recordings, and the public good that would come from the anthology outweighed the labels' legal claims). In 1947, he approached Moses Asch, who had just founded the Folkways label, to discuss issuing the anthology.

Asch's family had fled World War I Europe and settled in the Bronx, where they lived next door to Leon Trotsky. After the war, Asch studied electronics at a German university, and while on vacation in Paris, happened to come across the 1913 version of John Lomax's *Cowboy Songs and Frontier Ballads* in a bookstore on the Seine. Asch was deeply influenced by Teddy Roosevelt's introduction to the Lomax collection, in which Roosevelt described folklore as the "real expression of a people's culture." This tribute to folk culture stayed on Asch's mind in the years after his return to New York, where he worked as a sound engineer and designed amplifiers, including one for Franklin Roosevelt's truck so that FDR could amplify his voice when addressing crowds. Asch got his start as a record producer when, working as a sound technician on Broadway in 1939, he heard Lead Belly sing and was shocked to realize that only Alan Lomax had ever bothered to record the blues guitarist. Asch quickly set up a recording studio in his office, and three hours later, had recordings of eight Lead Belly songs, which he pressed and sold under the label "Asch Records." Asch's father told him that he should use his sound engineering skills to preserve elements of culture and "show what life is like." Albert Einstein, who was a friend of Asch's father, likewise encouraged Asch in his goal to document the important events and of his time and to capture the music of immigrant and disenfranchised populations in America, to have a record company through which he could "describe the human race, the sound it makes, what it creates" at a time when entire populations and their culture were being destroyed in Hitler's Germany.[21]

Asch Records, a one-man label run by Asch and his secretary, Marian Distler, then recorded Woody Guthrie, who, at Asch's urging, traveled to Massachusetts to visit the North End neighborhood of Boston where Sacco and Vanzetti had lived in the 1920s; Guthrie wrote an entire album of songs about the ill-fated radicals. In 1948, Asch and Distler founded Folkways Records. "The GIs were coming back from the war bringing songs,"[22] Asch said. His new Folkways label, which produced folk albums by Guthrie, Pete Seeger, and Bob Dylan, went on to become one of the most successful independent labels in the world.

Asch saw Harry Smith as a Woody Guthrie-like character, and, intrigued by Smith's collection of long-lost folk songs, agreed to issue the *Anthology* along with the twenty-eight-page book Smith had written about the songs. Asch said that Smith "knew the records' relationship to folk music, their relationship to English literature, to the world."[23] Smith's goal in getting the *Anthology* released by a commercial label was grandiose: he felt that "social changes would result" if Americans were confronted with the music of the impoverished and marginalized people of Appalachia and the Deep South, black and white. Hearing their powerful voices would awaken something in the hearts and consciences of complacent northern urban Americans who, in the "scared and satisfied reactionary freeze of the post-war period," were cut off from the hardships and injustices experienced generation after generation by people in the Mississippi Delta, rural Georgia, the mountains of Tennessee, and the prairies of Southwest Louisiana. The *Anthology*, Smith said, was "meant to distinguish those who responded from those who didn't"[24]; it was a declaration "of a weird but clearly recognizable America within the America of the exercise of institutional majoritarian power" at a time when, in Norman Mailer's words, the fear of "instant death by atomic war" coexisted with the fear of "a slow death by conformity with every instinct stifled."[25] Smith wanted to reveal the older, admirable, complicated America.

That older America had been characterized by the creativity and quirkiness of its folklore and the hardships and exiles of ordinary people, and Smith believed that "the folk," long excluded from representation in national cultural life, had, finally, to have their say, not as they had through FDR's federal aid programs as the hardscrabble recipients of national charity and sympathy, but as artists and bearers of ideas and conclusions arrived at through the course of long experience and hard-earned sentiment.

Deeply troubled by the way labels segregated the music of African-Americans on "race records," and by manufacturers' insistence on using terms like "Negro" to identify performers, Smith never, in his biography of any musician on the *Anthology*, identified a performer by race. "There isn't that much difference between one person and another," Smith said.[26] He delighted in "sowing a confusion" about whether a musician was black or white, and looked back with satisfaction on the fact that "it took years before anybody discovered that Mississippi John Hurt wasn't a hillbilly."[27] In Smith's version of America, citizens were not categorizable by race, and this is part of the message he hoped the *Anthology* would make dramatic, relevant and affecting. And indeed, for the young urban folk music lovers of the fifties and sixties, Smith's mixing of "hillbilly, race, and Cajun" performers exposed a "hidden republic" of music, an integration and mixing of black and white performances that had started out as separate events in a segregated series,[28] recorded in an America that was "simultaneously a seamless web of connections and an anarchy of separations."[29]

Despite the gravity of this political and social agenda, Smith's liner notes, decorated with drawings of down-home musical instruments like the banjo and autoharp, are comic in tone. In his telegraphic headline-style song descriptions, he summarized the plot of each song with a wry humor that illuminated the historical and social contexts of folk music: for a song recounting the sinking of the RMS Titanic, "When That Great Ship Went Down," performed by William and Versey Smith in 1927 for Paramount, Smith wrote: "Manufacturers Proud Dream Destroyed at Shipwreck. Segregated Poor Die First." Smith adds the remark "Wish we could get the news this way now," through song. The Carolina Tar Heels'

1932 "Got the Farm Land Blues," played on harmonica, banjo, and gui-
tar, is summarized as "Discouraging Acts of God and Man Convince
Farmer of Positive Benefits in Urban Life," and the story told in
"Drunkards Special" is annotated by Smith, "Wife's Logic Fails to Explain
Strange Bedfellow to Drunkard."

Woven in between songs by the Carter Family, Blind Lemon Jefferson,
and Mississippi John Hurt, are six songs from Southwest Louisiana divided
across albums titled "Ballads," "Social Music" and "Songs": the 1928
recording of Cleoma Breaux and Joseph Falcon's "*Le vieux soûlard et sa
femme,*" [The Old Drunkard and His Wife], the couple's 1929 "*C'est si
triste sans lui,*" [It's Sad Without Him], Columbus Fruge's 1929 "*Saut
Crapaud,*" [Jump, Toad!] music by the Breaux Freres, and Blind Uncle
Gaspard's "*La Danseuse.*" Smith describes Cleoma Breaux Falcon and Joe
Falcon as "Pioneer French Recording Artists" and explains that "the arcadian violin," with a melody rather foreign to the Anglo-American pattern,
is very typical of Louisiana, though seldom heard in the states to its north.
But this music belonged, Smith's inclusion of it insisted, in the category of
national folk music, along with the music of the Cincinnati Jug Band and
The Sacred Harp Singers. These were a more exotic, but also an entirely
American folk. As Asch remarked in his liner notes, "These are the songs
people listen to, the tunes and songs heard on these records, although
they listen to radio, watch movies and television, [these songs] are listened
to in the privacy of their homes, at gatherings, or for themselves, and are
still the intimate part of their lives rather than the commercial or classical
music heard and accepted by us urbanites."[30]

Many of the musicians have names that make them seem as if they
aren't strangers but long-lost neighbors from an earlier American rural
world—Mr. & Mrs. Stoneman, the Carter Family, Uncle Dave Macon,
Rev. F.W. McGee, the Bently Boys—although most of them would have
made unsettling neighbors and relatives, with their stories of train wrecks,
gun fights, the tragedies of thwarted courtship, and visions of Judgment
Day.

In the Cajun song "*Le vieux soûlard et sa femme,*" a woman wonders
what the meaning of love could possibly be if her husband keeps leaving
her to go off on a drinking spree. "*C'est Triste Sans Lui*" has heart-
wrenching lyrics, but Cleoma Breaux's exuberant vocal delivery, along
with Joe Falcon's boisterous, rousing performance style, belied the mournful lyrics, a juxtaposition that characterized many romantic ballads in the
French Louisiana tradition.

"*Saute, Crapaud*" is a whimsical children's song with nonsensical lyrics, described by Smith as "possibly the most widely known of any arcadian dance tune":

> *Ta queue va bruler*
> *Prends courage, a'va repousser*
> *C'est Jacques Pétrin, pas rien sur la tête*
> *En r'venant du Lac Charles en mangeant des bananes.*[31]
>
> [Jump, toad! You're going to burn your tail.
> Take heart—it'll grow back.
> There's Jacques Petrin, bareheaded,
> Coming back from Lake Charles, eating bananas.]

French Louisiana dance hall musicians had an ear for such silly, sometimes bawdy references: one traditional dance tune describes the way that Uncle Adam's banana fell to pieces at his feet the moment he peeled it; in another, the singer claims that it was "Uncle Edouard's daughter who rubbed my little washboard … Uncle Hilaire's daughter who touched my little spoon." In the Breaux Brothers' "*Les Blues Du Petit Chien*" [Little Dog Blues], recorded for Vocalion in 1934, the speaker tells a woman: "*Oh, laisse moi être ton p'tit chien/Jusqu'à ce que le gros chien vienne*" [Oh, let me be your little dog until the big dog comes]. Taken as a whole, the six Southwest Louisiana songs that appear on the *Anthology* represent the same cohabitation of hard times storyline and playful dance tune that characterized the music of the Cajun-Creole tradition.

The Smith collection had a life-changing effect on a cohort of Greenwich Village musicians who first heard the *Anthology* in the 1950s and early 1960s. John Cohen of the string band New Lost City Ramblers said the albums "gave us contact with musicians and cultures we wouldn't have known existed … artists who became like mystical gods to us …"[32] Cohen, whose photography documented the lives of traditional musicians in Appalachia and the congregations of African-American churches, found in Smith a kindred spirit. The *Anthology* was "our bible," said folk-blues guitarist Dave Van Ronk. "We knew every word of every song on it, including the ones we hated."[33] Folklorist Ralph Rinzler was "profoundly influenced by the *Anthology* when it was first released,"[34] and called it the "mother-lode" of the "strange, idiosyncratic, often exotic, sometimes … bizarre repertoire"[35] of old-time American music. The experience of listening to, and studying, Smith's collection, was the central formative musical experience of many in Rinzler's cohort: "As with *Moby-Dick*'s Ishmael, whose whale ship was his Harvard and Yale, that first generation of the Folk Song Revival made the *Anthology* their Indiana and UCLA: an education and initiation into the study and performance of traditional musical forms."[36] The newly canonical music seemed to be a message from an older America, one in which folk musicians "were cut off ... by a national narrative that never included their kind ... they appeared now like visitors from another world, like passengers on a ship that had drifted into the sea of the unwritten."[37]

Smith's anthology made the argument that the American national culture was in fact what Ralph Ellison would describe as "a fractured, vernacular-weighted intricate whole," that although the cultural old guard with its refined and tutored sensibilities curated a hierarchy of artistic goods, Americans' free-floating aesthetic sensibilities would naturally "transcend the lines of class, religion, region, and race—floating free, as it were, in the crowd"; that listeners would be drawn to the stories of other, previously unknown-to-them Americans. The "Americanness" of American culture had been a matter of wordplay, Ellison argued, but we were all "the inheritors, creators, and creations of a culture of cultures." The *Anthology* also made the point that Mississippians working the cotton fields, Appalachians working the mines, and Louisianans working the sweet potato fields were asserting their claim to being part of the integrative collective whole of untelevised American culture. It asserted that Ellison was right when he claimed that the oldest abiding American question was "What about me?"[38]

What was true of the French-language Louisiana music on the *Anthology* was also true of the whole of the selections: listeners found the music "emotionally shattering yet culturally incomprehensible," for it wasn't anything like the music that had been sold by the recording industry as "folk"—that is, not the Kingston Trio.[39] Although many of the musicians, young when they'd recorded in the 1920s and 1930s, were still living in the same small communities, Cohen, Seeger, and Van Ronk concluded that "All those guys on that Harry Smith anthology are dead. *Had* to be," because the unamplified singing and generations-old lyrics seemed to be coming from another century: "For this music sounded like it came right out of the ground. Songs like the clods of rich dark earth, fecund, timeless." Banjo player Clarence Ashley, who at the time he recorded in 1929 was in his mid-thirties, sounded, on the *Anthology*, "as if he'd died seventeen or one hundred and seventeen years before," but he clearly "wasn't as old as the song."[40]

Smith's *Anthology* became the founding document of the American folk revival, its "musical Constitution,"[41] partly because by studying and imitating the playing of old-time musicians, contemporary folk musicians could revive traditional playing styles rather than simply combining traditional lyrics with a modern folk-pop style: "Hearing all these people for the very first time, it was as if a veil was lifted, and I was finally aware of what seemed to me to be the heart of American music. That's what I was born to do, I thought. Play and sing like those guys."[42] "Those guys" were conceived of as "premodern, unrestrainedly emotive, and noncommercial," revered for their "Otherness" and admired for their ability to be "independent, proud in the face of hardship, straightforward, beholden to no special interests."[43] In other words, they were, in the imaginations of the young college students who avidly sought out their albums, exactly what many in the folk revival generation—those who came of age between the end of World War II and the end of the Vietnam War[44]—wanted to be themselves.

The music of the *Anthology* became the music against which folk would forever after be measured. It documented the fact that the "old, weird America" was the real America, its music sounding "like field recordings, from the Amazon, or Africa, but it's here, in the United States. It's not conspicuous, but it's *there*."[45] And the *Anthology*, taken as a "Rosetta Stone, a treasure map of an ancient and now-hidden America,"[46] became the canon in large part because key members of the folk movement, including Pete Seeger's half-brother Mike Seeger, wanted to reincorporate that "weirdness" into American music by tracking down and bringing into the national spotlight not only the music but the *Anthology* musicians themselves.

Seeger played in the New Lost City Ramblers, a traditional music revival band whose members had studied recordings of 1920s and 1930s string band music in order to recreate, or reinterpret, old-time music on period instruments for new, young audiences. Seeger's bandmate John Cohen was equally dedicated to "fidelity of instrumental and vocal styles in the performance of folk music by non-folk."[47] But when Seeger, Cohen, and their friend Ralph Rinzler realized that many of the *Anthology* musicians were likely still alive and well and residing in the same states listed in Smith's liner notes, they set out to locate the originals, traveling south, pilgrims on the route. Because the recording technology of the 1920s and 1930s had been so rudimentary, the *Anthology* recordings sounded ancient, the voices tinny and far-off, and deciding to hunt for the musicians on backwoods farms and in mountain cabins must have seemed like proposing to bring alive characters from a beloved classic novel—like finding *Moby-Dick*'s Ishmael, retired from his old occupation of working on a whaling ship.

This was how the blind guitarist Arthel "Doc" Watson, Virginia banjo player Dock Boggs, Tennessee-born banjoist Clarence Ashley, and blues guitarist Mississippi John Hurt ended up playing in Greenwich Village coffeehouses, at national folk music festivals in Chicago and Newport, and at Carnegie Hall—Harry Smith, "a polymath and an autodidact, a dope fiend and an alcoholic, a legendary experimental filmmaker and a more legendary sponger ... most notorious as a fabulist,"[48] had unscrolled the treasure map, and the folk revival generation, *Anthology* in hand, were converted from being documentary archivists who collected, documented and imitated traditional songs to being cultural interventionists determined to create new audiences for old-time music, both in its home regions and nationally.

Rinzler, playing banjo with the Greenbriar Boys at the Union Grove Fiddlers Convention in North Carolina in 1960, was "stunned" to come across Clarence Ashley, and, returning to North Carolina four months later to record Ashley for Folkways, he developed a plan for helping old-time musicians earn a living playing traditional music. Rinzler considered it a travesty that these musicians had been overlooked and forgotten, "that someone like Doc Watson should be playing in a VFW hall on an electric guitar, who had this potential.[49]" As a young man, Watson had played bluegrass and blues on an acoustic guitar and sung mountain ballads he'd learned as a boy, but had switched to playing commercial standards on an electric guitar when the sounds of amplified country music became popular. Rinzler convinced Watson that he could make a better living playing acoustic guitar and singing traditional music, and to demonstrate his point, invited Ashley and Watson to perform in concert at P.S. 41 in Greenwich Village at one of the first concerts staged by the non-profit Friends of Old-Time Music, a folk revival concert organization Rinzler founded with John Cohen and Izzy Young, who had opened the Folklore Center bookstore on MacDougal Street in 1957. The Friends of Old-Time Music was a response to a growing concern among Rinzler and his cohort that what was being promoted on the New York folk music scene was a commercial, contemporary popular folk sound, with bands like the Kingston Trio[50] defining the public understanding of "folk." He wanted to "take more meaningful music—or what I felt was the real stuff—and have it slowly replace the more sophisticated," meaning commercial, music.[51]

The organization invited Dock Boggs, Mother Maybelle Carter, Mississippi John Hurt and other *Anthology* musicians to perform in New York, and seeing Watson go, in a year and a half, from living on state aid for the blind to "supporting his family and wowing audiences all over the country" was convincing enough to make Rinzler believe almost anything was possible. Rinzler functioned as an Artist & Repertoire man to Watson, advising him on which songs to play and getting him gigs at colleges and in coffeehouses. Working with traditional musicians prompted Rinzler to abandon his career as a revival musician and devote himself to working with the musicians instead, including Bill Monroe, whose bluegrass music Rinzler had been playing with the Greenbriar Boys: "It didn't have any meaning for me to get on a stage and play imitation Bill Monroe when I was booking him. It seemed like a travesty ..."[52] Rinzler wanted to be an intermediary between artists and audiences,[53] and, as a musician, just get out of the way.

If the folklore revivalists have been accused of being obsessed with notions of authenticity, Rinzler had the virtue of declaring himself, relative to the living, breathing *Anthology* singers, inauthentic. Unlike Harry Oster, and indeed Lomax, who themselves performed the folk songs they admired, Rinzler gave up playing music professionally in order to better serve oldtime music. He was sensitive to the fact that he didn't really belong inside the venues where he did fieldwork. In his graduate school years, he had recorded in London taverns, and in his Camden Town Irish pub session liner notes, he explained how important it was to reproduce on the album the aural atmosphere of a pub filled with great Irish musicians, to preserve "text within context" rather than record in a "sterile studio": "When it [folk music] is removed from its habitual framework and [experienced or] exhibited apart from the whole, it loses that sense of urgency and direct communication which, along with style, improvisation and other characteristics, sets it happily apart from the world of art music."[54]

Rinzler's understanding of context, and his appreciation for a traditional music that was set apart from "the world of art music" were formed at the earliest age. Lomax's Library of Congress recordings, first released when Rinzler was seven, put the hook in him for traditional music: "I had ... firmly emblazoned on my mind the beauty of alternative esthetics ... And the sense that folklore was connected to something that was thousands of years old."[55] Rinzler grew up talking music with his uncle, who had studied with folklorist George Lyman Kittredge, Francis Child's successor at Harvard. As a music major, then a French major, at Swarthmore, Rinzler worked at the college's radio station, which organized the Swarthmore Folk Festival, and developed a friendship with Roger Abrahams, who would become a well-known academic folklorist of African-American and Afro-Caribbean cultures.[56]

Rinzler spent college summers in Greenwich Village watching Woody Guthrie play in Washington Square and teaching himself to play banjo. He became friends with Mike and Peggy Seeger, whose father, ethnomusicologist Charles Seeger, had been an administrator for the WPA's Federal Music Project. As a field worker, Charles Seeger had insisted that the relevant question for any folk song collector was not "What is good music?" but rather "What is music good for?"[57] Like Charles Seeger, Rinzler wanted to know how a particular song functioned in the social environment, whether there was historical information and moral reckoning embedded in its narrative, whether it was a song to call out the dancers or comfort the mourning. From Mike Seeger, Rinzler learned both the philosophy and techniques of ethnomusicology fieldwork and the practical, technical skill of how to record old-time music.

Rinzler's friendship with the Seeger family was deeply important. After Swarthmore, Rinzler left for Paris in 1957 to pursue a graduate degree in French, but moved to England a year later to study with British folklorist A.L. Lloyd, a devoted collector and researcher of British occupational folk songs. Lloyd, whose parents and two sisters had died in a tuberculosis epidemic in 1925, had been shipped off as a boy to Australia by the British Legion, in which his father had served, to work as a migrant laborer in the Australian bush lands, along with a host of other orphaned children sponsored by the Salvation Army and other charities. Sent by the Labor Exchange to work as a farm worker, Lloyd listened closely to the songs sung by the merino sheep shearers he worked among, and began to transcribe the tunes and lyrics, some for their "poetic vividness," or "some special quality of melody," and others because, given his own exile, he could feel as though he had directly experienced some part of the narrative. The songs called out to weary travelers who had wandered, destitute and alone, and taken up hard work in a far-off land.

Lloyd developed, as a lonesome young migrant worker, the motive that would inform his lifetime of song collecting, a motive that would inform his student Rinzler's work as well: "I was concerned mainly to take the songs into my own cultural baggage."[58] Lloyd wanted to experience the songs not as a stranger in a strange land making an explorer's discovery, but as artful expressions that had familiar and universal resonance, not as if he were eavesdropping on the music of the "other." He wanted the songs to feel congruent with some element of his own experience.

While Rinzler was studying with Lloyd in London, Peggy Seeger introduced him to Alan Lomax, who had expatriated himself in 1950 to escape McCarthy's anti-Communist campaign.[59] Lomax had been named as an alleged Communist in the list compiled by Martin Dies's Committee Investigating Un-American Activities, and an FBI investigation concluded that Lomax was a "Bohemian" who was "single-mindedly devoted to folk music," that he was "known to associate with a Negro by the name of 'Lead Belly' who was released from a southern penitentiary," that he was "always singing peculiar songs of a Western or Negro type," and that on three or four nights a week, there was "a great amount of singing and music emanating from his apartment."[60] In the spring of 1950, Lomax's name appeared in an article identifying members of Communist front groups because he had been one of the sponsors of a dinner given by the Civil Rights Congress to honor lawyers who had defended people accused of being Communists.[61] A group of former FBI agents issued a pamphlet, "Red Channels: The Report of Communist Influence in Radio and Television," accusing Pete Seeger, Civil Rights activist and blues guitarist Josh White, and Alan Lomax, along with 148 other musicians and entertainers, of being communists. However, Lomax's declared purpose for moving to England was to develop a library of recordings of world folk music for Columbia Records, the eighteen-volume Columbia World Library of Folk and Primitive Music[62]; he didn't return to the United States for eight years.

Suspicions about Lomax's motives in championing old-time music were especially outrageous because he saw folk music as a democratic cultural form that constituted its own argument against totalitarianism of any stripe. The fact that Louisiana "speaks and sings with a heavy French accent" was by itself a piece of evidence for the argument that folklore was a strong current in American life that ran counter to any authoritarian, Fascist tendency, Lomax said,[63] and he saw the post-World War II national interest in folklore as a sign that Americans, psychologically cut off from the heritage of the Western European tradition through the trauma of war, were beginning to appreciate and value their own "national cultural resources." "In folklore, you get a kind of rudimentary humanistic approach to life, a deep sense of values and something that deserves to have its place in the sun,"[64] he said. In the post-war years before his expatriation, Lomax had organized a concert series called "Midnight Special" at New York City's Town Hall and was heartened by the popular appreciation of the blues musicians in the series, which included performances by Sydney Bechet, Sonny Boy Williamson, and Big Bill Broonzy. Lomax's goal was to bring folk singers "of every race and nationality" to New York to play honky-tonk, blues, spirituals and mountain ballads: "[These musicians] have had experiences in the lost regions of American life," Lomax said. He put Piedmont blues guitarist Brownie McGhee, Appalachian ballad singer Jean Ritchie and Virginia banjo player Hobart Smith on stage for the "Ballads, Hoe-Downs, Spirituals (White and Negro), and Blues" program of Columbia University's "Annual Festival of Contemporary American Music," and concluded that the young, liberal audience "wanted to stay with these people forever."[65]

Yet he was troubled, when he returned a decade later from London to New York, to see the extent to which folk music had become a commodity marketed and sold to young, liberal audiences, with "city singers polishing their country personae" to present songs full of "home-spun imagery" on string instruments[66] at expensive festivals, more commerce than art, characterized by commercial production values that made it unlikely that any listener would experience a true engagement with the music of regional America. So when Boston entrepreneur George Wein, creator of the Newport Jazz Festival, decided to add a folk festival in 1959, Lomax was initially critical of the project, voicing his concerns at the Newport Folk Foundation's 1959 symposium on American Folk Music that the festival was a "publicity stunt" that presented folk music as "merely a type of entertainment,"[67] enriching promoters and sponsors and, in the process, "imposing a new sound" on regional cultures, ultimately destroying whatever was ostensibly being promoted. Lomax protested that the festival's board of directors were not folklorists or musicians, and that no money made from the folk revival was being directed back to the grassroots from whence it came. But in the years ahead, he came to see the festival as an opportunity to steer the folk movement back to the roots of traditional music.

In 1964, newly appointed, along with Pete Seeger, to the board of the Newport Folk Festival, Lomax wrote a letter to fellow members of the board urging them to focus less on showcasing young urban "smooth entertainers" who had learned to perform folk music, and more on finding those lonely performers, ignored by their own people, who were abandoning their traditional music in order to make a living, unappreciated by local audiences who had begun tuning in to hear pop music on commercial radio.[68] Previous Newport performers had included Joan Baez, daughter of an MIT professor and veteran of the Cambridge folk music scene, the former rock and roll-loving Bob Dylan, who worked the music clubs in Greenwich Village, and Tom Paxton, another Village habitué, who had a Bachelor of Fine Arts degree in theater. These weren't the "folk" that Lomax, ever the Romantic purist, had in mind when he thought about "tribal" and "regional" music, and he argued that it was high time the Newport organizers made a strenuous effort to find forgotten and struggling musicians whose work truly needed saving.

In "An Appeal for Cultural Equity," Lomax summarized the philosophy and strategies that had always driven his fieldwork and that he hoped would be influential on other music folklorists. He accused the music industry of putting local musicians out of work, silencing folk song and tribal ritual and imposing "a few standardized, mass-produced and cheapened cultures everywhere," replacing the "cultural constellations" of the American landscape with the phony uniformity sold by a centralized music industry whose only goal was to promote industry stars on blaring top-40 radio broadcasts. In losing regional music, the national culture lost not only "a way of viewing, thinking, and feeling" but a means of adaptation to a regional habitat, since music taught people how to live within a particular landscape and social system. In allowing a musical language to disappear, we "throw away a system of interaction," Lomax said, and he came to see the necessary equality of musical genres—of different systems of interaction—as a logical extension of the commitment to "the principles of political, social and economic justice" to which liberal, progressive society must be dedicated.

The goal of genre equality was threatened by modern technological and commercial systems that "blanketed the world" with standardized music and literature, like so many manufactured goods, Lomax warned, and the solution was to bring a counterbalancing outside interest—he considered himself to be that counterbalancing interest—to support local music communities. Local languages and local music deserved their fair share of radio airtime. If "country folk" heard their own music on the radio, they would develop a determination to preserve that music. Lomax held up the example of black orchestral music in New Orleans, which "flowered" because black musicians found steady work in New Orleans clubs, and their ability to make a living as professional musicians then gave them the time to record and export their music. "Nations do not generate music," Lomax argued. "They can only consume it. Indeed our new system of national consumption of music via national communications systems is depriving the musical creator of the thing he needs most next to money—a local, tribal or regional audience that he can sing directly for."[69]

Lomax urged the board to hire Rinzler to do fieldwork in the South to find the older musicians whose songs young middle-class folk musicians were imitating and commercializing. Then, money would be directed back to the musicians' communities through Newport-sponsored local festivals that would help sustain and revitalize traditional cultures. Music would be broadcast from the festivals over local radio, allowing traditional music to successfully compete with national pop music. Lomax insisted that he would only be involved if the foundation agreed to invest in the musicians themselves and in their communities, and that he would support the showcasing of urban, commercial folk singers only to the extent that it would benefit musicians who had learned their folk songs in "folk communities."[70]

Rinzler collaborated with Lomax and board member Mike Seeger to develop the bulk of his fieldwork strategy. As Rinzler recalled, Lomax went back over his 1930s trips: "He sat down with me in his living room and rambled over the continent in his mind and said, 'Back in the '30s I went here and I went there and the best stuff was in this town' and he just came up with an incredible number of things. 'Go see this person here and that person there.' I started with what Alan knew and went on to what I knew, and called all kinds of people on the phone and laid out a map, a route, and went out and found it."[71]

Lomax and Seeger recommended that Rinzler visit the Maritime Provinces in Canada, French Québec, the "foreign minority neighborhoods" of Detroit, Chicago and Pittsburgh, backwoods Alabama, and Cajun Louisiana. Traveling across the American South, Rinzler had a chance to unlock some of the mysteries of the *Anthology*, meeting Kentucky fiddlers, Sacred Harp Singers in northern Alabama, and French Louisiana musicians in Southwest Louisiana, whose race, unstated by Smith in his liner notes, was unknown to the albums' listeners. In the Civil Rights years of Southwest Louisiana, words that denoted ethnicity and race were in any case confounding to outsiders: Creole guitarist Clarence Garlow, known as a zydeco and R&B musician during his recording career, recalled how in his childhood near Lake Charles, because he used to play his father's old fiddle, "I was a black Cajun."[72] Clifton Chenier was affectionately referred to as "the blackest [Cajun],"[73] and New Orleans recording studio owner Cosimo Matassa noted that when young Cajun and Creole musicians sang in English, it was impossible to know whether the singer was black or white, since they both sounded the same.[74]

When Rinzler, who was of Russian-Jewish descent, died in July 1994, The *New York Times* obituary read: "Mr. Rinzler, who was black, was widely credited with nudging the Smithsonian toward expanding its activities beyond a focus on white American culture."[75]

"Mr. Rinzler, who was black": Harry Smith would have loved that.

Notes

1. Andrew Perchuk, "Struggle and Structure" in *Harry Smith, The Avant-Garde in the American Vernacular*, ed. Andrew Perchuk (Los Angeles: Getty Publications, 2010), 12.
2. Albert C. Barnes in *They Taught Themselves, American Primitive Painters of the 20th Century*, Sidney Janis (New York: The Dial Press, 1942), 7–8; 187.
3. Sidney Janis, *They Taught Themselves*, 232–233.
4. Sidney Janis, *They Taught Themselves*, 76–77.
5. Jonas Mekas in *American Magus, Harry Smith, A Modern Alchemist*, ed. Paola Igliori (New York: Inanout Press, 1996), 83.
6. Harry Smith, *Anthology*, liner notes, 10.
7. Allen Ginsberg, "Allen Ginsberg on Harry Smith," *Harry Smith Anthology*, liner notes, 55.
8. Ginsberg, *Anthology* liner notes, 56.
9. Marcus, *Anthology* liner notes, 9.
10. Marcus, *Anthology* liner notes, 21.
11. Moses Asch, "The Birth and Growth of the Anthology of American Folk Music," *Anthology* liner notes, 33.
12. Asch, *Anthology* liner notes, 32.
13. Asch, *Anthology* liner notes, 37.
14. Chuck Pirtle, *Anthology* liner notes, 52.
15. Marcus, *Anthology* liner notes, 10–11.
16. Harry Smith in "A Rare Interview with Harry Smith," John Cohen, in *Sing Out! The Folk Song Magazine*, Volume 18/Number 1, April/May 1969, reprinted in *American Magus Harry Smith: A Modern Alchemist*, ed. Paola Igliori (New York: Inanout Press, 1996), 26.
17. Smith, *Sing Out! The Folk Song Magazine*, 40.
18. Marcus, *Anthology* liner notes, 7.
19. Marcus, *Anthology* liner notes, 8.
20. Marcus, *Anthology* liner notes, 5.

21. Gene Bluestein, *Poplore* (Amherst: University of Massachusetts Press, 1994), 109–118.
22. Asch, *Anthology* liner notes, 32.
23. Moses Asch, "The Birth and Growth of Anthology of American Folk Music," in *American Magus*, 94.
24. Marcus, *Anthology* liner notes, 10.
25. Marcus, *Anthology* liner notes, 25.
26. Smith, *Anthology* liner notes, 22–24.
27. Marcus, *Anthology* liner notes, 11.
28. Rosenberg, *Anthology* liner notes, 37.
29. Marcus, *Anthology* liner notes, 11.
30. Asch, "General Notes on this Series," *Anthology* liner notes.
31. Francois, *Yé Yaille*, 273.
32. John Cohen, *Anthology* liner notes, 5.
33. Van Ronk, *Anthology* liner notes, 5.
34. Anthony Seeger and Amy Horowitz, "Introduction," *Anthology* liner notes, 3.
35. Cantwell, "Smith's Memory Theater," 365.
36. John Pankake, "The Brotherhood of the *Anthology*," *Anthology*, liner notes, 26.
37. Marcus, *Anthology* liner notes, 6.
38. Ralph Ellison, "The Little Man at Chehaw Station," reprinted in *The American Intellectual Tradition, Volume II*, fourth edition, ed. Charles Capper and David A. Hollinger (New York: Oxford University Press, 2001), 425, 433, 435.
39. John Pankake, *Anthology* liner notes, 27.
40. Marcus, *Anthology* liner notes, 17.
41. Robert Cantwell, "Smith's Memory Theater: The Folkways Anthology of American Folk Music," *New England Review*, Vol. 13, No. 3/4 (Spring–Summer 1991): 364.
42. Pete Stampel, *Anthology* liner notes, 22–23.
43. Filene, *Romancing the Folk*, 63–65.
44. Jeff Todd Titon, "Authenticity and Authentication: Mike Seeger, the New Lost City Ramblers and the Old-Time Music Revival," *Journal of Folklore Research*, Vol 49, No, 2. (May–August, 2012): 228.
45. Marcus, *Anthology* liner notes, 6.
46. Luis Kemnitzer, "West Coast Record Collector," *Anthology* liner notes, 30.
47. Joseph C. Hickerson, review of Friends of Old Time Music, *Ethnomusicology* Vol. 10, No. 3, Sep., 1966: 371.
48. Marcus, *Anthology* liner notes, 7.

49. Richard Gagné, "Ralph Rinzler, Folklorist: Professional Biography," *Folklore Forum* 27:1 (Bloomington: Folklore and Ethnomusicology Department, Indiana University, 1996): 26.
50. Alan Lomax, *Alan Lomax: Selected Writings: 1934–1937* (London: Routledge, 2005), 155.
51. Alan Lomax, *Selected Writings*, 173.
52. Gagné, "Ralph Rinzler," 28.
53. Gagné, "Ralph Rinzler," 39.
54. Gagné, "Ralph Rinzler," 40.
55. Gagné, "Ralph Rinzler," 21.
56. William S. Walker, "A Living Exhibition: The Smithsonian, Folklife, and the Making of the Modern Museum" (PhD diss., Brandeis University, 2007): 125.
57. Robert R. Grimes, "Form, Content and Value: Seeger and Criticism to 1940," in *Understanding Charles Seeger, Pioneer in Musicology*, ed. Bell Yung and Helen Rees (Champaign: University of Illinois Press, 1999), 80.
58. Andrew Lloyd, Interview with Mark Gregory, published in Overland Literary Journal, 1970. http://folkstream.com/reviews/lloyd/
59. Gagné, "Ralph Rinzler," 22–24.
60. John Szwed, *Alan Lomax, The Man Who Recorded the World* (New York: Viking, 2010): 203–204.
61. Szwed, *Alan Lomax*, 249.
62. Szwed, *Alan Lomax*, 251.
63. Lomax, *Selected Writings*, 90.
64. Lomax, *Selected Writings*, 114–116.
65. Szwed, *Alan Lomax*, 225; 234.
66. Szwed, *Alan Lomax*, 315–316.
67. Brauner, "The Newport Folk Festival," 61.
68. Szwed, *Alan Lomax*, 348–349.
69. Alan Lomax, "An Appeal for Cultural Equity," 1972, reprinted in 1985 Festival of American Folklife Program Guide, Smithsonian Institution.
70. William S. Walker, *The Smithsonian and the Transformation of the Universal Museum* (Amherst: University of Massachusetts Press, 2013), 124.
71. Brauner, "The Newport Folk Festival," 183.
72. Broven, *South to Louisiana*, 105.
73. Broven, *South to Louisiana*, 113.
74. Brauner, "The Newport Folk Festival," 179.
75. *The New York Times*, "Ralph Rinzler, 59, Smithsonian Official and Folk-Life Expert," July 8, 1994.

BIBLIOGRAPHY

Asch, Moses. "The Birth and Regrowth of the Anthology of American Folk Music." Liner notes for "*Anthology of American Folk Music*," edited by Harry Smith. Folkways Records FP 252, 1997, compact disc.

Bluestein, Geene. *Poplore*. Amherst: University of Massachusetts Press, 1994.

Brauner, Cheryl Anne. "A Study of the Newport Folk Festival and the Newport Folk Foundation." M.A. thesis, Memorial University of Newfoundland (Canada), 1986, ProQuest (MK68253).

Broven, John. *South to Louisiana, The Music of the Cajun Bayous*. Gretna: Pelican Publishing Company, 1983.

Cantwell, Robert. "Smith's Memory Theater: The Folkways Anthology of American Folk Music." *New England Review* 13.3/4 (Spring–Summer 1991): 364–397.

Capper, Charles, and David A. Hollinger. *The American Intellectual Tradition, Volume II*, fourth edition. New York: Oxford University Press, 2001.

Cohen, John. Liner notes for "*Anthology*."

Ellison, Ralph. "The Little Man at Chehaw Station" in *The American Intellectual Tradition*, Volume II, fourth edition, edited by Charles Capper and David A. Hollinger. New York: Oxford University Press, 2001.

Filene, Benjamin. *Romancing the Folk, Public Memory & American Roots Music*. Chapel Hill: University of North Carolina Press, 2000.

François, Raymond E. *Yé Yaille, Chère!* Ville Platte: Swallow Publications, 1990.

Gagné, Richard. "Ralph Rinzler, Folklorist: Professional Biography." *Folklore Forum* 27:1. Bloomington: Folklore and Ethnomusicology Department, Indiana University (1996): 20–49.

Ginsberg, Allen. Liner notes for "*Anthology*."

Hickerson, Joseph C. Review of Friends of Old Time Music. *Ethnomusicology* 10.3 (Sep., 1966): 371.

Janis, Sydney. *They Taught Themselves, American Primitive Painters of the 20th Century*. New York: The Dial Press, 1942.

Kemnitzer, Luis. "West Coast Record Collector." Liner notes for "*Anthology*."

Lomax, Alan. *Alan Lomax: Selected Writings: 1934–1937*. London: Routledge, 2005.

Lloyd, Andrew. "A.L. Lloyd Folklore and Australia." Interview with Mark Gregory. Published in Overland Literary Journal, 1970. http://folkstream.com/reviews/lloyd/.

Marcus, Greil. Liner notes for "*Anthology*."

Mekas, Jonas in *American Magus, Harry Smith, A Modern Alchemist*, edited by Paola Igliori. New York: Inanout Press, 1996.

Obituary of Ralph Rinzler. *The New York Times*, July 8, 1994, national edition.

Pankake, John. "*The Brotherhood of the Anthology*." Liner notes for "*Anthology*."

Perchuk, Andrew. "Struggle and Structure." In *Harry Smith, The Avant-Garde in the American Vernacular*, edited by Andrew Perchuk. Los Angeles: Getty Publications, 2010.

Pirtle, Chuck. Liner notes for "*Anthology*."

Rosenberg, Neil. Liner notes for "*Anthology*."

Seeger, Anthony and Amy Horowitz. "Introduction." Liner notes for "*Anthology*."

Smith, Harry. "A Rare Interview with Harry Smith," John Cohen, in "Sing Out! The Folksong Magazine," Volume 18/Number 1, April/May 1969, reprinted in *American Magus*.

Stampel, Pete. Liner notes for "*Anthology*."

Szwed, John. *Alan Lomax, The Man Who Recorded the World*. New York: Viking, 2010.

Titon, Jeff Todd. "Authenticity and Authentication: Mike Seeger, the New Lost City Ramblers and the Old-Time Music Revival." *Journal of Folklore Research* Vol 49.2 (May–August, 2012): 227–245.

Van Ronk, Dave. Liner notes for "*Anthology*."

Walker, William S. "A Living Exhibition: The Smithsonian, Folklife, and the Making of the Modern Museum." PhD diss., Brandeis University, 2007, ProQuest (3274388).

CHAPTER 6

"I Want You to Be/Just like You Used to Be, Darling": Choreographing the Newport Waltz

Anxiety over the relationship between authenticity—the real, immediate, organic object or image—and imitation—the manufactured, packaged, approximated commodity—has been a "recurring metaphysical preoccupation" in American civilization, according to Americanist Miles Orvell, inspiring an obsession with the folk, the organic, the original, and the natural, and driving a "consuming effort to restore contact with real things."[1] This tension was driven by the mass-manufacture of consumer goods, each one of which was an exact duplicate of every other, and by the dominance and pervasiveness of the machine, which replicated, reproduced, and standardized. Orvell's argument can be elaborated into the domain of sound and expression to locate a cultural anxiety about the authenticity and idiosyncrasy of musicians and performances, an anxiety that Rinzler, like Lomax, learned to live with.

The relationship between the performers of French Louisiana music and the patrons who wished to promote the music to a national audience became one of mutual ambassadorship in unfamiliar territory. Tentative forays by older Southwest Louisiana musicians onto the national stage developed into ambitious projects to record and expand the listening audience for French-language music and attract a younger generation of musicians back home into apprenticeship in the genre. The popularization of the regional sound led French Louisiana musicians to experiment with more commercially popular instruments and styles. Civil rights era folklorists working in Lyndon Johnson's Washington began to discern the socio-

© The Author(s) 2019
P. Peknik, *French Louisiana Music and Its Patrons,*
https://doi.org/10.1007/978-3-319-97424-8_6

political utility of showcasing the genre's genesis in collaborations between white and black musicians. And so, at the national music festivals that would feature some of the most talented practitioners of old-time French Louisiana music, it was never simply about the music.

Rinzler got caught in the contradictions of trying to sustain and preserve a traditional culture, which is a conservative objective, while working from a set of liberal, progressive principles within the boundaries of a commercial event. He wanted the music culture of Southwest Louisiana to benefit from outside funding, marketing and appreciation, while protecting the culture of Southwest Louisiana itself from change. "Life there is like nowhere else," he said, "and in some ways, it should remain that way."[2] Thus, even if younger and commercially oriented musicians wanted to experiment with new genres, Rinzler did not want them to want that. His goal was not to help regional musicians become what they wanted, but to help them remain what they had been. His work for the Newport Folk Festival was evidence both of how deeply committed he, like Lomax and Smith before him, was to the ideals of racial egalitarianism and cultural equity, and of how difficult it was to neatly package and promote these cultural politics. Rinzler saw the folk revival movement itself as predicated on the existence of an elite urban privileged class who could idealize "the peasantry" and their roots in "the romance of the pastoral" only because they were separated from "the folk" by "education, social position, and economic resources."[3] Rinzler was interested in both the instrumental composition of traditional bands, with their old-fashioned folk banjos and fiddles, and in the lyrical content of the songs, which told the stories of the grievances and triumphs of the socially marginalized, and he thought there was an important, and progressive, message in the music about the value of old-fashioned community life.

But Rinzler had to contend with the same fact that Lomax had grappled with, which was that, in spite of Lomax's deeply felt conviction that musicians could be "provided with a socio-political rationale for their musical activity,"[4] traditional old-time musicians were nothing like their revival counterparts. They didn't have, or need, or want to be given, a sociopolitical rationale for their performance. They were musicians by avocation or by profession, community entertainers. The first American folk music festivals, including North Carolina's Mountain Dance and Folk Festival in 1928 and the National Folk Festival held in St. Louis in 1934, had been completely non-political events organized in a tourist and recreational framework,[5] and Rinzler became frustrated by how difficult it was to achieve his goal of popularizing traditional music, making it marketable in the service of progressive political ideals, and still protect old-time musicians from the innovations and pressures of the contemporary urban music scene—in fact, he had to persuade certain old-time musicians that they shouldn't find those innovations or opportunities appealing.

The field work that Rinzler did to locate those musicians in the first place brought him back not just to the same communities, but to some of the same houses that Lomax and Oster had visited. Harry Oster provided Rinzler with information about the towns where he had done research and introduced him to local singers and musicians. Rinzler's field work in Louisiana, across several southern states and into French-speaking Canada, transformed the nature of the Newport Folk Festival, as well as folklorists' assumptions about the possibilities of field work, Rinzler explained: "People had sort of coasted on the assumption that the Library of Congress had really covered the field in the '30s and '40s and that there really wasn't that much left—it was slim pickings. Individuals like Mike Seeger had all looked into different regional traditions wherever they happened to be, or in areas that they happened to be interested in. They'd come back with a wealth of material, just really good musicians and good instrumentalists. And it was evident that if you looked, you could find materials anywhere."[6]

In April 1964, Rinzler traveled to Diamond in Plaquemines Parish on the banks of the Mississippi, where he recorded Creole singer Alma Barthelemy, whose voice had been recorded by Oster in 1957, singing "*En me promenant*" [While Out Walking] and "*Beau Cavalier*," [Handsome Cavalier] songs that were characteristic of the a capella "home music" wives and mothers performed on their front porches and at family gatherings.[7] Also in Barthelemy's repertoire were the songs "*Par derrière chez mon père*" [Out In Back of my Father's House], a song sung by Cajuns to commemorate their ancestors' experience of exile from French Canada, along with "*C'est la Sainte Marguerite*," a ballad commemorating the martyred Christian Saint Margaret, persecuted for her religious faith by her pagan father, "*Un jour dedans Paris*" [A Day in Paris] and "*Il y a une Allemande*," [There is a German Lady]. Barthelemy, whom Rinzler considered an extraordinary vocalist, was a Creole singer, and the songs, rooted in the Cajun historical experience, provided explicit evidence of the shared Cajun-Creole musical tradition.

Many in Barthelemy's extended family were rice farmers or fishermen, and many of the songs her father used to sing came from a songbook of the music of Pierre-Jean de Béranger, an early nineteenth-century French songwriter who composed poetic songs about French history, the monarchy and the Catholic church, including songs critical of Napoleon and supportive of the revolutionary and democratic movements of eighteenth-century and nineteenth-century France.[8] That was exactly what Rinzler was looking for: songs from the French continental tradition sung by Cajun and Creole singers in their homes, not because those songs were peculiar artifacts of an incomprehensible past, but because even though they had their origin in the generational or cultural past, they still did a kind of work—storytelling, entertaining—that a contemporary song could not do as beautifully, like the grandfather clock whose weights and pendulum lyre make the passage of time visible, and through whose grinding gears and bells the arrival of a new hour is dramatized. Modern-day society did not preclude folk expression any more so than it precluded the heirloom watch or the mortar and pestle; folk expressions about needles in haystacks have endured in contemporary spoken English.

Rinzler and Barthelemy discussed the origins and narratives of some of the twenty-nine songs Barthelemy performed, with Rinzler keen on identifying those that had been least altered over time or were always sung the same way by everyone in the community and by people of different generations. "*Toujours la même chose,*" she said ["Always the same thing"]. This reveals Rinzler's definition of the folk tradition as constituted by the ritual performance of a piece of ancestral or community music. Indeed, throughout his fieldwork in Southwest Louisiana, Rinzler was keen on identifying those songs that performers had learned from their parents and grandparents rather than from public performances, radio or records. Forty years after radio had come to some Southwest Louisiana homes, Rinzler saw these third-generation radio audiences as the bearers of the music traditions of their grandparents, and this view seemed to be borne out whenever informants said that they had learned a certain song from grandparents or elderly neighbors.[9] But the oral tradition is both conservative and innovative, certain melodies and lyrics preserved while others are revised and adapted, not only from generation to generation but also from one singer to the next. The folk tradition is also constituted by the creative acting upon of ancestral or community music by an individual performer who embellishes and particularizes the song, or who borrows a storyline from one song to create another entirely different song. Columbus Fruge's "*Valse de Bayou Teche*" has an entirely different melody than Nathan Abshire's "*Valse de Bayou Teche,*" even while in both Fruge's song and Abshire's song, a man laments that his lover's family has interfered in their courtship:

Si t'aurais voulu m'écouter, chère,
Toi tu s'rais au Bayou Teche avec ton nèg' chérie !
T'as écouté ton papa et ta maman, chère
Les embarras de ton papa et ta maman, chère. (Frugé)

[If only you'd listened to me, darling
You'd be in Bayou Teche with your sweetheart, my dear
But you listened to your mother and father, dear
And they are keeping us apart, dear]

J'ai roulé, j'ai prié, pour t'avoir, chère;
Pour t'avoir avec moi dans ma chambre.
Mon beau frère, mon beau frère, viens donc m'voir, cher
Viens donc m'voir près d'mourir au Bayou Teche (Abshire)[10]

[I wandered, I prayed to see you, my darling
To have you here in my room.
Dear brother-in-law come to Bayou Teche and see
Come and see how it's killing me]

Thus there are themes and characters, lyrical fragments and melodic lines that form a core vocabulary in the music, but "*Toujours la même chose*" has to be understood as Barthelemy's conclusion, which oughtn't to have become Rinzler's. Barthelemy was a singer of the "home music" songs sung only by women in their own homes[11]; she likely wouldn't have traveled far beyond her community and heard other versions of the songs. What Rinzler was after was those songs in the folk tradition that had been sung the same way across generations and communities, figuring that they that were important enough to have been transmitted nearly whole cloth, that their form had been fixed. But a song that was important enough to have been performed and adapted and interpreted over time by many people in neighboring communities into their own versions was evidence of its having been well used over time, such that each community had made it its own, that each singer had made it their own. Adaptations and revisions happen naturally and improvisationally. Only the publishing of sheet music and the recording and broadcast of a single version of a song arrest this process. The recorded version of a song takes on an authority that compels the individual performer who has heard that same version repeatedly broadcast or played on a jukebox less likely to alter the musical or lyrical phrasing. This happens across all folk genres, just as it did with the blues: "Before the jukebox, and way before blues radio, the way a person played a particular song could reveal the town or plantation where they'd learned it …. Recordings … etched a permanence to lyrics that had previously been mutable."[12]

As is clear from Rinzler's transcriptions of the lyrics of "*Cadet Roussel*," as sung by Barthelemy—who says she knew it from childhood—this is not the same song, despite the title, as the "*Cadet Roussel*" that appears on Harry Oster's *Folksongs of the Louisiana Acadians,* sung by Mamou carpenter Isom J. Fontenot. In Fontenot's song, a young man outdoes even the king because he has finer possessions than the king has:

> *C'est un bon jeune homme*
> *C'est un vaillant beau*
> *Il a des chiens que la roi n'a pas si bons….*
> *Il a un habit que le roi n'a pas si bel*

> [Cadet Roussel] is a good young man
> He's a brave and handsome lad
> The dogs he has are even better than the king's
> And he has an outfit more beautiful than the king's.]

Barthelemy's version, which she told Rinzler her family sang on Christmas, is comical and bawdy:

> *Oh Cadet Roussel avait trois souliers*
> *Deux qu'il met dans les deux pieds*
> *Et le troisième n'a pas de semelle*
> *C'est pour lui chausser sa belle*

> *Cadet Roussel avait trois bons chiens*
> *Qui n'y voient goutte et qui jappent bien*
> *Oh quand tu les appelles, ça fout le camp*
> *Mais que dites-vous de Cadet Roussel?*[13]

> [Cadet Roussel had three shoes
> Two that he put on his two feet
> And the third didn't have a sole
> But it fit his girlfriend well

> Cadet Roussel had three good dogs
> Who were blind and loudly barked
> Oh when you called them to come they always ran away
> What do you think about Cadet Roussel?]

French Louisiana music was traditional folk music in the sense that musicians were self-taught, having learned by imitating other musicians in the family or immediate community, and in the sense that the music was valued for its social, not its commercial, attributes. But "remaking" the songs was a rite of passage for accomplished musicians, who made the changes that best suited the purposes of their immediate communities. It isn't sufficient to define French Louisiana folk music the way Irish folk music, for example, has been defined, as "a body of tunes held in common by members of a national group,"[14] since in the case of French Louisiana music, it's the fact that the instrumentation and language are common to all the songs, and that the French language was uncommon in the larger culture, that is more consequential than the fact that there is a "body of tunes."

Why does it matter that Rinzler was looking for songs that had been transmitted whole cloth, in which melodies and storylines had been preserved, pieces that were passed as finished and unchanging artifacts from parent to child and neighbor to neighbor, when in fact, no such songs truly existed? It matters because the real nature of folk music transmission in Southwest Louisiana—participatory, collective, improvisational—was a more compelling model of democracy and racial and cultural politics than any other, and certainly a more compelling model than the presentation of folk music as a relic from the lives of a traditional population that had simply memorized received forms, and taught their children to do the same. The dynamic social engagement that created French Louisiana music, with white and black musicians working from common texts, was more novel and radical to most Americans than any of the protest music Columbia Records proudly advertised as the soundtrack of "all the revolutionaries."[15]

The Southwest Louisiana promoters of French-language music were hardly motivated by a revolutionary political sensibility. Rather, the French language, and French Louisiana cultural traditions, were what Paul Tate championed in a speech at the Opelousas Yambilee Performance in October 1964 when he told an audience that included Rinzler and Mike Seeger that Southwest Louisianans should be proud that the Newport Folk Foundation had taken an interest in their "French music."[16] Tate sometimes represented local recording artists (some of whom, unable to read English, had relied on handshakes) in their contracts with labels and studios,[17] so was a trustworthy spokesman among musicians, and his allegiance was to the language and the community. Revon Reed had begun broadcasting an old-time French-language music program over KEUN from Fred's Lounge in 1962. Now Tate and Reed would have a chance to shape the Newport Folk Foundation's understanding of French Louisiana music and its rightful place in the folk revival.

Reed introduced Rinzler to local musicians, bringing in Nathan Abshire and Edward and Elby "Bee" DesHotels, whose father was a violinist, accordionist and teller of French folk tales, setting up auditions for his friends Cyprien and Adam Landreneau and their neighbor Edius Naquin, whose repertoire consisted exclusively of folk songs that had originated in Normandy, Brittany and Gascony, and arranging recording sessions, including one in which Reed played triangle accompanying the Landreneaus and Dewey Balfa. Tate traveled throughout Southwest Louisiana with Rinzler and Seeger, introducing them to local musicians and arranging their performances at local festivals, including the Ville Platte Cotton Festival, which had been established in 1953 by World War II veterans, and the Crowley Rice Festival.

Tate was a talented organizer and committed Democratic party activist with a gift for seeing how local cultural issues connected to the larger political and social picture. In 1959, he arranged the appearance of Senator John F. Kennedy at the 1959 Crowley Rice Festival. Kennedy was looking to generate Southern support leading up to his announcement of his presidential candidacy. The alliance between Massachusetts and Louisiana Democrats had been formed during the 1956 Democratic National Convention in Chicago, when Louisiana's delegates, including Crowley native Judge Edmund M. Reggie, were seated across the aisle from the Massachusetts delegates throughout the week-long convention. Reggie, who had persuaded his fellow Louisiana delegates to support Kennedy as Adlai Stevenson's vice presidential candidate,[18] hosted JFK's visit to Crowley, where he met with Democratic State Senator Edwin Edwards, who made much of his Cajun heritage in his many campaigns for public office, from Crowley City Council to the governorship. The French-speaking Catholic crowd of 135,000 at the International Rice Festival was won over when the Catholic Senator Kennedy's French-speaking wife, Jacqueline Bouvier Kennedy, addressed them in French: "So she gets up there and, in French, she recounts a story about how when she was a little girl, her father had told her that Louisiana was way down south, but it … was a little part of France, and she had been in love with it ever since. Well, what do you think? I mean, the house comes down."[19] Democratic political organizer Philip Desmarais recalled in a 1966 interview that the enthusiastic crowds that came out to see the Kennedys prompted Louisiana

Supreme Court Judge John Fournet to remark to him, "My God; Huey [Huey P. Long] never got anything like this."[20]

Kennedy's pre-campaign stops in Louisiana were savvy political theater, as Catholics, who comprised one-third of the state's population, were disproportionately represented in the ranks of active voters. Kennedy's Louisiana supporters also organized stops at the Opelousas Yambilee Festival—another festival that was organized in the immediate post-war period (1946), and another one of the festivals Rinzler and Seeger attended—and in Lake Charles, then in New Orleans, where Kennedy met with NAACP leader Alexander Pierre Tureaud. In the 1956 election, seventy-five percent of black Louisianans had voted for Eisenhower, but Kennedy appealed so strongly to Catholic, Creole and African-American voters in Louisiana that in the 1960 election, seventy percent voted for Kennedy. Judge Reggie, who had been a longtime friend of Joseph Kennedy, Sr., managed Kennedy's campaign in Louisiana in 1960, and maintained close bonds with the Kennedy family for decades (his daughter, Victoria, married Senator Edward Kennedy of Massachusetts); Philip Desmarais was appointed by Kennedy to serve as Deputy Assistant Secretary for the Department of Health, Education, and Welfare in 1961. The festivals that were such important stops for Kennedy were also key stops for Rinzler and Seeger.

Rinzler and Seeger compiled forty-eight reels of tape of Southwest Louisiana music during their trips in 1964, 1965 and 1966, recording musicians in their homes, at Fred's Lounge, where Revon Reed's KEUN broadcasts of old-time music featured news and advertisements in French, at a jam session in Mamou's Hotel Cazan, and at festivals, where the Newport Folk Foundation offered prize money to the winners of traditional music competitions. The Foundation sponsored contests at the Louisiana Folk Festival in Ville Platte, the Yambilee Festival in Opelousas (where Revon Reed gave out the prizes), the Dairy Festival in Abbeville, and the Cotton Festival in Ville Platte, where Mrs. Charlton Guillory performed "*La Marseillaise*" in the singing contest.

The tunes Rinzler recorded during the Louisiana sessions constitute a perfect set list from the French Louisiana repertoire, from adaptations of Old World songs composed in seventeenth- and eighteenth-century France ("*Auprès de ma blonde,*" "*Chanson de Bonaparte,*" "*La fille du roi*"), to songs that emerged from the New World experiences of white and black settlers in the Acadian parishes ("*J'ai passé devant ta porte,*" "*Jolie blonde,*" "*Allons à Lafayette,*" "*Allons danser, Colinda,*" "*J'ai été au bal hier soir"*). Rinzler found one of the old-time recording artists still performing (Preston Manuel, who had recorded in 1937),[21] while the younger generation was experimenting with "a little electric music."

Rinzler's work in Southwest Louisiana differed significantly from his projects in other parts of the South, where he saw the Newport Folk Foundation in a revivalist role, persuading blues and bluegrass musicians to perform again and creating local audiences for roots music. In Southwest Louisiana, however, old-time musicians were still performing every weekend at dance halls throughout the region. In 1960, there were a dozen radio stations that played French-language music and a number of local record labels recorded traditional music, including the *La Louisiane* label, founded in Lafayette in 1959.[22] What Rinzler wanted for Southwest Louisiana was a national audience that would allow old-time musicians' work to continue to be vitally important at a time when the younger generation was less interested in apprenticing themselves to traditional musicians than they were in experimenting with the sounds of New Orleans and Memphis rhythm and blues. Younger musicians were putting aside the fiddle and accordion in favor of using new instrumentation, including piano, saxophone, electric guitar and full percussion kits, to play swamp pop music.

Swamp pop had developed in the nightclubs of Lafayette, Ville Platte, Opelousas and Lawtell where both young Cajun and Creole musicians performed, and these musicians collaborated in recording studios, including Eddie Schuler's, and J.D. Miller's Crowley studio, whose session band included both black and white musicians. The young generation reworked songs from the traditional canon and popularized them with younger listeners, although "*Colinda*," "*Jolie blonde*," and "*Hip et taïaut*" were mostly in English ("an attempt to appeal to a wider, non-francophone audience").[23] The "golden age of swamp pop" was short-lived—1958 to 1963—and largely generational, with young musicians looking to New Orleans musician Fats Domino's 1956 "Blueberry Hill" as a model for how to combine Creole-French vocal phrasings with the rhythms of the new rock.[24] Those old-time musicians who concluded that there wasn't any longer a big demand for their music were responding to the popularity of rhythm and blues and rock with teenagers ("I had to put my accordion on the armoire because they all wanted rock and roll," Creole musician Bois Sec Ardoin said),[25] not to the fact that their own generation had abandoned old-time music ("People want to hear the old style, they don't like the new music too much," Cajun performer Aldus Roger insisted.)[26]

The most important facts about swamp pop in the context of the discussion of traditional French-language music in Louisiana is that some of the local labels that had been recording old-time music began investing instead in swamp pop. Swamp pop provides yet another example of collaboration between Creole and Cajun musicians in Louisiana post-war culture: "The musical integration in swamp-pop was facilitated by a racial climate that was more relaxed in Southwest Louisiana than in much of the South," swamp pop guitarist Earl King remembered. "I used to hear a few bands had racial problems ... I think it was in certain areas of the South, but South Louisiana, no. They're just fine, these people are just so interwoven into one another." Swamp pop performer Ron Bernard had similar memories: "We never thought of it as being a black-white thing," Bernard explained. "There was just good music that everybody played."[27]

Alan Lomax made a similar, perhaps overstated observation about race relations after visiting a horse racing track on a summer day: "The thing that surprises most people about this scene is the fact that black people and white people meet on these horse race tracks and have fun and there's no problems and everybody hollers and everybody jumps up and down and they call each other names. I'm a southerner and I never saw anything like that in my whole life until I went to Carencro on weekends. This is the one place where the whole race stuff just never did work," Lomax said.[28] But time and again, Lomax put "the whole race stuff" to work in telling the story of American music history. For "Folksong 59" at Carnegie Hall, he had presented bluegrass and gospel, country and blues, proclaiming to the audience that the folk movement was a success not only because the music of the Mississippi Delta poured out of jukeboxes across the nation, but also because, hearing ballad singers in the city subway, "When I closed my eyes I couldn't tell a Negro from a white singer."[29]

Rinzler had a strong liberal commitment to progress in the Civil Rights movement, and his fascination with race relations in Southwest Louisiana is reflected in the kinds of questions he asked in his fieldwork interviews. One of the first questions he posed to Joe Falcon is whether he remembered many black musicians playing music during his childhood, and after Falcon explained that Creole musicians played "the same thing we was playing," with the same kind of rhythm, Rinzler pursued the same line of questioning with Cajun fiddler Leo Soileau:

Rinzler: Did you ever hear any colored people play French music?
Soileau: I played for years with Amédé Ardoin.
Rinzler: Did they call the music the Negros played the same name?
Soileau: They didn't talk about it differently….
Rinzler: In one band of musicians, they'd have white and colored musicians together.
Soileau: Yeah.
Rinzler: That's something you don't see nowadays.
Soileau: Now they [in this country] want to kill [blacks].
Rinzler: Do you believe [this music] is kind of dying out or this kind of music will stay around for a while.
Soileau: Oh, I believe it'll stick. There's more people recording now.
Rinzler: What did they call music in those days? Did they call it Cajun music? Creole music?
Soileau: French music.[30]

Rinzler developed a set of questions to ask each of the musicians he recorded, and their answers create a portrait of Southwestern Louisiana musicians engaged in community and professional music and variably exposed to or ignorant of developments in mainstream popular music. Dewey Balfa, whose father farmed cotton, sweet potatoes and corn, stated his occupation as superintendent of sales for an insurance company. Asked whether he played in order to earn extra money, he said, "Would rather be top notch pro than anything in the world." Rinzler's line of questioning reveals his concerns about the provenance and authenticity of the music and its performers. Balfa was the only one of Rinzler's informants who asserted an interest in becoming a revered professional. The others, asked whether they played for the money, said, "*Plutot pour la musique*" [More for the music], "Yes, but I still enjoy it" or "No, just for the music." Rinzler had a series of questions about race and genre that stumped some of the musicians: "Do you know any Negroes who play French music? If so who? Where do they live? What is the music that French-speaking Negroes play? Is their music different from other French music?" Cajun musician Roy Fuselier, who lived on 2nd Street in Mamou, reported that yes, he had heard Creole performers play French music, and when asked where, he said, "My house in Mamou." He described the Creole style as "rough time," and said that, whether played by whites or by Creoles, the music was called Cajun, and that he had been most inspired by Amédé Ardoin. Rice farmer Wallace James "Cheese" Reed stated that he knew "many" Creoles who played the same music as Cajuns, and he attributed its origins to the mixing of the music of formerly enslaved African-Americans with "French and Cajun." Bois Sec Ardoin insisted that the name of the genre of music that French-speaking Creoles played was simply "French music." Isom Fontenot reported that he had heard Bois Sec play in Mamou, and that no, the French music he played wasn't different from the French music white musicians played. He had heard Creole harmonica players and heard Creoles play the blues, but had never tried to play like them, he told Rinzler.

Rinzler was also interested in knowing what non-local musical influences informed the musicians' repertoire and performance style, and must have been surprised when Dewey Balfa listed his "favorite non-Cajun musicians" as Johnny Cash and George Jones. Isom Fontenot said that he listened to the Grand Ole Opry and Louisiana Hayride, and liked hillbilly and country music. Belton Richard learned new music and new styles of music from records and from the very occasional Grand Ole Opry broadcast, while Roy Fuselier liked Bill Monroe and Hank Williams. Bois Sec Ardoin, however, said that he wasn't influenced by any recording artists as a child because his family had no records ["*On n'avait pas des discques*"] and that as for genres other than French Louisiana music: "*Ne sait pas beaucoup de ce genre de musique*" [I don't know much about that kind of music]. As for his favorite non-French Louisiana musician, Aldus Roger said, "Not interested."

Had the musicians been influenced by music they'd heard in Texas? The most Rinzler could get in affirmative response was Wallace "Cheese" Reed's "Not exactly. Perhaps learned a little different style." Travel to Southwest Louisiana from other regions was "too difficult," Fuselier explained, so the only live music he'd heard in childhood was local. All of the musicians recalled having learned music at a very early age from family members: Isom Fontenot, who grew up a carpenter's son on South Street in Mamou, learned harmonica from his brother-in-law when he was nine, and recalled hearing his father sing "old songs." Fontenot, who was born in 1908, said that his favorite musician when he was a child was a Creole musician. The songs that were being played in Southwest Louisiana in the mid-1960s still had the same tunes, he explained, though there were different lyrics here and there. "They're still playing the same tunes. They've changed the words," Roy Fuselier said.

Dewey Balfa painted a portrait of a music-filled childhood home in which his talented father played fiddle three or four nights a week, as did his oldest brother (until his brother left home to get married, and took his fiddle with him), and he recalled the invitation-only Saturday night *bals des maisons* at which he first performed. Belton Richard's father and six uncles all played accordion. Most musicians said they had not composed original music. When asked who taught them to play, some of the musicians responded "No one." Though most of the questions had to do with the musicians' early exposure to music and the development of their craft, Rinzler persisted in posing a series of questions about alcohol use: Do you play/sing better if you drink when you play? Do you ever play without drinking? Do most musicians play best when they drink? The answers were either yes, or a little, or that it wasn't necessary to drink, or that it depended on the person. At the end of the interview, Bois Sec told Rinzler: "It's like being admitted to prison, this questionnaire."

Rinzler's informants testified to the history of a shared repertoire and cross-racial artistic collaboration, and that is part of what Rinzler wished to put on stage at Newport. For the 1964–1967 festivals, he arranged for both Cajun and Creole musicians to perform, including Canray Fontenot and Alphonse "Bois Sec" Ardoin, Clifton Chenier, Isom Fontenot, and Adam and Cyprien Landreneau. Rinzler's goal was to generate a sincere and enduring interest in old-time music on a national scale so that regional music could reap the benefits, with a proportion of the proceeds of the Newport Folk Festival to be directed back into field work, local festivals, and grants to organizations and projects that supported folk music. He saw these performers as organic bearers of a folk tradition, and hoped that national exposure would get people "back in the swing of the music which they loved for years but abandoned for poor reasons."[31]

But the first-time ever national presentation of an ages-old American folk music created by black and white musicians who had lived and worked together for centuries was also a powerful symbol, in the weeks just after President Lyndon Johnson signed the Civil Rights Act of 1964, of the kind of society Rinzler imagined was finally possible during a year that the nation was, in historian Terry Anderson's words, at "the pinnacle of liberalism."[32] Harry Smith may have made his point about race by omitting biographical information in his liner notes, but Rinzler would make it through the very visible medium of the festival stage. Expressed through the polished songs of Joan Baez and Peter, Paul and Mary, the appeal to a sense of the common humanity of all Americans seemed to be the brand-new message of the young generation; delivered through the music of Cajun and Creole accordionists, fiddlers, harmonica players, and vocalists, it was the sage and rugged common sense wisdom of an older generation who grew up in the

American past. The theme of racial equality was, in some sense, a kind of festival motif, as *New York Times* journalist Robert Shelton noted in his coverage of the festival: "There was a democratizing spirit about this fusion of white and Negro musical forms and about the people who are the conveyor belts of these traditions that was little short of utopian."[33]

Mike Seeger brought a different liberal politics to his vision of the festival lineup, suggesting in a letter to the board of directors of the Newport Folk Foundation the following year that subsequent festivals include more female performers[34] and more songs in foreign languages. Seeger had, from his first involvement with Newport, advocated that a broader range of American musical forms be featured, including American Indian, Hawaiian, Eskimo, Dutch, German, Jewish, Italian, and Polish. John Cohen explained that bringing southern white performers like Tennessee banjoist Clarence Ashley, bluegrass guitarist Doc Watson, and Virginia bluegrass musicians Ralph and Carter Stanley to the stage of northern festivals was never simply about the music: "The act of finding linkages between people who would otherwise be opposed to one another was interesting and political. We were putting our stamp of approval on these white guys who until that time had been stereotyped as racists, lynchers, and all those nightmarish things about the South. We were trying to turn Ashley and Watson and the Stanleys into real people ... acknowledging these people and their culture was political..."[35]

In 1964 and 1965, when Alan Lomax, Ralph Rinzler, Mike Seeger and Pete Seeger were all on the board of the Newport Folk Foundation together, Pete Seeger argued that the foundation should direct funds back to local communities to support young musicians' playing of old-time music: "I'm very concerned with the slow dying-out of some very wonderful musicians who are not being replaced, so I'd like to cast my vote for any project however humble, by which some one or another tradition can be kept alive in its home grounds." At the 1964 festival, Lomax was unhappy that the festival still featured many urban folk performers. Although one of the financial strategies of the festival was that well-known folk musicians would draw the crowds who would then be introduced to grassroots musicians—"the good unknown performer"—Lomax found it impossible to bite his tongue when confronted with the "inauthenticity" of the polished commercial bands. He compared the Chicago electric Paul Butterfield Blues Band unfavorably to "the old-time farmer who played blues for himself and his friends on a box with an ax handle glued to it, and homemade strings."[36]

Lomax's exhortation to a workshop audience to go beyond the music and "collect the people and learn about their lives and needs"[37] has the exhibitionary ring of P.T. Barnum. And some of the old-time musicians were frustrated and confounded by the patronizing applause of audiences that, acutely aware of the performers as travelers from a different socioeconomic world, seemed to be not only clapping for the music but also patting themselves on the back for their enlightened class and racial politics. Fiddler Clayton "Pappy" McMichen made his contempt clear: "What are you people doing here? You don't know anything about the music," he told the audience. "You're the easiest audience in the world to play for, because you don't want anything from us. I could play the worst fiddle in the world, and you'd still applaud. You just like us because we're old."[38] McMichen, who was sixty-four when he appeared at Newport, had recorded for Decca in the 1930s and 1940s, and was skilled at playing jazz, original compositions, and Tin Pan Alley standards. The question "What are you people doing here?" was a cultural and a sociological question, and McMichen didn't want anything to do with the audience's desire to experience the strange, "authentic" rural South—that haunted world of field-work poverty and racial violence and despair—in the privileged, controlled environment of a New England seacoast music festival. He was aggravated at the public fascination with hillbillies and mountaineers, but was gracious with Rinzler about it in a letter later that summer: "We were both happy and glad for you that the Festival was the success it was meant to be. If you should ever happen to be in our neck of the woods, please let us hear from you so that we can try to return some of the wonderful hospitality we received."

For the 1964 festival, Rinzler invited Revon Reed's friends, Cajun accordionists Gladius Thibodeaux and Louis "Vinesse" LeJeune (a cousin of Iry LeJeune). Paul Tate and Revon Reed accompanied the group to Newport, with Reed playing triangle in the ensemble, which included the last-minute addition of fiddler Dewey Balfa, substituting for a musician who couldn't get permission from his parole officer to leave Louisiana. The band opened with "Grand Mamou" and received a standing ovation. Balfa, who was used to playing for an audience of one or two hundred, was shocked by the roaring applause of the crowd of 17,000 at Newport.[39] Not long after, Balfa would pen "Newport Waltz," whose lyrics told other Cajun musicians about the welcome reception the Louisianans had received at the festival:

C'est là bas à Newport on a été
On s'est fait un tas de bon amis.
J'aimerais dire à tous les Cadiens
Si tu veux un bon temps, va au festival, yaie.[40]

[We went to Newport
We made a lot of good friends
I'd like to tell all the Cajuns
If you want to have a good time, go to the festival (loud yell)]

Paul Tate, seeing Joan Baez dancing to Balfa's music, and hoping that her interest would inspire high school and college kids in Southwest Louisiana to take an interest in traditional music over "the current fads such as rock and roll," wrote her a letter asking her to perform a concert in Lafayette and include at least one Acadian song in French, for which he promised to send her the lyrics. "The Acadian music has not yet been reduced to sheet music," Tate wrote.

Balfa's presence at Newport turned out to be consequential for the future of traditional music in Louisiana, and if, as the Newport Folk Foundation directors concluded, the revival of interest in traditional Cajun music in southwest Louisiana was the most successful of the Foundation's many revival projects in small communities in North Carolina, Arkansas, Mississippi, Louisiana, and Georgia,[41] then that success also flowed from Balfa's response to the standing ovation and his determination to bring "the echo of that applause" back to his home.[42] Balfa had learned to play fiddle from his father, accordionist Charles Balfa, a sharecropper in Bayou Grand Louis near Mamou whose songs had come from Normandy and Nova Scotia.[43] During the 1940s, Balfa and his brothers Will and Rodney were playing eight shows a week in dance halls,[44] though music was still a pastime and not a living for Balfa, who drove a school bus, raised cattle, and worked as a salesman for a New Orleans-based insurance company. Balfa and his generation of old-time musicians had been waiting in dismay for heirs to the tradition to come forward, but the youngest musicians in Southwest Louisiana had directed their talents to swamp pop and rock, dismissing old-time music as the outdated music of the older generation at the same time that the nation's youth as a whole began to embrace the new sound of the Beatles and the British Invasion. Balfa had no idea what a festival was before going to Newport, and the invitation for Southwest Louisiana musicians to perform nationally had been met with skepticism and even derision in local newspapers, with an Opelousas journalist dismissing old-time music as an anachronistic, and unappealing, genre. "Everybody knows that it sounds like a bunch of cats fighting in an alley," the article read.[45] But surprisingly for these naysaying locals, the appearance of Cajun musicians at Newport "brought the young back into the fold,"[46] providing a cohort of role models outside of rock music.

Rinzler had worked with other Newport performers to be sure that the traditional musicians would play traditional songs at Newport. Finding himself on a national stage for the first time, Doc Watson wanted to play Eddie Arnold and Chet Atkins songs, believing that popular Nashville tunes were what the audience wanted. This was a "classic problem" for folklorists working with traditional musicians, Rinzler said: "A craftsperson can make something that looks like something he's just seen in a newspaper, thinking that that's what's the latest thing. So he'll copy a crockpot that's mass produced and sold at K-Mart because that's what he sees in the paper…" Rinzler had to convince Watson and some other old-time musicians that the way to become popular was to "take the deepest cut of tradition that they were in contact with through their family or community" and play "those songs … the grassroots stuff that was unique and distinctive regionally and familially."[47]

LeJeune, Thibodeaux, Reed, and Balfa were committed traditionalists who, rather than changing their music to suit the times, wanted the new times to embrace old-time music. As Paul Tate wrote in a letter to the board of directors of the Newport Folk Foundation, "The invitation of the Cajun band to Newport had the desired effect of giving stature to traditional Acadian music played on traditional instruments."[48] Balfa returned to Louisiana determined to use the success of Cajun music at Newport as an argument to the younger generation that their cultural heritage was an asset rather than a liability. Rinzler encouraged Balfa's activist approach, and the Newport Folk Foundation, on Rinzler's initiative, designed and funded the Louisiana Folk Foundation to support the cultural preservation work of Balfa and other local musicians, academics, and state and local politicians devoted to raising the stature of local culture.

Reed, Tate and a core group of local activists organized traditional music contests and concerts at local agricultural fairs in Crowley, Abbeville, and Opelousas, giving people the chance to hear old-time music outside a dance hall setting.[49] When Rinzler returned in October 1965, he found that the Louisiana Folk Foundation's interest had expanded to include a focus on the preservation of the French language. On that trip, Rinzler and Seeger recorded forty more reels of tape of French-language music sung by Cajuns, Creoles and the Houma Indians, and invited Canray Fontenot, Bois Sec Ardoin, Adam Landreneau, Cyprien Landreneau and Isom Fontenot to play at the Newport festival in 1966.[50] Rinzler described the Landreneaus, in a letter to John Pankake of the New Lost City Ramblers, as "two doughty old rice farmers," and counted on Revon Reed to "keep them together and sober." The letter perfectly captures Rinzler's perspectives and objectives:

> The older gents are perhaps the most picturesque looking pair you will ever have the pleasure of seeing on a stage. The fiddler looks like he stepped right out of a Bruegel country scene while the accordion player defies description but is basically rotund, bald, scarlet-faced with burning eyes, a fierce visage and a phenomenal sense of humor. Both men sing well in an all but extinct style; the fiddler is one of the finest traditional singers I have ever heard in terms of style. He is a hoarse, wild, strident tenor who ornaments his lines with yelps, whines and enthusiastic shouts. His fiddling style matches his singing. It sounds strangely like a thermin, always on pitch and quite sweet in sound but marked by a curious wheeling vibrato. ... The two older guys speak French most of the time but can get on well enough in English. They are not, however, really articulate in English. Further, they are experienced performers in the down home sense, but are far more relaxed when performing to strangers if Revon can introduce them and their songs for them. If not Revon, perhaps Paul Tate, an affluent lawyer, French speaker, and literature neighbor, can come and do the honors. Tate is a charming man who has devoted a great deal of time to the study of Cajun history and culture.[51]

As a patron of traditional music, Rinzler constantly worried about whether the dynamic, compelling sounds he'd heard on field recording trips, music he described as "brilliant, compelling ... wild and primitive" would translate to the stage. He wanted performers to be seen as rugged, earnest, unpolished and worthy because he had such a devout appreciation for traditional music, describing the way the sound of the voices of Gaelic singers on Cape Breton Island "still rings in my ears and delights my soul," and conscientiously wary of doing anything that would seem "selfish or political" as a patron of traditional music. He fretted over Bill Monroe's "depressing morass" of personal and financial problems: "I can understand the relationship of his music to his lonely life," Rinzler wrote in lobbying Pankake to book Monroe to perform. "I take no commission on his bookings for I feel he has given more than he received in the many years that he has been performing and creating. Flatt and Scruggs have monopolized the small bluegrass field and there is little left for Monroe (an entertainment has-been in Nashville terms) except to continue to create and inspire those who follow music rather than pop-record charts. Dammit...." Getting traditional performers gigs that would keep them "in the public eye," was paramount, and difficult, Rinzler explained to Pankake, describing the Kentucky banjo player Cousin Emmy as "having a habit of either not showing up or cancelling on short notice. But I feel she's worth a risk." He explained that a Louisville fiddler, bass, and jug group is "great if you can get them to do old stuff ... but they are not hip to the folk scene. This is ideal in many ways, and I prefer this situation to the traditional guy who is over-instructed and squared off to some city-folk guy's ideas of what tradition he feels the guy should represent."

Dewey Balfa was Rinzler's model performer, and Balfa would return to the Newport festival in 1967 with his brothers Will, Rodney, and Harry on fiddles, guitars, and triangle and Hadley Fontenot on accordion in the Balfa Brothers Band, the group he had formed after returning from his first Newport festival. The appreciative Newport audience motivated Balfa to approach Floyd Soileau of Swallow Records in Ville Platte to record the music of the Balfa Brothers and use his label to promote old-time music. Soileau, skeptical about the commercial potential of the Balfas' traditional sound, with the fiddlers dominating and the accordion in the background, hesitated, thinking the fiddle was outdated and that only an accordion-heavy sound would sell. Balfa explained that while his family band had several offers of recording contracts from out-of-state companies, he preferred to record the band's first sessions at home. "Floyd, we're going to be on somebody's label for sure, and the first song we're going to record is" *La valse de bambocheur* "[The Drunkard's Sorrowful Waltz]," Balfa explained. Floyd had been looking, without any luck, for a band to record that very song.[52] The popular success of French Louisiana music at Newport had also gotten the attention of Chris Strachwitz, who wrote to Rinzler, "Who were the members of the Cajun band you brought to Newport—everyone told me how good they were but no on knew any names."

Encouraged by the response to the Balfa Brothers' first single and album, Soileau began to record more old-time Cajun musicians, including Dennis McGee, Ed and Bee DesHotels, and the Landreneaus. Balfa wasn't surprised that Soileau and other local labels had lost faith in traditional music, since many locals had predicted that the Louisiana musicians would

153

be rejected at Newport. Balfa summarized expectations back home as "They're going out there to get laughed at."[53] Soileau acknowledged that it took the interest of outsiders to reignite his own interest in traditional music: "There were a lot of people away from here who were learning about Cajun music, they wanted that root sound. They would come in and inquire about some of the musicians and then later—I could still kick myself about this—it took fellows like Chris Strachwitz who came out of California to discover Joe Falcon, who was still alive at the time and living in Jennings—I didn't know about this—and some other talented musicians that they dug up and recorded." Most of the older musicians weren't playing dances anymore, and were not approaching local labels to record, but national labels had taken note of what happened at Newport: "Fortunately somebody had the foresight to come and dig around and find these people and record them," Soileau said, "And now they've got a good representation of some of the early Cajun things ... We've got a good spread now for future generations to be able to know what Cajun music was all about."[54]

Eddie Shuler of Goldband Records in Lake Charles was still recording traditional Cajun music because he knew it would always sell in that part of the country, if nowhere else, but he hadn't tried to promote it outside of Southwest Louisiana because he assumed the language barrier would be too great for a national audience to tolerate. "You couldn't understand what they were saying," he explained. But Soileau was respectful of the genre as a part of Louisiana's cultural heritage: "Here I was in the richest country in the world, you know, technologically speaking, monetary, ... and we have right here in our midst this truly authentic, truly undiscovered music.... Nobody knew it was here.... But I said, 'Well, I can preserve the music, supposing the world changes tomorrow and there won't be any Cajuns around to play this music.'"[55]

Fiddler Canray Fontenot and accordionist Alphonse "Bois Sec" Ardoin were indeed the last of their generation of old-time Creole musicians. Rinzler invited them to perform at the 1966 Newport festival, with Revon Reed as their guide. They were so afraid of losing him amid the throngs of people that they walked closely behind him through the crowds, Ardoin said: "*On marchait si près qu'on a tout écorché ses talons de souliers*"[56] [We walked so close we wore down the backs of his shoes]. In anticipation of the festival that year, Rinzler wrote to the editor of *Sing Out! Magazine*, the folk music journal, regarding a story on French Louisiana music: "I have some decent photos of Negro Cajun musicians and Harry [Oster] probably has some good photos of both white and Negro musicians. I think the article should cover both the Negro of 'zaidego' (sp?) and the white ('fais do do') traditions. There are other terms for the two depending on which area you're working in." Rinzler explained that there was no need to look back at "the good old days" or "golden age" of the music, holding that "the tradition of the music and language is still incredibly vital."

Ultimately, Rinzler's mission to educate middle-class urban listeners about the virtues of old music was out of step with younger listeners' understanding of the festival as a purely social event. By 1967, Rinzler had become disenchanted with the spectacle and hedonism of the festival. "There was something about bringing the best of tradition into the midst of an entertainment-oriented scene with a lot of kids drinking beer or smoking pot that was just really offensive to me,"[57] he said.

The 1964 festival attendance was over 70,000, and the traffic and noise were overwhelming for local residents and business owners. College students without tickets congregated on the streets of Newport, and city officials posted signs on major roadways leading into town asking that the unticketed "Keep Out of Newport."[58] This was hardly an environment in which the public could develop a sympathetic understanding of the integrity of regional music, and Rinzler worried that young middle-class college students were coming to the festival in the same spirit as the society rich had come to Newport in the Gilded Age, "passing fanciers" in a place of summer leisure.[59] Rinzler was frustrated that the festival compartmentalized and showcased only one aspect—music—of complex cultural traditions, presenting it within the boundaries of a commercial event, divorced from material culture and from the other creative activities within the culture that made the music expressive of an entire way of life.

In 1967, Rinzler accepted a job organizing the Smithsonian Festival of American Folklife, eager to combine music with the presentation of craftwork by harness makers, wheelwrights, and weavers and to provide opportunities for the public to talk with festival participants. Rinzler invited Dewey Balfa, "Vinesse" LeJeune's band, and two dozen other Southwest Louisiana musicians to perform. Balfa told the audience that he was amazed that the music of an isolated region had gained a broad audience, and in between songs he explained Cajun culture and history. The music of the Old World was presented alongside the music of the New World: Lulu Landry, like Alma Barthelemy a "home music" ballad singer from Louisiana, performed her version of "*La Chanson de la Mariée*" [The Bride's Song], immediately followed by Louise Reichert, from Auvergne, France, singing a version of the same song.[60]

Alma Barthelemy appeared at the festival in 1968, along with Doc Watson and Lightnin' Hopkins, and the festival program guide included an explanation of folk tradition quite at odds with Rinzler's view of folk arts as playing a still-vital role in contemporary culture: "Folklife in America is essentially a condition of the past; even where it still exists it belongs to the past." In a modern world where geographical distances were less important and popular culture had a homogenizing influence, folklife was "a vanishing anachronism which no amount of artifice can cause to endure." Even when folk traditions were still practiced, the stimulus for their temporary survival was "an urban, sophisticated market" that appreciated folk traditions as a popular trend, but modern technology, communication, and social attitudes would soon make the preservation of folk forms impossible: "While today's city-bred customers thus help to prolong traditional skills, the motivation changes and the product becomes a different one. Today, true folklife and folk expressions, fragile and flickering in a few belated cultural pockets, are like stubs of candles guttering in the breeze.... In the brief, dying interval in which they still exist, however, we are making haste to observe them and see, as it were, the past still living,"[61] the text concluded. Though these words may have expressed the academic analysis of folk culture, Rinzler never surrendered his view of folk music and crafts as an integral, dynamic aspect of the American cultural landscape, and his success in organizing the Festival of American Folklife on the National Mall would inspire the passage of the American Folklife Preservation Act.

This act, introduced by Democratic Texas Senator Ralph Yarborough, stated that each American participated in the distinctive "ways" of his family, ethnic group, region and occupation, all of which comprised "his traditional or folk culture," which had been learned orally and "maintained without institutional direction." In addition, each American shared with all Americans the customs and traditions of the national culture. The federal government had a legitimate interest in studying and supporting American folklife, including music, language, "wisdom" and lore, because the nation's constituent cultures fostered "a sense of identity and individuality" within that national culture. The bill proposed to fund the presentation of folklife programs which met "standards of authenticity" and were of such "significant merit" that they could encourage a greater public awareness of American cultural diversity.[62] Cultural diversity meant, most explicitly, racial and regional diversity, and the inclusion of French Louisiana music allowed Rinzler to fold in ethnic and linguistic diversity.

Rinzler subscribed to folklorist Benjamin Botkin's belief in folklore as "germinal rather than vestigial,"[63] as coherent and present system rather than as driftwood thrown up by the nationalizing and standardizing tide of mass culture: "This is the American rhythm," Botkin wrote about American folk music, "the American declamation, the American experience."[64] The foundational tradition of French Louisiana music as one part of that American national experience could be nurtured, praised, funded and promoted, Rinzler argued, as a way of generating and regenerating, not memorializing, Southwest Louisiana French culture. And Rinzler found the rapport between Cajun and Creole musicians instructive at a moment when Americans were grappling with the politics of race: for the 1969 festival, he introduced the Balfa and Ardoin families by saying, "There's a large body of French language music.... and both white and black musicians play a lot of the same tunes and then in each family or community there's a lot of material that is distinctive with only the family or the community." Mike Seeger hosted an evening concert by the Ardoins and Canray Fontenot, which was listed as "Louisiana-French Black Music" in the program. But the rapport between Cajun and Creole musicians couldn't be understood or appreciated by some festival attendees: an audience member criticized Rinzler for putting the Balfas on stage first, before the Ardoins. "Now, let's not make a preposterous issue out of this," Rinzler said. "We would have started with the blacks if there had been amplifiers for them here. They weren't here. That's the only reason we didn't start with them."[65]

The idea of an integrated Southern folk band contradicted the regional stereotypes that Washington festivalgoers brought to the venue. The Civil Rights movement in Southwest Louisiana was a relatively quiet and orderly affair, and the region experienced relatively little racial conflict over voting and desegregation, particularly in Catholic parishes. By 1956, twice as many blacks were registered to vote in Louisiana's French Catholic parishes as in its Anglo-Protestant ones. In St. Mary Parish, black candidates garnered white support and even ran on integrated tickets, and in an area around Opelousas, one Congress of Racial Equality worker organized a farmers' market cooperative whose two hundred members included thirty-five whites. Some NAACP branches in southern Louisiana began to attract a significant number of white members by the mid-1960s.[66] What was true of Louisiana in general was true of Southwest Louisiana a dozen times over: among blacks and whites there was always, said NAACP field secretary Harvey Britton said, "an underlying feeling of comradeship."[67] The Balfas and the Ardoins were cultural evidence of the potential for productive collaboration.

But that sense of comradeship would be challenged by a new focus by state and local activists on the French language and French-American ethnicity. In October 1964, Rinzler sat in on a meeting at the University of Southwestern Louisiana (now the University of Louisiana at Lafayette) organized by French professor Hosea Phillips, at which state education administrators, state politicians, members of the Louisiana Folk Foundation and representatives from the *Société de France Amérique* discussed a long-term strategy for strengthening Louisiana French culture: bringing the French language, which had been banished from the schools and government offices in the 1920s, back into education and civic life.[68] In 1934, Alan Lomax had recorded Phillips and two other Louisiana State University students, Erastre Vidrine and Hart Perrodin, singing traditional songs they had learned in their native Evangeline Parish, including "*Grand Basile*," and "*J'ai passé devant ta porte.*"[69] Phillips developed a life-long scholarly interest in the history of colonial French Louisiana, publishing a book on Cajun French in 1945. Encouraged by the attention of federal folklorists and national festival organizers, Phillips and other local activists launched a French-language movement that, with the support of state politicians, funding from the federal government, and the personnel resources of the French and Canadian governments, would greatly contribute to the endurance and acclaim of French Louisiana traditional music. But the story of the creative collaborations of Creoles and Cajuns in the music tradition of their Francophone region would get lost along the way, drowned out by the rhetoric of the ethnic revival and the exigencies of politics and marketing. Rinzler would struggle with how best to present musicians he thought of as down-home traditional performers in the most unnatural, commercial context of a festival.

Discussing the Newport roster for 1967, Revon Reed anticipated the effect Dewey Balfa would have on the audience. Dewey is "so sympathetic and emotional (without empathy and pathos and dramatics)—humble is the word," Reed said, "that I know the folkniks will love them." Meanwhile, back at Fred's Lounge, out-of-town young musicians flocked to the newly hip, post-Newport Mamou bar to crash Reed's radio show and ask that their bands be allowed to perform. "How do I turn down a bunch of kids who drive thirty to forty miles to play one or two numbers with their band—which includes non-traditional instruments?" Reed wrote, referring to arguments with Tate over the invasion. "I'm more chicken-hearted than traditional-hearted to refuse—and so they play and sing and make merry, and Paul gets disturbed about it!! And then we compromise and start all over again." Rinzler struggled with such compromises for the rest of his tenure with Newport. He wanted to showcase on the commercial Newport festival stage musicians whose relationship to music would be seen as so non-commercial, organic, communal and unselfconscious that national organizations would pour money into state and local music programs back in Louisiana so that those same musicians could sustain their relationship to the music. The most effective and dedicated patron of French Louisiana music, Rinzler watched the genre become a commercially successful cultural product with an international consumer base, but in his private papers, he focused on the music's little-known, self-taught performers. One of the most detailed stories Rinzler preserved was Aubrey DeVille's account of his childhood fascination with music, which became a consuming obsession and inspired a nearly religious sense of reverence. "It's a deep and true sound," DeVille said. "I'm not a professional, you know—I don't know all them things. I didn't study with no books or nothing like that. When I hear a song I like, it enters my head and I think about it. Then it enters my heart and I feel it enter my fiddle and I play it."[70]

NOTES

1. Miles Orvell, *The Real Thing, Imitation and Authenticity in American Culture* (Chapel Hill: University of North Carolina Press, 1989), xvi, xxiv.
2. Ralph Rinzler, Forward to *Cajun and Creole Music Makers*, Ancelet, 9.
3. Ralph Rinzler quoted in "From the 30s to the 60s: The folk music revival in the United States," Ron Eyerman and Scott Barretta, *Theory and Society*, Vol. 25, No. 4 (August, 1996): 501.
4. Alan Lomax quoted in "From the 30s to the 60s," Eyerman and Barretta, 513.
5. Eyerman and Barretta, "From the 30s to the 60s," 538.
6. Ralph Rinzler, quoted in Brauner, "The Newport Folk Festival," 182.
7. Lisa Richardson, "Women and Home Music in South Louisiana," in *La Musique de la Maison*, Origin Jazz Library, 2008, compact disc, liner notes, p. 4.
8. Arthur Arnould, *Béranger, Ses Amis, Ses Ennemies et Ses Critiques*. Volume 1 (Ann Arbor: University of Michigan Library, 2009), 148.
9. Edium Nacquin, for example, told Rinzler she had learned one song from her grandmother, whose brother had been a soldier in the Confederate Army, and who lived to the age of 99, and another from Ulyses Picrottie, an eighty-year-old resident of Mamou.
10. Francois, *Yé Yaille*, 39–42.

11. Lisa Richardson, "Women and Home Music," 4.
12. Robert Gordon, *Can't Be Satisfied: The Life and Times of Muddy Waters* (New York: Back Bay Books, 2003), 62.
13. Alma Barthelemy, lyrics transcribed by Ralph Rinzler. Library of Congress, Louisiana Collections in the Archive of Folk Culture, Ralph Rinzler Louisiana Recordings, AFC1972/026.
14. Sally K. Sommers Smith, "Irish Traditional Music in a Modern World," *New Hibernia Review* 5.2 (2001): 111.
15. Eyerman and Barretta, "From the 30s to the 60s," 534.
16. Paul Tate, 10/17/64. The Archives of Cajun and Creole Folklore, University of Louisiana at Lafayette, CRI1.004. Audio recording.
17. Broven, *South to Louisiana*, 240.
18. Philip H. Des Marais, interviewed by Charles T. Morrissey, March 9, 1966, Washington, DC, John F. Kennedy Oral History Collection, JFK #1, 3/9/1966.
19. *Times-Picayune*, November 18, 1953.
20. Philip H. Desmarais, Oral History transcript, 31.
21. Rinzler, UL archives, field notes to Reel 2B 10/65/3, 4.
22. Brauner, "Newport Folk Festival," 287.
23. Bernard, *Swamp Pop*, 85.
24. Bernard, *Swamp Pop*, 180.
25. Tisserand, *Kingdom of Zydeco*, 83.
26. Savoy, Cajun Music, 196.
27. Earl King and Ron Bernard quoted in Broven, *South to Louisiana*, 181–182.
28. Alan Lomax, "Cajun Country," DVD.
29. John Szwed, Alan Lomax, The Man Who Recorded the World (New York: Viking, 2010), 310.
30. Leo Soileau, interviewed by Ralph Rinzler, USL archives, R12. Audio recording.
31. Brauner, "Newport Folk Festival," 189.
32. Terry H. Anderson, *The Sixties*, 4th edition (Saddle River: Prentice Hall, 2012), 41.
33. Robert Shelton, "Symbolic Finale: Folk Festival Winds up with Songs of the Negro Integration Movement," *New York Times*, August 2, 1964, Sec. 2, 9.
34. Brauner, "Newport Folk Festival," 123.
35. Cohen, John. Quoted in Szwed, "Alan Lomax," 337.
36. Brauner, "Newport Folk Festival," 66; 102; 161.
37. Brauner, "Newport Folk Festival," 107.
38. Brauner, "Newport Folk Festival," 122.

39. Ron Yule, Louisiana Fiddlers (Jackson: University Press of Mississippi, 2009), 6. Szwed, Alan Lomax, *The Man Who Recorded the World*, 337.
40. Dewey Balfa, "The Balfa Brothers Play Traditional Cajun Music," Swallow Records, 1965, compact disc, liner notes, 3.
41. Brauner, "Newport Folk Festival," 159.
42. Blanc and Strachwitz, "*J'Ai Eté au Bal.*"
43. Will Spires, The Balfa Brothers: They Carried Cajun Music to the World, *Frets Magazine* (May 1982): 30–33.
44. Broven, *South to Louisiana*, 243.
45. Barry Jean Ancelet interview with Dewey Balfa, USL archives, AN1.
46. Cajun guitarist D.L. Menard in "*J'ai eté au bal,*" Les Blank, Chris Strachwitz, DVD (1998).
47. Brauner, "Newport Folk Festival," 185–186.
48. Brauner, "Newport Folk Festival," 194.
49. Barry Jean Ancelet, *Cajun Music: Its Origins and Development* (Lafayette: Center for Louisiana Studies, University of Southwest Louisiana, 1989), 38.
50. Brauner, "Newport Folk Festival," 195.
51. Ralph Rinzler, Letter to John Pankake, Oct. 1, 1965, Mamou, Louisiana. Ralph Rinzler Papers Fieldwork Box 4 Louisiana, Correspondence 1–3, Smithsonian Center for Folklife and Cultural Heritage, Washington, DC.
52. Spires, "The Balfa Brothers," 30–33.
53. Brauner, "Newport Folk Festival," 195.
54. Floyd Soileau, quoted in Broven, *South to Louisiana*, 245.
55. Soileau, quoted in Broven, *South to Louisiana*, 260.
56. Canray Fontenot, in *Cajun and Creole Music Makers*, Ancelet, 86.
57. Gagné, "Ralph Rinzler," 28.
58. Brauner, "Newport Folk Foundation," 86.
59. James, *American Scene*, 211.
60. Walker, *Transformation of the Universal Museum*, 192–193.
61. C. Malcolm Watkins, "The Historic Roots of American Folklife,"1968 Festival of American Folklife, The Smithsonian Institution, Program Guide, 10–11.
62. American Folklife Preservation Bill, March 20, 1969, S. 1591.
63. Benjamin A. Botkin, quoted in *Romancing the Folk*, Filene, 139.
64. Botkin, quoted in Delaina Sepko, "The Archive of American Folk Song, The Library of Congress Recording Laboratory and Notions of American Identity," *Fontes Artis Musicae* 62/2, 98.
65. Walker, *Transformation*, 104–105.
66. Fairclough, *Race & Democracy*, 383.
67. Fairclough, *Race & Democracy*, xx.
68. Brauner, "Newport Folk Festival," 195–196.

69. Joshua Clegg Caffery, *Traditional Music in Coastal Louisiana: The 1934 Lomax Recordings* (Baton Rouge: Louisiana State University Press, 2013), 50–53.
70. Aubrey DeVille, Ralph Rinzler Papers Fieldwork Box 4 Louisiana, Correspondence 1–3, Smithsonian Center for Folklife and Cultural Heritage, Washington, DC.

BIBLIOGRAPHY

Ancelet, Barry Jean. *Cajun and Creole Music Makers*. Jackson: University Press of Mississippi, 1999.

Anderson, Terry H. *The Sixties*. 4th ed. Saddle River: Prentice Hall, 2012.

Arnould, Arthur. *Béranger, Ses Amis, Ses Ennemies et Ses Critiques*: Volume 1. Ann Arbor: University of Michigan Library, 2009.

Bernard, Shane K. *The Cajuns, Americanization of a People*. Jackson: University Press of Mississippi, 2003.

Blank, Les, and Chris Strachwitz. *"J'ai eté au Bal."* 1998, DVD.

Botkin, Benjamin, quoted in Delaina Sepko, "The Archive of American Folk Song, The Library of Congress Recording Laboratory and Notions of American Identity," *Fontes Artis Musicae* 62/2.

———.Quoted in Romancing the Folk, Public Memory & American Roots Music. Chapel Hill: University of North Carolina Press, 2000.

Brauner, Cheryl Anne. "A Study of the Newport Folk Festival and the Newport Folk Foundation." M.A. thesis, Memorial University of Newfoundland (Canada), 1986, ProQuest (MK68253).

Broven, John. *South to Louisiana, The Music of the Cajun Bayous*. Gretna: Pelican Publishing Company, 1983.

Caffery, Joshua Clegg. Folklife Lecture on Louisiana Music, Library of Congress, Washington, DC, December 11, 2013. http://www.loc.gov/today/cyberlc/transcripts/2013/131211afc1200.txt

DeMarais, Phillip H. Interview by Charles T. Morrissey, March 9, 1966, Washington, DC, John F. Kennedy Oral History Collection JFK #1, 3/9/1966.

Fairclough, Adam. *Race & Democracy, The Civil Rights Struggle in Louisiana, 1913–1972*. Athens: University of Georgia Press, 1995.

Ron Eyerman and Scott Barretta, "From the 30s to the 60s: The Folk Music Revival in the United States," *Theory and Society*, Vol. 25, No. 4 (August, 1996): 501–543.

François, Raymond E. *Yé Yaille, Chère!* Ville Platte: Swallow Publications, 1990.

Gagné, Richard. "Ralph Rinzler, Folklorist: Professional Biography." *Folklore Forum* 27:1. Bloomington: Folklore and Ethnomusicology Department, Indiana University (1996): 20–49.

Gordon, Robert. *Can't Be Satisfied: The Life and Times of Muddy Waters.* New York: Back Bay Books, 2002.

Lomax, Alan. "Cajun Country," American Patchwork, 2006. DVD.

Orvell, Miles. *The Real Thing, Imitation and Authenticity in American Culture.* Chapel Hill: University of North Carolina Press, 1989.

Savoy, Ann Allen. *Cajun Music: A Reflection of a People, Vol. 1.* Eunice: Bluebird Press, 1984.

Spires, Will. "The Balfa Brothers: They Carried Cajun Music to the World," *Frets Magazine* (May 1982a).

Richardson, Lisa. "Women and Home Music in South Louisiana." Liner notes for *"La Musique de la Maison,"* Origin Jazz Library, 2008, compact disc.

Rinzler, Ralph, quoted in "From the 30s to the 60s," Eyerman and Barretta.

———. Quoted in "A Study of the Newport Folk Festival," Brauner.

Shelton, Robert. "Symbolic Finale: Folk Festival Winds up with Songs of the Negro Integration Movement," *New York Times*, August 2, 1964.

Soileau, Leo. Interview by Ralph Rinzler, Audio Recording. USL Archives, R12.

Sommers Smith, Sally K. "Irish Traditional Music in a Modern World." *New Hibernia Review* 5.2 (2001): 111–125.

Spires, Will. The Balfa Brothers: They Carried Cajun Music to the World. *Frets Magazine* (May 1982b): 30–33.

Szwed, John. Alan Lomax, *The Man Who Recorded the World.* New York: Viking, 2010.

Tate, Paul. Audio recording. Archives of Cajun and Creole Folklore, University of Louisiana at Lafayette, CRI1.004.

Times-Picayune, November 18, 1953.

Tisserand, Michael. *The Kingdom of Zydeco.* New York: Avon Books, 1998.

Walker, William. *The Smithsonian and the Transformation of the Universal Museum.* Amherst: University of Massachusetts Press, 2013.

Watkins, Malcolm C. "The Historic Roots of American Folklife," 1968 Festival of American Folklife, The Smithsonian Institution, Program Guide.

Yule, Ron. Louisiana Fiddlers. Jackson: University Press of Mississippi, 2009.

CHAPTER 7

Utter Strangers: The English and French Language Movements

National recognition of the soulful, raucous music of Southwest Louisiana prompted a new regard in Louisiana for the paramount importance of the French language in the state's history and culture. But because the movement to restore French in Louisiana's public life was modeled after French Canadian efforts to protect a minority language in a majority English-speaking nation, when the state of Louisiana began to try to reestablish the French language, its efforts focused on the history of French Canadian migrants to Louisiana, and Creoles, who were ancestrally French Caribbean Africans, dropped out of the state's narrative. The band was broken up. The story was fractured.

And while French Louisiana music had been promoted by Southwest Louisianans for music's sake, and by Rinzler and Lomax for American society's sake, the French language was promoted by the state of Louisiana for the economy's sake, in an effort to connect Louisiana to new opportunities in an economic network of tourism and global partnerships. If one of the triumphs of the story is that French Louisiana music had finally gotten the place it deserved in the national folk music story, one of the ironies is that that music became the sole repository of a version of French that was then legislated out of Louisiana history in favor of continental Parisian French, and some of the Creole actors in Louisiana's complicated history got upstaged by the descendants of a romanticized French Canadian past.

© The Author(s) 2019
P. Peknik, *French Louisiana Music and Its Patrons*,
https://doi.org/10.1007/978-3-319-97424-8_7

While the project to fund and sustain traditional music had been part of a national program directed by the Library of Congress, the Newport Folk Foundation, and the Smithsonian Institute, the French language preservation movement had various constituencies and was also an international project, participated in and promoted by French and French Canadian organizations. In the decades after World War II, as France lost its former colonies, including Indochina, Algeria and Tunisia, Senegal and the Ivory Coast, the French government of Charles de Gaulle, seeking to restore French "cultural grandeur"[1] and anxious that the French language would not survive decolonization, sought to reunite its former colonies under the concept of a French-speaking "Commonwealth of Nations"[2] in which European, African and North American peoples would be psychologically and sentimentally connected to France as well as economically connected through favorable trade agreements. Ideas for this global "Francophone community," in which a former political community—the global French empire—would be transformed into a cultural community of shared language and historical and cultural affinity, began to be widely and seriously discussed in France in 1965, and a range of governmental and private organizations were quickly established to facilitate cultural, technological, and educational exchanges.[3] The members of this community included not only the continental francophone populations of Belgium and Switzerland and the ex-colonial French populations of Africa and Indochina, but, however historically distant the colonial relationship, Haiti, the Canadian provinces of Québec and New Brunswick, New Orleans and the Acadian parishes of Southwest Louisiana.

The global Francophone movement reached into Louisiana at a moment when the attention of activists like Paul Tate and Revon Reed had long been focused on language and culture preservation, but the philosophical and resource support of the French and Canadian governments gave the grassroots movement a traction and allure it would otherwise have lacked, until finally, the state of Louisiana began to recognize the significance and potential economic benefits of its francophone culture.

It was the French Canadian plan to observe the bicentennial of the *Grand Dérangement* that prompted Louisiana to organize and fund its own Acadian Bicentennial Celebration. The state calculated that the bicentennial commemoration would bring in an additional fifty-five to seventy-five million dollars in tourism revenue in 1955.[4] Cajun singers and dancers from St. Martinville performed during half-time ceremonies at that year's Sugar Bowl in New Orleans. One hundred and thirty-five delegates from

French Canadian cultural organizations, including *Le Conseil de la Vie Française en Amérique* [The Council on French Life in America] and *Le Comité Permanent de la Survivance du Français en Amérique* [The Permanent Committee for the Survival of French in America] attended the inaugural festivities in January,[5] and a bicentennial delegation left New Orleans by train in February headed for Montreal, Québec City, and New Brunswick. A Lafayette journalist predicted that the state would benefit a hundred-fold in advertising and promotion from the delegation's pilgrimage to Canada. Folklorist Sarah Gertrude Knott organized St. Martinville's celebration of the music and folktales of Acadia. Accordionist Cyprien Landreneau played traditional Cajun dance hall music, and Revon Reed and Paul Tate brought from Mamou a contingent of over forty costumed horseback riders to demonstrate the traditional *courir de Mardi Gras.* The success of the bicentennial inspired the state Department of Education to publish a guide for teachers titled "Our Acadian Heritage: Let's Keep It!"

Controversies erupted over which version of the French language the state should keep. One of the assumptions of the global French language and culture movement was that language and culture are inextricably linked, that the French language is more than a mere means of communication; rather, the language inevitably leads to "a special way of thinking, even a way of life."[6] Southwest Louisiana's French language movement was premised on this conception of language as promoting and sustaining a way of life, but political battles were fought over exactly which French—standard Parisian French, Cajun French or Creole French—needed to be preserved, and which "way of life" was at stake. The textbook continental French of "genteel Acadians" who "thought like Anglo-Saxons" and saw the *Grand Dérangement* as an interesting "migration" was opposed to the "authentic" French of rural Cajuns who considered the expulsion from Canada a tragic crime.[7] The controversies over who was running the bicentennial, and which parishes would most benefit from the profits, generated a rhetoric in which Louisianans of French Canadian descent existed in an oppositional category to the majority culture, a category that encompassed social class (the not-genteel), ethnicity (those who "think like" French-descended Catholics rather than like Anglo-Saxon Protestants), and education (those who don't speak textbook continental French). This sorting out was the beginning of a public rhetoric in which Cajuns were a distinct cultural group separate from French-speaking Creoles. Likewise, the French language movement in Louisiana divided the word "French" into subcategories of standard, proper textbook French, Cajun French, and Creole French. Standard continental French won the day, with Cajun and Creole French increasingly spoken only in stores, in family homes, and in the music.

The historical connection between French Canada and Southwest Louisiana, reanimated by the bicentennial, was crucial to the French language movement in Louisiana. Support for a global French linguistic and cultural movement had been building throughout the 1960s in Canada. In 1961, Quebec established a delegation in Paris that functioned as an embassy for French-speaking Canada.[8] In July 1967, French President Charles de Gaulle thrilled Quebecois nationalists when, on a visit to Montreal, he proclaimed "*Vive le Québec libre.*"

Just as France had made agreements with newly independent African republics committing France (which sought above all else priority in purchasing natural resources and favorable tariff rates) to "aid in education, while French was recognized as the official language of the African states," similar agreements were made with the Quebec government in 1965, 1967 and 1969 to support francophone culture in the province. The *Francophonie* movement led to the creation of a variety of governmental and private agencies and organizations dedicated to the preservation of the French language and global French culture: the *Association des Universités Partiellement ou Entièrement de Langue Française* (AUPELF) was founded in September 1961 and based in Montreal; the Paris-based *Association de Solidarité Francophone* (ASF) was founded in November 1966; the *Association Internationale des Parlementaires de Langue Française*, headquartered in Paris, was founded in May 1967; the *Conseil International de la Langue Française* was organized in September 1967; the *Association des Communautés de Langue Française* was founded in 1959 as the *Association Européenne de l'Ethnie Française*.[9]

When the *Agence de Coopération Culturelle et Technique* [Agency for Cultural and Technological Cooperation], established in February 1969 at a conference in Niamey, Niger, sought the participation of Louisiana at the 1970 conference, Paul Tate was chosen to attend. The *Times-Picayune* covered Tate's visit to the Republic of Niger in a March 6, 1970 story headlined "Tate Will Visit in West Africa." Tate, who had brought his early activism in Mamou to the Louisiana Historical Society, first went to Paris to meet with other delegates, then on to Niger as the representative of the state's new Council for the Development of French in Louisiana, in the hopes that Francophone Louisiana could gain "additional contacts throughout the world and … additional help and assistance for the movement in its early stage of development."[10]

In Niamey, participants established the Francophone Agency, with a provisional secretariat based in Paris, to organize common action in cultural, economic, technical, and even political spheres, including "multilateral cooperation in French education … arts and letters." The cost of the agency's programs was not disclosed, but was estimated by French journalists at *Le Devoir* to be $1,300,000 and by *Le Monde* at $6,000,000, with France contributing forty-five percent of the budget, Canada thirty percent, and other countries, including Belgium, twenty-five percent.[11] Thus, the French language preservation movement in Louisiana was part of a larger global movement. But the fear that the French language was disappearing was an old fear in Louisiana, with stories of the decline of French appearing regularly in Louisiana newspapers from the time of Reconstruction.

The status of the French language in Louisiana has been a subject of debate since Louisiana's admission as a state into the federal Union.

As a new state, Louisiana had retained its civil law system rather than adopting the common law system of the US state and federal governments, but in order to interact with other state legal systems and the federal courts, Louisiana's courts were compelled to conduct judicial proceedings in English. This introduction of English into official proceedings of state government was the *coup de grâce* to the legal status of French in Louisiana, which had previously enjoyed "equal, if not favored status" with English.[12] The fight to regain that equal status would go on throughout the Civil War years and into the early twentieth century. Every generation sounded the alarm that French was dying and that young people couldn't communicate with their grandparents, that French wasn't being taught in the schools, and that French Louisiana was losing to the forces of Anglophone commercialism.

In a July 1879 article, "*L'Avenir de la Langue Française en Louisiane*" [The Future of the French Language in Louisiana] in the *Pioneer of Assumption* newspaper in Napoleonville, the author lamented the decline of French—which, although it was the mother tongue of one third of the population of the state and the language of a mother country celebrated for its accomplishments in the sciences, arts and politics—was being "exiled by its enemies from the public schools of the state" so that the poor, "with their wallets emptied by the Civil War and its disastrous consequences," were not able to learn French. In other words, language was a civil rights issue, and impoverished children were being deprived of the right to speak, and therefore to think, in French. Instead, the children, educated in English in the schools, brought English back into the family home, becoming so alienated from their elders that they would not even know how to read the French inscriptions engraved on the tombstones of their ancestors. Yet French was still an essential tool in commerce, industry and intellectual culture, the writer said, essential not only for ambitious young people aspiring to become lawyers and judges—the source of public law was the Napoleonic Code—but also for revolutionaries, who could arm themselves with all weapons *"pour la lutte des prolétaires"*—the struggle of the working classes, which apparently this author considered best fought in French. The writer imagined the shame young Louisianans would feel if they traveled to Paris and, despite having a French last name and having been brought up in a former French colony, didn't speak a word of French.[13]

A May 1893 article in the *Opelousas Courier* encouraged readers to support new tax policies that would fund French language education in the Acadian parishes: "Why this neglect, this abandoning of the language our ancestors spoke ... this language that has become precious to us and has given us a great advantage over Americans who speak only English..."[14] But of the thirty-three French-language newspapers published in 1860, only seven remained in 1900, and of the twenty-six bilingual English-French newspapers in 1860, only five survived the end of the century, all of them in the Acadian parishes and New Orleans.[15]

For each move toward the preservation of French, there was a subsequent move in the opposite direction. Louisiana's Reconstruction constitutions stridently required that English be the only language used in Louisiana public school instruction, but the state Constitution of 1879 stated that although elementary school instruction was to be in English, grade schools could teach in French in those parishes where the French language predominated.[16] In any case, because there were not yet compulsory education laws, Cajuns and Creoles were able to avoid assimilation into English, and despite the new laws, in 1900, Lafayette (fifty-one percent) and Thibodaux (sixty percent) had French-speaking majorities.[17]

Then, in 1915, the State Education Committee adopted an English-only education policy, fearing that Louisiana's low English literacy rates would hurt the state economy.[18] Louisiana's Compulsory Education Act of 1916, combined with 1918 congressional hearings on a proposed federal Americanization Bill, would aggressively change French language culture in Southwest Louisiana.

The premise of the Americanization Bill, introduced by Georgia Senator Hoke Smith and Iowa Representative Horace Mann Towner,[19] was that up until 1885, immigrants to the United States had been of "Teutonic and Celtic origin, possessing ideals, customs, standards of living, modes of thought, and religion the same general tenor as those of the early (Anglo-Saxon) settlers," but that the new Southern and Eastern European immigrants, who had different religious beliefs, customs, habits, and ideals, manifested "no desire of becoming Americans," and were unable to "speak, read or write the English language."[20] And there was a concomitant decrease in the percentage of immigrants who became naturalized citizens. Wartime industries were dependent on immigrant labor, yet many foreign workers and draft-age men could not understand English; foreign-born soldiers arrived at boot camp not comprehending the simple commands "Forward," "Halt" and "March."[21]

In 1918, the American Council on Education in Washington, DC, commissioned a report on the Americanization movement and the proposed bill, and the report concluded that the federal government did indeed need to take an active role in assuring that states were teaching English to non-English speaking immigrants and their children. In a somewhat fragile line of legal reasoning, the bill's sponsors concluded that because immigrants tended to move from one state to the next seeking work, their education was a federal matter. Presumably, then, the federal government's involvement in the state public school curriculum was justified under the Commerce Clause of the US Constitution, under which the federal government could regulate interstate commerce.

Under the proposed bill, the federal power would provide the states with funding to provide English language and civics education to non-English speakers. Secretary of the Interior Francis K. Lane described the Americanization project as best accomplished by "teaching American history in the American tongue ... by letting American boys and girls know that the history of the United States is not a mere series of fugitive incidents, remote, separate, unrelated, but is a philosophy..."[22]

Many state and municipal agencies and private organizations, including churches, civic clubs and settlement homes, already had programs designed to promote the Americanization of the laboring immigrant population, who lived in crowded urban enclaves that were "intensely alien," The *New York World* newspaper reported.[23] Some manufacturing interests, including the Ford Motor Company in Detroit, where workers spoke over one hundred different languages and dialects, had established in-house schools to teach them English[24] in an effort to increase occupational productivity, discourage labor unrest, and promote industrial safety, since many immigrant factory workers couldn't understand simple posted signs warning them about the dangers of operating machinery. Herbert Kaufman, Special Assistant to the Secretary of the Interior, in Charge of Americanization, declared that "13 percent of the folk in Lawrence and Fall River, Mass. (two cities with large French Canadian communities) are utter strangers in a strange land."

But in congressional hearings on the Americanization Bill, it became clear that the Americanization project would be directed not only at these utter strangers but at all persons "unable to understand and use the English language." The bill's proponents emphasized that white southerners were one of the key targets of the legislation, and that finally, the illiterate men of Kentucky, who spoke a "very pure, Shakespearean English" would be able to read the Bible. Cotton farmers would be able to read Department of Agriculture bulletins on crop diversification and thereby save themselves from overplanting cotton. Illiteracy was not merely the mark of the immigrant, Kaufman said, but was highest in rural communities and "the open country," where in some places, "books were looked upon as a mysterious curiosity."

According to the census data presented at the hearings, Louisiana and South Carolina had the highest percentages of illiterates in proportion to population in the entire nation, at more than twenty-five percent, and the highest percentage, along with New Mexico, of native whites with native parentage who were illiterate. The number of illiterate people in each state was of course much higher than the census recorded.

Under the Americanization bill appropriations scheme, Louisiana, Texas, and Georgia were to receive the largest share of federal aid of any southern states, with money going to teacher training and teacher and administrative salaries. In Georgia, the money was directed to teaching impoverished black and white southerners—the "native illiterate"—to read and write; in Texas, to teach Spanish-speaking Mexican immigrants—the "foreign illiterate"—to speak, read and write English, and in Louisiana, to teach speakers of Cajun and Creole French, who were not foreign-born but may have seemed to be utter strangers, to speak, read and write English. To the bill's supporters, the terms "foreign-born" and "non-English speaking" appeared to be synonymous descriptors of northern urban immigrants, just as the word "illiterate" referred to an English-speaking but illiterate black or white southerner. Louisianans who spoke only French, even if they could read and write in French, were an anomaly in the appropriations scheme: native-born of native parentage, but speakers of a foreign language.

Southern illiteracy was understood as one of the circumstances of poverty: in the 1910 census, Alabama reported 352,710 residents over the age of 10 who were illiterate in English, but only 3048 of those could not speak English. This was the southern pattern. But in Louisiana, of the 352,179 illiterate residents, 20,147 could not speak English. These statistics made Louisiana a key target of the English-only policies of the Americanization bill.[25] To secure its full financial benefits, each state was required to invest an amount equal to its federal appropriation. Louisiana would be required to provide for the education of non-English-speaking minors between the ages of sixteen (the age at which compulsory public schooling ended) and twenty-one.

Although the Smith-Bankhead Americanization Bill did not become law, newspapers from Cadillac, Michigan to Atlanta, Georgia called for "radical state measures" and "remedial legislation" to support Americanization at the state level, and as a direct response to the Americanization bill, the 1921 Louisiana State Constitution banned French from the public schools: "Article XII, Section 12. The general exercises in the public schools shall be conducted in the English language."[26]

Thus Dewey Balfa and other musicians of his generation, who referred to English speakers as "Americans," attended school at a time when French was forbidden on school grounds and children were severely punished for speaking it, even in casual conversations with classmates. As a result, the percentage of Cajun children who spoke French as their primary language declined from eighty-three percent for those born around 1900 to twenty-one percent for those born between 1956 and 1960. Of the 13,200 Cajun GIs who served in the Korean War, sixty-seven percent used French as their first language.[27] Only thirty-six percent of the 22,700 Cajun GIs who served in Vietnam spoke French as their first language.[28] This decline rallied Southwest Louisianans to a stance of nostalgia for what had been the only language of many Cajun and Creole grandparents, and some parents. In the 1970 Census, more than a half million Louisianans responded that French was the language spoken at home when they were young.[29] When the global Francophone movement reached into North America, there were many instant converts to the cause, including among Louisiana business organizations and politicians. The Lafayette Chamber of Commerce established the French Heritage Committee in 1967, whose slogan for small business owners was "Look French, Speak French,"[30] and the following year, several state legislators crafted State Act 409 establishing the Council for the Development of Louisiana-French, an agency whose very name began yet another political controversy over the role of French in Louisiana life.

Folklorists and musicians embraced the idea of preserving all the varieties of French spoken by Cajuns, Creoles, and New Orleanians. The Louisiana French spoken in New Orleans was quite similar to standard continental French and was mostly spoken by older people who had been educated in private schools run by the Catholic Church, using catechisms published in France or Québec. The syntax, grammar, and vocabulary of Louisiana French were such that a speaker would perhaps be assumed by Parisians to be from a village in northern or western France. The most widespread version of French in Louisiana was Acadian French, which had retained more archaic forms of pronunciation, including some seventeenth-century French grammatical features, for example, with possessives, and had more simplified verb conjugations. Acadian French borrowed vocabulary from English, African, Spanish, and Indian languages.

Creole French further simplified phonetic, syntactical and grammatical structures.[31] Creole French and Cajun French, both descended from colonial French, either in the Maritime Provinces of Canada or the Caribbean, especially Haiti, and then developing over many decades of co-existence, were mutually intelligible languages to Creoles and Cajuns in Southwest Louisiana, and there were black and white speakers of both Cajun French and Creole French.[32] Neither was a written language. Neither corresponded syntactically or grammatically to continental or Canadian French, and both contained borrowings from Native American and New World Spanish. Many French-speaking Canadians had left Canada for Saint-Domingue and for Martinique, Saint Lucia, and Guadeloupe, even before the Seven Years War began, in a "small but constant immigration," and many of those driven out of Canada in the *Grand Dérangement* sought refuge in Saint-Domingue.[33] This may explain some of the linguistic concurrences between Cajun and Creole French. When Ivory Coast President Félix Houphouet-Boigny's cabinet chief, Koffi Gervais, visited Lafayette, he was struck by the fact that both black and white Southwest Louisianans spoke essentially the same "Creole French," as he labeled it.[34]

Despite the variety of French-derived languages in Louisiana, including among the Houma Indians, the new state agency Council for the Development of Louisiana-French, created by a unanimous vote of the

Louisiana Legislature, quickly changed its name to the Council for the Development of French in Louisiana. The mission of the French government and French and French Canadian cultural organizations was, of course, to preserve French, not to support the teaching of a variety of non-written forms of colonial French. Thus while CODOFIL's mission was to "do any and all things necessary to accomplish the development, utilization and preservation of the French language as found in the state of Louisiana for the cultural, economic and tourist benefit of the state" (Act 209, Louisiana State Legislature, 1968), the organization had little use for the language "as found in the state," and much more use for standard continental French.

CODOFIL was created by a piece of legislation authored by Southwest Louisiana's four-term State Senator Dudley LeBlanc, who began his political career in 1923 giving campaign speeches in Cajun French, and who, in 1928, led a delegation of French Canadians, along with Mamou's French Canadian priest Father Fidele Chiasson, to a Massachusetts conference on North American Acadians. Over the next decades, LeBlanc led a series of trips to French-speaking Canada and hosted a series of visits by Francophone Canadians designed to strengthen connections between Southwest Louisiana and other Francophone communities in North America. In 1946, LeBlanc toured Southwest Louisiana with his "Evangeline girls," who performed Acadian folk dances to old-time tunes.[35]

The first chairman of CODOFIL, James Domengeaux, had, as a member of the Louisiana House of Representatives in 1941, and then as a US representative, argued for French as a second language in the United States,[36] believing Louisiana's adoption of French as an official language of government to be a necessary political and economic step to boost the state's economy and international visibility. In an October 11, 1977 letter to President Jimmy Carter, Louisiana Senators Russell B. Long and J. Bennett Johnson and US Representative John B. Breaux argued that Domengeaux was ever the ideal representative of the cause of the French language in America by noting that "his law firm has a noted reputation for handling hopeless murder cases, helping small landowners manipulated by big corporations, as well as assisting the free poor of charge."

As CODOFIL chair, Domengeaux oversaw the drafting of a formal agreement between Canadian Prime Minister Jean-Jacques Bertrand of Quebec and Louisiana Governor John McKeithen on "cultural cooperation" between the two entities: "Aware of the historic ties which bound them in the past, and of the common ancestry of part of their respective populations ... of the role which the Government of Quebec means to play in expanding French culture in America, [the] importance which the Government of the United States of America attaches to the dissemination and teaching of second languages, and the French language in particular, [and] the role which Louisiana can play in expanding French culture in the United States of America, have decided to enter into the present Agreement." Under "Co-operation in Cultural Matters," Louisiana and Canada agreed to arrange artistic and literary exhibitions on each other's territory, to establish media for the expression of French culture on their own territory, and to encourage exchanges of artists, writers, musicians, and lecturers."[37]

It was a non-Louisianan, University of Southwestern Louisiana political science professor Raymond Rodgers, who proposed to the State Superintendent of Schools that Louisiana model its own language programs on the successful programs of New Brunswick. Rodgers had spent most of his adult life in Canada, where he had developed an interest in French as a minority-culture language, and he concluded that, given that there were more Acadians in Louisiana than in Canada,[38] if the language renaissance failed in Louisiana, it would fail in Canada, too, dismantling the emerging separatist movement. Crafting a Cold War domino theory metaphor, Rodgers said that Acadiana was the "South Vietnam of French Canada."[39] Rodgers argued that restoring the French language in Louisiana required international co-operation, state action, and the support of the business community, churches, and the media. The Quebec government opened an office in Lafayette in 1969, and Rodgers continued his advocacy of the French language movement in Louisiana after returning to Canada to teach at the University of Winnipeg in Ottawa. As Jacques Henry has noted, the mobilization phase of the French language movement developed without public pressure or demands from the French-speaking population to defend or promote its language, but rather, was organized by key elites and outsiders, including not only Rodgers and Domengeaux but France's new emissary of the French language, Philippe Rossillon, and a coterie of French Canadian activist officials.[40]

The French language movement could hardly have been sustained in Louisiana without the contribution by the governments of Canada, France, and Belgium of French language teachers sent to work in Louisiana schools. In order to establish bilingual education, the state would have to import teachers who would be paid by the federal government through Title VII of the Elementary and Secondary Education Act's Bilingual

Education Act signed into law in 1968 by President Lyndon Johnson. Eventually, the federal government would spend millions on French education in Louisiana, not only through the Bilingual Education Act but through Title VII of the Emergency School Aid Act, also known as the Bilingual/Bicultural Act, signed into law in 1972 by President Nixon.[41]

As part of state's efforts to persuade the US Department of Education that such funding should be allocated, Southwestern Louisiana faculty member Marie Diane Rodgers, a French Canadian, wrote a policy paper titled "The French Heritage in Acadiana: The Fundamental Course of Action Necessary to Preserve the French Language" in which she explained that the renewal of French in Louisiana was "in the domestic and international interest of the U.S." because "Acadiana could look French and attract tourists from the French-speaking world…" and "Job opportunities abound for people with special language abilities in the foreign service, education and the armed forces." Rodgers argued that Louisiana could borrow "used" media content from French Canadian radio and television broadcasts, and adopt French Canadian textbooks for the teaching of French in schools, explaining that New Brunswick had preserved its French heritage only with the help of "the French network."

The French language movement in Louisiana generated press coverage in dozens of international newspapers and magazines, including the Paris newspaper *Le Monde*, the French news magazine *Jours de France*, Montréal's *Le Devoir*, and Belgium's French language *Le Soir*, and was lauded as a sign of the enduring strength of the French language in an increasingly Anglophone global economy. By the end of the 1950s, tourism had become Louisiana's largest industry, and Rodgers emphasized the economic boost the Lafayette area would derive from restoring historical buildings to "give a French flavor to downtown." In fact, Rodgers had a sweeping vision for the "new-old" architectural, design, linguistic and gastronomical character of Lafayette: "The 'look French' aspect of the program should be emphasized to attract tourists … Stores, restaurants, hotels and other public buildings should have French names, menus and décor…. Historical buildings and cities should be restored."[42] After World War II, Cajun cuisine had become the region's primary cultural export. Cajun cookbooks, first published in the early 1950s, standardized recipes and introduced the cuisine to the rest of America, much the way recorded music standardized and disseminated the region's complex musical heritage.

Rather than focus on a boost in tourism revenues, Domengeaux's vision was even more grandiose. He explained in an October 1968 speech to the Council board that the French renaissance movement would "outlast General de Gaulle"[43] as educated bilingual Louisianans went abroad to represent the interests of the United States in the French-speaking world. In remarks to the House of Representatives in 1974, Louisiana Congressman F. Edward Hebert agreed that Louisiana bilingualism would attract investments from France, French-speaking Canada, Belgium, and Switzerland, and he lauded Domengeaux for his "vision of what the United States could be in a world whose political, psychological, and sociological coordinates were changing radically." Hebert, as chairman of the House Armed Forces Committee, had concluded that second language development was "extremely serious for the security of the nation," and pointed out that the Soviets trained language technicians to increase their global reach in foreign policy. Hebert was speaking during an era in which the US military had used thousands of French-speaking interpreters and translators to prosecute the Vietnam War.[44]

Most Louisiana advocates of French language education had more circumscribed motives. Some wanted to create a bridge between younger and older generations by restoring French as a common social language. Returning World War II veterans had brought back home the realization that French was viewed in Europe as a language associated with great cultural pride and prestige.[45] Veteran Elmo Authement, who was born the year the Louisiana constitution banned French in the schools, remembered: "I was put on my knees in the hallway at school on grains of corn because I spoke French in the playground and got caught."[46] Authement, who was co-vice president, along with Paul Tate, of CODOFIL at its founding, became president of the French-language Television-Louisiane,[47] a non-profit French broadcasting corporation established under new state law. The station broadcast local content as well as France's TV5 news and entertainment.

Hosea Phillips, the University of Southwestern Louisiana faculty member who had organized the language renaissance meeting that Rinzler attended in Lafayette, recalled his punishment for speaking French in grammar school: "I was sent home on the first day at school to write 200 times 'I must not speak French on the school grounds'."[48] Revon Reed explained that in Mamou, children went on speaking French in schools despite punishments. He was kept after school with a dozen other children who persisted in speaking French. Yet French remained their preferred language, with no hard feelings against English.[49] Paul Tate, however, had much sterner views, describing the prohibition against speaking French as a violation of civil rights and personal dignity: "Those egotistical English speakers were the enemy for one reason: because they wanted to completely kill the French language, making them guilty of the crime of culturcide."[50]

The movement to restore French in public schools in Louisiana was launched in a remarkably short period of time.[51] Thirty teachers arrived from France in the program's inaugural year, 1969. The French government had authorized young men to teach in Louisiana's elementary schools as a form of public sector service in lieu of French military service, and within a few years, CODOFIL employed over three hundred French teachers, the vast majority from France, with a small number from Quebec and Belgium, and administered French programs in more than half the state's parishes,[52] teaching 40,800 children. In 1972, Domengeaux traveled to France with a group of students studying in a French program at the Université Catholique d'Angers, and met with French President Georges Pompidou: "M. Pompidou interrogated me about the situation of French in Louisiana. He was openly interested in the drama of a population, having kept its language, its customs, and traditions for two centuries, that was now having more and more difficulties. He declared himself ready to support our action with indispensable credits and exchanges to carry out the task."[53] Pompidou's administration sent hundreds of French instructors, with funding and materials, to teach French in the Louisiana public schools.

In New England, with its historically large population of French Canadian mill workers, a sister organization, the Council for the Development of French in New England (CODOFINE) was founded. The French initiative intersected at a moment in American culture when Americans were newly interested in the intergenerational continuity of ethnic identity and non-English languages, and Louisiana's French revival movement must also be understood in this national context. The number of Americans who indicated on the US Census in 1970 that their native language was a language other than English increased dramatically between 1960 and 1970, reversing a downward trend that had begun after World War II.[54] The increase in "mother tongue claiming" was very substantial, independent of immigrational and family growth factors, and was accompanied by an increase in the number of mother-tongue schools in the United States, a boom in foreign language broadcasting, the introduction of ethnic festivals and pageants in local communities, and the establishing of ethnic studies courses at American colleges.[55] As Americans weathered the traumas of the Vietnam War, the Civil Rights movement, the counter-culture, and disenchantment with national politics, many sought solace and meaning in a more exclusive sense of community, turning to ideas of ancestral identity, a "sidestream ethnicity" that was evidence of a psycho-logical, emotional drive to identify with the "otherness" of non-White Anglo-Saxon Protestant mainstream culture.[56]

Sidestream ethnicity came to play a public role very similar to that of religion in American life, "humanizing and strengthening ... a 'good influence' that makes for a more interesting, colorful, rooted life": "The ethnic revival in the United States succeeded in bringing sidestream eth-nicity out of the family and neighborhood closet ... and made it salon-worthy. It could be revealed (and gratified) in college and in church, in public places rather than merely in private ones.... [It] came to be viewed as the spice of life without which all would be anglobland, tasteless and inert."[57] Dewey Balfa confessed this same belief in the "angloblandness" of mainstream culture: "Once you've taken the Cajun language, you've taken the Cajun culture away from me, away from my grandchildren, then who are they? They're an American plastic card with a number on it."[58]

International, national, state, and local support for French in Louisiana succeeded impressively: between 1960 and 1970, there was a 120 percent increase in the number of Americans who claimed French as their mother tongue.[59] But although French was one of the "big six" languages that accounted for the lion's share of non-English mother-tongue claiming between 1960 and 1970, along with Spanish, German, Italian, Polish and Yiddish, scholars who write on mother-tongue claiming and ethnicity do not engage on the topic of French in Louisiana, since again, there's the old anomaly: Louisianans were native-born Americans whose great, great grandparents were also native-born Americans. And the French language movement, with its global context, had a different character and mani-fested different concerns. The French ethnic press was more fixated than the Spanish, Yiddish and German presses, for example, on the extent to which the ethnic mother tongue was spoken in the home, and the French language itself was the second most frequent topic discussed in print. The Hispanic press included many stories about the political and economic advances made by Spanish-speaking Americans, but the French ethnic press cast its gaze back to the *Grand Dérangement*, referring to either France or Canada as the old country.[60]

This is a population whose relationship to language, and perhaps to history, should be compared not with the history of German immigrants but with the history of Amish speakers of German. The precipitous decline of the number of Pennsylvania German speakers between 1900 and the 1950s conjured up "the specter of language death" as Pennsylvania German was increasingly learned only from grandparents; after World War I, "the ultimate extinction of Pennsylvania German" seemed inevitable. Although there was a resurgence of interest in Pennsylvania German in the 1930s, when WPA scholars were eagerly documenting every aspect of American folklife, the 1950s seemed to have marked the final turning away of children and adolescents from the ancestral dialect; in 1957, Pennsylvania German was given another twenty years. Many adults of the day had endured ridicule for speaking Pennsylvania German as children, and suffered under legal prohibitions against the language, and they embraced English because they thought it offered more advantages to their children. One informant said: "I did not speak anything but Pennsylvania German till I went to school, and I promised myself I would not do that to my children." By the 1960s, the switch to English seemed complete, and the last vestiges of Pennsylvania German could be found only in the leisure activities domain. Yet it was these activities that inspired language restoration efforts that resulted in "a renewed appreciation of Pennsylvania German as an integral part of the Pennsylvania German history and tradition."[61]

Likewise, the "leisure activities" domain became the essential, and then nearly the only, domain in which Cajun French could survive: in the lyrics of traditional songs. The French that was taught in Louisiana schools was standard French, and if Domengeaux was earnest in his desire to use French to boost Louisiana's tourism revenues from France and its political status in the Francophone world, it could not have been otherwise, since it was standard French that would make Louisiana the American corridor to the French-speaking world.[62] But Louisiana folklorists who study old-time French Louisiana music and Louisiana storytelling traditions were baffled by the state's devotion to standard continental French, arguing that there was no point in teaching an "academic, purist and elitist" form of continental French, since the only form that could preserve a continuity with the past was the particular French that had been spoken in Southwest Louisiana: "We can't just regenerate a generic French, we have to regenerate this one," Louisiana folklorist Barry Ancelet argued. "There's a whole aural poetics that operates. It's not only the language, but it's the way we see the world, the way we conceive of the way things work, the way we move through the world ... all of those things are expressed in the language. If that's not what we're trying to preserve, I quit."[63]

The unfortunate outcome of the French language movement is that its rhetoric was so intently premised on Cajun identity as to exclude Creoles altogether. Marie Rodgers' policy paper summarizing efforts to revive French in Southwest Louisiana describes the Acadian as a settler who disappeared "behind a barricade of swamp and distance," to recreate his life as it was in Nova-Scotia, and who lived "happily" until "the intrusion of American life." Absent from her account are any references to French-speaking Creoles in Southwest Louisiana, or the ways in which American life historically "intruded" on that population, until she acknowledges that, of the 400,000 Louisianans said to speak French daily, "This, I think, probably includes the Negroes, since they have a place in the 'French' culture."[64] This is the only time that Rodgers puts the word "French" in quotes. Cajuns were, in the words of anthropologist Dorice Tentchoff, "carefully put through a sieve separating white from black ... reworked in the image of Longfellow's poems into many pristine Evangelines and Gabriels... speaking contemporary French."[65]

Domengeaux, too, only briefly acknowledged that both Creoles and Cajuns inhabit Southwest Louisiana and had spent centuries speaking French to one another, despite the fact that some parishes had majority black populations: in St. John the Baptist and Pointe Coupée parishes, fifty-two percent of residents were Creole; in Iberville Parish, forty-nine percent.[66] The black population of Southwest Louisiana in its entirety was twenty-eight percent. In a February 1968 speech to the Louisiana Association of Fairs and Festivals, Domengeaux described Louisiana French culture as having been brought from the French Caribbean as well as from France and Quebec, though it is clear that Cajuns, not Creoles, are the model French-speaking Louisianans: "...and, of course, some degree of the French language and heritage is to be found in our colored population as well."[67] "*Some degree*" is the weakest term available to refer to common linguistic, religious, social, culinary, and musical traditions. In a January 22, 1973, letter to Dr. Ray Authement, President of the University of Southwestern Louisiana in Lafayette, Domengeaux reiterated this mild concession: "The culture of the French-speaking black Louisianan is unique in the world and is intimately identifiable with the history of the State and the French language. I therefore suggest that the proposed cultural and educational endeavor [the new Center for Acadian and Creole Folklore at the college, established with funding from the Rockefeller Foundation secured by Rinzler] include the folklore of the Black French-speaking Louisianans, as well as that of the French, Acadian and Creole."

The French language movement in Louisiana, predicated on the rhetoric of the shared French Canadian ancestry of all Southwest Louisianans, even got its own flag for the ten-year anniversary of the bicentennial. The flag, designed by a University of Southwest Louisiana dean who had been inspired by the Acadian flag of New Brunswick, and borrowing from the college's seal and the emblem of *France-Amérique de la Louisiane-Acadienne*, featured three silver *fleurs-de-lis* against a blue background, symbolizing the Cajuns' origins in France, a gold castle on a red field, symbolizing the Acadian exiles' settlement in Spanish colonial Louisiana, and a gold star on a white field symbolizing the patron saint of the Acadian people, Our Lady of Assumption.[68] Introduced in 1965, the flag was ubiquitous in Southwest Louisiana by 1968, where it proclaimed to Creoles that the history and culture of the region belonged exclusively to those whose ancestors claimed descent from eighteenth-century Canadians—and if not, well, never mind. Historically, the Creole population had been more likely than the Cajun population to be monolingual French speakers,[69] likely because of far more restrictive access to public education and its English-language curriculum, and not a single Creole could trace their ancestry to New Brunswick, but the rhetoric of the French language movement was strenuously predicated on Cajun identity.

The new French language programs in Louisiana were seen by traditionalists as being the final death knell of Cajun and Creole French, which from then on would only exist in old-time music. Dewey Balfa's daughter Christine told the *Times-Picayune* that a policy to teach standard French was "better than nothing," but that Cajuns no longer sounded like Cajuns; instead, they sounded like French-speaking Americans.[70] But old-time music did indeed benefit greatly from Louisiana's French language movement as a new generation of these "French-speaking Americans" grew up speaking French, studied French culture, wrote French language lyrics, and gained audiences for their music not only in the United States but in France and Canada.

The "French reality" of Southwest Louisiana, so historically complex and interconnected, was, in the years after the language revival movement, reimagined romantically and represented categorically as a story of persecuted French Canadian immigrants living out their lives together, developing their art and their folkways as a culturally isolated people. The old-time Creole musical tradition was subject to its own myth-making as well, as its most important musicians were retrospectively labeled zydeco musicians, even though they had played old-time music and sang centuries-old songs. The etymological connection between the word *genre* for a kind of music and the French *gens* for a kind of people is instructive: the rhetoric of ethnic revival and the Civil Rights movement took the traditional musicians of Southwest Louisiana and put them through the sieve, so that when Old-Timey Records released Amédé Ardoin's 1928–1938 recordings in 1983, the label described Ardoin as "the first Black zydeco recording artist," while Arhoolie called Ardoin "the First Black Cajun Recording Artist," and referred to Bois Sec Ardoin and Canray Fontenot as "an African American" band.[71] Alan Lomax would have been confounded, Harry Smith angered, and Ralph Rinzler must have been a little heartbroken. But the splintering of French Louisiana music into Cajun and Creole music produced a second wave of French language music composition in which Cajun musicians intently and very successfully focused on the history and politics of a distant, romanticized French Canadian past, and its Creole innovators, reacting to the growing movement toward a white francophone cultural transnationalism, moved away from that exclusionary version of history toward the electric sounds of urban African-American rhythm and blues.

NOTES

1. Jeffrey Robert Rosner, "Francophonie" as a Pan-Movement: The Politics of Cultural Affinity (Ph.D. diss., The John Hopkins University, 1969), 46.
2. Aonghas St-Hilaire, "North America and the Francophonie: Local and Transnational Movements for the Survival of French-Speaking North America," *Language Sciences*, Volume 19, Issue 4 (October 1997): 372.
3. Rosner, "Francophonie," 46.
4. Shane K. Bernard, "Acadian Pride, Anglo Conformism: The Acadian Bicentennial Celebration of 1955," *Louisiana History: The Journal of the Louisiana Historical Association*, Vol. 41, No. 2 (Spring 2000): 163.
5. Bernard, "Acadian Pride," 165–166.
6. Rosner, "Francophonie," 73.
7. Bernard, "Acadian Pride," 162.
8. St-Hilaire, "North America and the Francophonie," 374.
9. Rosner, "Francophonie," 71.
10. *Times-Picayune*, March 6, 1970, 49.
11. Rosner, "Francophonie," 94.

12. Roger K. Ward, "The French Language in Louisiana Law and Legal Education: A Requiem," *Louisiana Law Review*, Volume 57, Number 4 (Summer 1997): 1284–1285.
13. "*L'Avenir de la Langue Française en Louisiane*," Pioneer of Assumption Newspaper, July, 1879.
14. The Opelousas Courier, May 6, 1893.
15. Lawrence E. Estaville, Jr., "The Louisiana French," Journal of Historical Geography," 14, 4 (1998): 353.
16. Ward, "The French Language in Louisiana," 1298.
17. Estaville, "Louisiana French," 347.
18. Natsis, "Legislation and Language," 326.
19. Dewey W. Grantham, *Hoke Smith and the Politics of the New South* (Baton Rouge: Louisiana State University Press, 1967), 334.
20. Howard C. Hill, "The Americanization Movement," *The American Journal of Sociology*, Volume XXIV, Number 6 (May 1919): 612.
21. Americanization Bill: Hearings Before the Committee on Education and Labor, United States Senate, Sixty-ninth Congress, First session on S.17, September 11, 1919, transcript, 6.
22. Hill, "The Americanization Movement," 631.
23. Americanization Bill, hearings, transcript, 27–28.
24. Hill, "The Americanization Movement," 633.
25. Americanization hearings, Exhibit C, 25.
26. Constitution of the State of Louisiana Adopted in Convention at the City of Baton Rouge. Louisiana, 1921.
27. Bernard, *The Cajuns*, 27.
28. Bernard, *The Cajuns*, 34; 66.
29. St-Hilaire, "North America and the Francophonie," 377.
30. Marie Diane Rodgers, "The French Heritage in Acadiana: The Fundamental Course of Action Necessary to Preserve the French Language," May, 1968, 17.
31. Phillips, "Spoken French," 174–177.
32. Dorice Tentchoff, "Ethnic Survival under Anglo-American Hegemony: The Louisiana Cajuns, *Anthropological Quarterly*, Vol. 53, No. 4 (Oct., 1980): 236–237.
33. Gabriel Debien, trans. Glen Conrad, "The Acadians in Santo Domingo: 1764–1789," in *The Cajuns: Essays on Their History and Culture* (Lafayette: University of Southwestern Louisiana, 1978), 21.
34. James Domengeaux interview by Barry Ancelet, April 23, 1972. AN1.052. The Archives of Cajun and Creole Folklore, The University of Louisiana at Lafayette. Audio recording.
35. W. Fitzhugh Brundage, "*La Reveil de la Louisiane*: Memory and Acadian Identity, 1920–1960," *Where These Memories Grow: History, Memory, and*

Southern Identity (Chapel Hill: The University of North Carolina Press, 2000), 281–282.

36. Domengeaux interview, AN1.166, archives of the University of Lafayette. Audio recording.
37. "Agreement Between the Government of Quebec and the State of Louisiana on Cultural Co-operation." University Archives & Manuscript Collections, University of Louisiana at Lafayette.
38. James Domengeaux, Speech to the Louisiana Association of Fairs and Festivals, February 10, 1968, transcript, 4. University Archives & Manuscript Collections, University of Louisiana at Lafayette.
39. Bernard, *The Cajuns*, 89.
40. Jacques Henry, "The Louisiana French Movement, Actors and Actions in Social Change" in French and Creole in Louisiana, ed. Albert Valdman (New York: Plenum Press, 1997), 185–186.
41. Bernard, *The Cajuns*, 83.
42. Rodgers, "The French Heritage," 13–21.
43. James Domengeaux, Speech as Council Chairman, October 17, 1968, transcript, 2. University Archives & Manuscript Collections, University of Louisiana at Lafayette.
44. "The New Louisiana Story," 93rd Congress, Second Session, Congressional Record, Volume 2, Part 5 (March 7, 1974, to March 18, 1974), 5417–5422.
45. James J. Natsis, "Legislation and Language: The Politics of Speaking French in Louisiana," *The French Review*, Vol. 73, No. 2 (Dec., 1999): 326.
46. Natsis, "Legislation and Language," 326.
47. The Acadian Museum, Erath, Louisiana, exhibit.
48. Natsis, "Legislation and Language," 326.
49. Reed, *Lâche Pas*, 30.
50. Reed, *Lâche Pas*, 30.
51. Natsis, "Legislation and Language," 327.
52. Bernard, *The Cajuns*, 84.
53. Natsis, "Legislation and Language," 328.
54. Joshua A. Fishman, "Mother-Tongue Claiming in the United States Since 1960: Trends and Correlates," in *The Rise and Fall of the Ethnic Revival: Perspectives on Language and Ethnicity*, ed. Joshua Fishman, et al (Berlin: De Gruyter Mouton, 1985), 129.
55. Fishman, "Epilogue," *The Rise and Fall*, 489.
56. Fishman, "Epilogue," *The Rise and Fall*, 509.
57. Fishman, "Epilogue," *The Rise and Fall*, 510–511.
58. Dewey Balfa in Alan Lomax's *Cajun Country*, DVD.
59. Fishman, "Mother-Tongue Claiming," *The Rise and Fall*, 134.
60. Gertner, et al, "Language and Ethnicity" in *The Rise and Fall*, 309–314.

61. Wolfgang W. Moelleken, "Language Maintenance and Language Shift in Pennsylvania German: A Comparative Investigation," *Monatshefte*, Vol. 75, No. 2 (1983): 172–182.

62. Henry, "The Louisiana French Movement, Actors and Actions in Social Change," 189.

63. Ancelet has been one of the most activist figures in the language preservation movement in Southwest Louisiana. These remarks appear in in Pat Mire's *Mon Cher Comrade.*

64. Rodgers, "The French Heritage," 2–5.

65. Dorice Tentchoff, "Ethnic Survival under Anglo-American Hegemony: The Louisiana Cajuns," *Anthropological Quarterly*, Vol. 53, No. 4 (Oct., 1980): 238.

66. Bernard, *The Cajuns*, 53.

67. Domengeaux, Fairs and Festivals speech, transcript, 3.

68. Bernard, *The Cajuns*, 81–82.

69. Fairclough, *Race & Democracy*, 124.

70. Melissa Hartmann, "Le cri du bayou: the status and promotion of the French language and Cajun music in Louisiana" (M.A. thesis, Colorado State University, 2012): 6.

71. Améde Ardoin, "Louisiana Cajun Music Vol. 6: Amadé Ardoin—The First Black Zydeco Recording Artist (1928–1938)." Old-Timey Records, LP 124, 1983; Bois Sec Ardoin and Canray Fontenot, "La Musique Creole." Arhoolie Records, CD 445, 1996, compact disc.

BIBLIOGRAPHY

"Agreement Between the Government of Quebec and the State of Louisiana on Cultural Co-operation." University Archives & Manuscript Collections, University of Louisiana at Lafayette.

Bernard, Shane K. *The Cajuns, Americanization of a People.* Jackson: University Press of Mississippi, 2003.

———. "Acadian Pride, Anglo Conformism: The Acadian Bicentennial Celebration of 1955." *Louisiana History: The Journal of the Louisiana Historical Association* 41.2 (Spring 2000): 161–174.

Brundage, W. Fitzhugh. "*La réveil de la Louisiane*: Memory and Acadian Identity, 1920–1960," *Where These Memories Grow: History, Memory, and Southern Identity*. Chapel Hill: The University of North Carolina Press, 2000.

Constitution of the State of Louisiana Adopted in Convention in the City of Baton Rouge, Louisiana, 1921.

Debien, Gabriel, trans. Glenn R. Conrad. "The Acadians in Santo Domingo: 1764–1789." In *The Cajuns: Essays on Their History and Culture*, ed. Glenn R. Conrad. Lafayette: University of Southwestern Louisiana, 1978.

Domengeaux, James. Interview by Barry Ancelet, April 23, 1972. AN1.052. The Archives of the University of Louisiana at Lafayette. Audio Recording.

———. "Speech as Council Chairman," October 17, 1968. Transcript. Archives at UL.

———. "Speech to the Louisiana Association of Fairs and Festivals, February 10, 1968. Transcript. Archives at UL.

Estaville, Lawrence E., Jr. "The Louisiana French." *Journal of Historical Geography* 14.4 (1998): 342–359.

Fairclough, Adam. *Race & Democracy, The Civil Rights Struggle in Louisiana, 1913–1972*. Athens: University of Georgia Press, 1995.

Fishman, Joshua A. "Epilogue: The Rise and Fall of the Ethnic Revival in the United States." In *The Rise and Fall of the Ethnic Revival*, Michael H. Gertner, Joshua A. Fishman and Esther G. Lowy. Berlin: De Gruyter Mouton, 1985.

Grantham, Dewey W. *Hoke Smith and the Politics of the New South*. Baton Rouge: Louisiana State University Press, 1967.

Hartmann, Melissa. "Le cri du bayou: the status and promotion of the French language and Cajun music in Louisiana." M.A. thesis, Colorado State University. Photocopy. Ann Arbor, MI: UMI Dissertation Pub., ProQuest. In French. The Historic New Orleans Collection, Research Center, New Orleans, Louisiana.

Henry, Jacques. "The Louisiana French Movement, Actors and Actions in Social Change." In *French and Creole in Louisiana*, edited by Albert Valdman. New York: Plenum Press, 1997.

Hill, Howard C. "The Americanization Movement," *The American Journal of Sociology* 24.6 (May 1919): 609–642.

"*L'Avenir de la Langue Française en Louisiane*," Pioneer of Assumption Newspaper, July, 1879.

Mattern, Mark. "Let the Good Times Unroll: Music and Race Relations in Southwest Louisiana." *Black Music Research Journal* 17.2 (Autumn, 1997): 159–168.

Moelleken, Wolfgang W. "Language Maintenance and Language Shift in Pennsylvania German: A Comparative Investigation" *Monatshefte* 75.2 (1983): 172–186.

Natsis, James J. "Legislation and Language: The Politics of Speaking French in Louisiana." *The French Review* 73.2 (Dec., 1999): 325–331.

Phillips, Hosea. "The Spoken French of Louisiana." In *The Cajuns: Essays on Their History and Culture*, edited by Glenn R. Conrad. Lafayette: University of Southwestern Louisiana, 1978.

Reed, Revon. *Lâche Pas La Patate: Portrait des Acadiens de la Louisiane*. Montreal: Éditions Parti pris, 1976.

Rodgers, Marie Diane. "The French Heritage in Acadiana: The Fundamental Course of Action Necessary to Preserve the French Language." May, 1968. http://files.eric.ed.gov/fulltext/ED022145.pdf

Rosner, Jeffrey Robert. "'Francophonie' as a Pan-Movement: The Politics of Cultural Affinity." Ph.D. diss., The John Hopkins University, 1969, ProQuest (7216827).

St-Hilaire, Aonghas. "North America and the Francophonie: Local and Transnational Movements for the Survival of French-Speaking North America." *Language Sciences* 19.4 (October 1997): 369–380.

Volume 2, Part 5 (March 7, 1974, to March 18, 1974).

Tentchoff, Dorice. "Ethnic Survival under Anglo-American Hegemony: The Louisiana Cajuns." *Anthropological Quarterly* 53.4 (Oct., 1980): 229–241.

The Times-Picayune, March 6, 1970.

US Congress. Congressional Record. 93rd Congress, 2nd session, 1974. Vol. 2, pt. 5.

US Congress. Senate. Committee on Education and Labor. Americanization Bill: Hearings before the Committee on Education and Labor. 69th Cong., 1st sess., September 11, 1919.

Ward, Roger K. "The French Language in Louisiana Law and Legal Education: A Requiem." *Louisiana Law Review* 57.4 (Summer 1997): 1283–1324.

CHAPTER 8

"Les metamorphoses": Civil Rights, Ethnic Revival, and New Regional Sounds

In a region bathed in its mythology of itself—Evangeline Parish having been named for the ill-fated romantic heroine of Henry Wadsworth Longfellow's poem—race and genre were also the stuff of myth-making. As the sounds of urban African-American culture drew the younger generation of Creole musicians away from traditional music and Creole accordionists began to imitate, and to identify with, the highly amplified Texas zydeco sound they heard on records and on the radio, the music culture of Southwest Louisiana fractured along generational as well as racial lines. Younger Cajun musicians, drawn to rock much the way those of an earlier generation had incorporated country and western instrumentation and styles into their sound, had less interest in old-time music traditions. Ultimately, those younger Cajun musicians found their way back to old-time music through the experience of traveling to France and to French-speaking Canada, much as an earlier generation had found its way to cultural pride through their experiences in wartime France, while younger Creole musicians assimilated into the music culture of the urban African-American South. The national mood on racial and ethnic politics and the generational divide between sixties generation young people and their elders played a decisive role in the history of music.

Music journalists and historians of Louisiana culture struggled to describe and categorize French Louisiana music in light of new ethnic and racial sensibilities, labeling Amédé Ardoin's singing and accordion styles "very much white Cajun," and referring to the Creole Carrière brothers,

© The Author(s) 2019
P. Peknik, *French Louisiana Music and Its Patrons*,
https://doi.org/10.1007/978-3-319-97424-8_8

fiddler Bébé and accordionist Eraste, whose 1974 Arhoolie album was titled "Cajun Fiddle Styles," as "important practitioners of the early, primitive zydeco sound."[1] French Louisiana music was claimed as Creole music by Creoles, and as Cajun music by Cajuns, with one musician insisting that he could tell the difference between the music of Amédé Ardoin and the music of Dennis McGee because "I could tell the difference between a black fiddler and a white fiddler."[2]

The record men who recorded Cajun and Creole musicians, the folklorists who studied the culture, and the musicians themselves disagreed over questions of proprietorship, relationships between the old and the new, the desire for authenticity and the demands of the market. Chris Strachwitz had become intrigued by the tenacity of southern cultural traditions when he was stationed in Austria while serving with the US Army in the mid-1950s. He was already aware of Creole culture because of the Louisianans who had poured into California during World War II to work in defense industry jobs, and on the army base abroad, he noticed the way Louisianans and other regional and cultural minorities stuck together in the barracks and reminisced about and guarded their southern folkways: "The Texans realized they had something good down there. The Cajuns, too, missed their own culture. No one paid them any attention except their own kind of people."[3] Back in the States, Strachwitz was eager to see those regional cultures first-hand. On a road trip through Louisiana in the summer of 1960, he asked a gas station attendant where to find Cajun music and was sent to the Midway Club in Lafayette where Aldus Roger's band was playing, men and women dancing counterclockwise in a circle. "Cajun country has had its mojo hand on me ever since," he said. He was determined to "catch" and document, not produce, the music of the vernacular tradition, and reached out to Paul Tate and Eddie Shuler as he set his mind to putting out as many authentic folk music records as he could. Strachwitz was particularly fascinated by the fact that the producers of the music were not, like the Amish, a propertied separatist population but a marginalized and unpropertied cultural group, and he was astonished by the fact that this cultural group was interracial.

On a road trip across Louisiana through Alabama, Georgia, and the Carolinas in the summer of 1962, Strachwitz become aware of the extent and depth of southern segregation as well as by the matter-of-factness with which Southerners spoke of it, casually, as an intractable fact of life. He and blues historian Paul Oliver met with the Clarksdale, Mississippi head of the NAACP, who explained that because Strachwitz was from Germany and Oliver was from England, they could get away with going anywhere they wanted despite racial boundaries, but, the NAACP official explained, "I can't go anywhere I want." Strachwitz was shocked and moved by that revelation.

On a trip to Texas two years later, Strachwitz was drawn to the music of Louisiana-born musician Clifton Chenier because he considered Chenier a Creole musician performing in the tradition of old-time French Louisiana music, playing entirely for "his own Creole people in that neighborhood in Houston, in a language only they could understand," but in a language which he knew would also appeal to white college-educated blues fans. When Lightnin' Hopkins sent Strachwitz to hear Chenier playing in one of southeast Houston's Frenchtown neighborhood beer joints, Strachwitz fell in love with Chenier's bluesy piano key accordion music and Creole singing, and called Bill Quinn the next day to arrange a recording session with Chenier at Gold Star Studio. But Chenier, who thought of his music as rhythm and blues with an accordion, showed up for the session with a full band, telling Strachwitz, "I gotta have an orchestra." He wanted the full electric guitar, bass, piano, saxophone and drum sound, not an old-time acoustic performance.

Asked to name his early influences, he named blues celebrities B.B. King, Muddy Waters and his cousin Lightnin' Hopkins, not traditional Creole or Cajun musicians, and told Strachwitz that the music market was all about soul and rhythm and blues, that his goal was to best Ray Charles with young listeners. "I'm going to whip that goddamn Fats Domino," Chenier boasted.[4] Just as Rinzler had intervened and implored Doc Watson to play roots music on an acoustic guitar rather than country standards on an electric guitar, Strachwitz had to cajole and negotiate with Chenier to persuade him to play down-home songs and sing in French. "I wanted to capture the sound of that Creole or 'French' music that I'd heard at that beer joint in Houston, but Clifton wanted to make it rock and roll," Strachwitz said. "I was lucky to have met him under circumstances in which he was singing in French."

Chenier had made his first recordings for the Hollywood, California blues and gospel label Specialty Records in 1955, the same year that label signed Little Richard, and the ambitious Chenier thought of himself as belonging in a cohort of blues and rock stars that included Percy Mayfield, Chuck Berry, and T-Bone Walker. When Strachwitz met him several years later, Chenier was set on recording mostly rock and roll numbers, and he and Strachwitz argued over the fact that Chenier "wasn't going to do any more of that goddamn French," despite the fact that the French songs were all Strachwitz wanted to record. "I just thought he sounded so much better singing in Creole," Strachwitz said.[5]

Despite his insistence to Strachwitz that he was done with French-language music, when Chenier's "*Tous les jours la même chose*" [Every day the same thing], released as "Louisiana Blues," became Chenier's first Arhoolie hit, and he saw the appeal of French-language music among young African-Americans and Creoles, he reversed course and started on the path to becoming a promoter of the Creole French language and the old accordion-rubboard combo. On one Arhoolie recording, his uncle Morris "Big" Chenier accompanied him on an old beat-up fiddle playing Ardoin's "Eunice Two Step," released as "Sweet Little Doll." Asked whether he was pleased to see the French language being promoted through the work of the Center for the Development of French in Louisiana, Chenier replied, "I love that. Cause you see, like I say, there's a lot of people holding back on French, you know, but me, I never was ashamed of French and I never will be."[6]

But just the presence of an accordion in a multi-instrument blues-and-rock band, with a few French lyrics punctuating the English, didn't make Chenier a classic Creole performer, just as the popularity of this new zydeco sound didn't retroactively transform old-time Creole musicians into old-time zydeco musicians. Canray Fontenot and "Bois Sec" Ardoin were perplexed when people began to talk about zydeco music's early twentieth-century origins in the music of Amédé Ardoin. "Now they're talking about zydeco music," Fontenot said in an interview in the 1980s. "They never had that. I never known that. They don't even know what it means. If you was black, you was playing Creole. If you was white you was playing Cajun." Ardoin agreed: "For me, I don't know much for the zydeco music, I never played that. I was born with Creole music ... Creole music is my music."[7] Zydeco was merely the name given to the way Chenier played, Ardoin said. "It's just a word that's been made up," Cajun fiddler Marc Savoy agreed.[8] "Bois Sec" Ardoin described zydeco music as a genre that did not have the melodic or rhythmic complexity or require the technical virtuosity to be considered a form descended from Amédé Ardoin's mastery: "*Pour moi, c'est du tonnerre et des éclairs*"[9] [To me, it's just a bunch of thunder and lightning].

Chenier presented zydeco both as a musical form that he had invented and one that he had revived: "I'm the one that started zydeco, well the old generation had it a long time ago."[10] By Chenier's accounts, the old-time

Creole accordionists Sidney Babineaux, who was born in the 1880s, and Claude Faulk, born in 1908, had played "old-timey" zydeco music. Because Chenier adapted some of the songs of Creole accordionist Claude Faulk, and performed some music from the old-time French Louisiana repertoire, including "*Jolie blonde*," "Louisiana Two-Step" and "Lafayette Waltz," he was comfortable claiming that all old-time Creole music had just been an earlier form of zydeco, and that traditional Creole accordionists like Amédé Ardoin were zydeco musicians, which is the like saying that since the Rolling Stones covered Muddy Water's "Can't Be Satisfied," Muddy Waters was a rock and roll musician. Zydeco had been developed in the Creole neighborhoods of Houston when French Louisiana music collided with urban blues, and then, in the 1970s, when rapidly rising oil prices brought new jobs to Southwest Louisiana, bringing Louisiana Texans back across the border, the faster-tempo accordion sound became popular in Lafayette and Lake Charles dance halls and thought of, in time, as a Louisiana music.

The beginning of Creoles' identification with African-Americans and their steady movement toward mainstream urban black music began in the World War II era, Nicholas Spitzer has argued. "The loss of French and Afro-Caribbean aspects in [Creole] music both reflected and reinforced this assimilation," according to Spitzer: "The Louisiana Cajun French and Afro-French musical traditions were being pulled apart because of the tendency of the population as a whole to affiliate more readily with the national black/white ethnic dichotomy rather than the more fluid aesthetic and social circumstances of French Louisiana."[11]

The appeal of this contemporary urban music, and the promotion of an invented tradition of zydeco as an indigenous Southwest Louisiana form, threatened the endurance of older Creole music.[12] At Lafayette's "A Tribute to Cajun Music" in 1974, Ralph Rinzler broached the topic with an audience that had come to hear Dennis McGee, Nathan Abshire, the Balfa Brothers, "Bois Sec" Ardoin and Canray Fontenot and Clifton Chenier: "There is a tradition longstanding in Cajun communities where musicians, black and white, have performed and recorded together," Rinzler said in his introductory remarks, explaining how the music of Southwestern Louisiana had flowed across the border from Louisiana to Texas, and even reached into Houston, "where Clifton Chenier has played his brand of Cajun-derived music called zydeco since 1958." It had been Rinzler's idea for Lafayette to host a music festival to showcase "Acadian Creole music." "The term zydeco has been used to describe a style of Cajun music played by black musicians, but it is clear that Chenier's music is very personal and bears little resemblance to the music of the Ardoins and Canray Fontenot," he concluded. Ardoin and Fontenot were the last of their generation of old-time Creole musicians. "The French music went down amongst us blacks,"[13] "Bois Sec" Ardoin recalled. Musing on the labeling of Amédé Ardoin's old-time music as zydeco, zydeco accordionist Rockin' Sidney Simien said, "When I first heard his music, I said it was Cajun music. ... I thought it [the term 'zydeco' in the title] was a misprint." When Nicholas Spitzer did field work in Southwest Louisiana in the 1980s, older Creoles complained about the Afro-Americanization of their music, and considered Chenier an aspiring rock and roll musician who had turned his back on old-time Creole music.[14] Zydeco, which became a symbol of Creole ethnicity for the younger generation, was "neither Cajun, blues, nor necessarily even Creole," but in the same mood of ethnic revivalism in which Cajuns raised their Acadian flag, the term "zydeco" was generically applied to all Creole music, and "anachronistically applied to Creole musical styles antedating zydeco's appearance by decades or more" as a way to invent a centuries-old romanticized rural past for a newly developed urban Texas musical style.[15]

The insistence that zydeco music was a folk style being revived rather than a contemporary form being invented was part of its appeal. Zydeco was promoted as having emerged from rural folk culture, and entered popular consciousness as the folk music of Louisiana's rural black Creoles, "a self-sufficient, nonindustrial, geographically isolated collective of kith and kin, cooperatively producing only what they consumed, consuming only what they produced, communicating exclusively through oral/aural conduits," whereas in fact, zydeco style was coherent with urban popular music, and was developed "by urban wage earners, professional musicians, whose technological and musical sophistication ... geographic and socioeconomic mobility, and more general relations to urban industrial ... consumer economies are all more consistent with mass popular music than they are with local folk tradition."[16] The struggles of the Civil Rights movement then informed and intensified the popular appreciation of Chenier's music, so that the young white college students who saw Chenier at a 1966 University of California-Berkeley blues concert performing on a bill with Muddy Waters were listening not just to a popular musician but also to a popular black folk musician, a distinction that was meaningful not only on the Berkeley campus but in the larger national culture.

When zydeco proved to be not really folk enough, Strachwitz continued on his hunt for local folk tradition, recording the Ardoin family in their home performing old style two-steps and waltzes. Like Rinzler, Strachwitz wanted not just to document and preserve, but to intervene at a moment in time when the last generation to have grown up playing old-time French Louisiana music still had time to pass the tradition on. Rinzler had pulled Canray Fontenot out of retirement to bring him to Newport. By 1966, Fontenot no longer even owned a fiddle, and hadn't played for eight years. "A person gets tired of all that, just like anything else," Fontenot said. The fiddle he used at Newport had been dug out of the trash by a city worker, and Fontenot restrung it and brought it to the festival. Nor had Fontenot only ever played old-time music. He had been in a string band in the 1940s, playing hillbilly music. "Bois Sec" Ardoin and Canray Fontenot had no similarly renowned Creole successors, but Fontenot taught generations of fiddlers to play. When he died in 1996, *The New York Times* memorialized him in the parlance of the day as "a synthesizer of cultural identities,"[17] a phrase that would have baffled him as well as generations of old-time French Louisiana musicians. Fontenot and "Bois Sec" Ardoin, who played together for forty years, received the National Heritage Fellowship from the National Endowment for the Arts in 1986 for their contribution to traditional arts, and when Ardoin died in 2007, *The New York Times* credited him with having "stalwartly sustained" South Louisiana tradition by performing with "a younger generation of Creole traditionalists, notably Balfa Toujours, led by Dewey's daughter Christine."[18]

The younger generation of traditionalists, brought up to speak standard continental French as taught by French, Canadian and Belgian school teachers, and then, eventually, Louisiana teachers, included accordionist Zachary Richard and fiddler Michael Doucet, founder of the traditionalist band Beausoleil. Richard, who had studied history at Tulane in the early 1970s and aspired to become a successful country-rock songwriter and singer, had his mind changed about the French language when he traveled to France to perform at music festivals at the invitation of a French musician he had met in Louisiana. Richard moved to Quebec, where his French-language music found an appreciative audience, and was drawn to the radical politics of the separatist movement. Pondering the history of the Acadians in New Brunswick, Nova Scotia, and New Orleans, he wrote what he described as militant songs about his newly discovered Acadian heritage. In "*Réveille*," Richard tells the story of British soldiers burning the crops and homes of Acadian villagers in the eighteenth century: "*Mon grand,*

grand, grand grand-père/Est v'nu de la Bretagne, Le sang de ma famille a mouillé l'Acadie" [My great, great great-grandfather/Came from Brittany/ The blood of my ancestors was spilled in Acadia]. Richard describes the Acadians being driven like cattle and cast to the wind, imprisoned, impoverished, and separated from family members. As the women weep, the men, led by Beausoleil, take up arms to resist British tyranny, and then the exiled people of Canada resettle in Louisiana, separated from their homeland, parents, and children, "orphans of Acadia:" *C'est les goddams qui viennent/ Voler les enfants*" [The goddamned (British) are coming/To steal our children]. The song's title is a rallying cry "*pour sauver l'héritage*" [To save our heritage.]

Richard's song captured, and perpetuated, the myth of a direct migration from Canada to Louisiana beginning in 1755, although there was no such immediate, overland migration. In fact, many Acadians went to New England and Philadelphia, Maryland and New York, Saint-Domingue and other islands in the French West Indies, or to England and France, returning after the Treaty of 1763 to Quebec, the Falkland Islands and Louisiana. Even the 1906 *An Historical Sketch of the Acadians: Their Deportation and Wanderings* by George Potter Bible documents the Acadians' experiences in Georgia and the Carolinas, an experience through which the exile "lost his identity as an Acadian": "They (many of them) avoid all reference to Acadians, and would be pleased to be known exclusively as Americans," Judge Joseph A. Breaux of the Supreme Court of Louisiana was quoted as saying.[19] Many Cajuns felt estranged from the grand historic tale of the Acadian dispersal from Canada and the distant Acadian past in New Brunswick and Nova Scotia, which was "a state-imagined connection with a disjunct past ... [that imposed] a 'recollection' of a past that was not truly knowable, ownable, or memorable to these Cajuns. L'Acadie became an ethereal trace of a past with no ground."[20]

Yet people like to create myths that are larger than themselves, Richard said.[21] And the stories they told themselves inspired not only sorrow and longing, but also anger. Songs about the Acadian experience in French Canada began to fill the Cajun repertoire. Richard's "*Dans le nord canadien*" [In the Canadian North] describes British soldiers coming to burn the homes of Acadians; in the years ahead, Dewey Balfa would write "1755," one of dozens of songs by Cajun musicians about *Le Grand Dérangement*: "*En 1755, on a été epaillé/Comme des veaux et des vaches*" [In 1775, they took everything from us/Like we were cows and calves]. The expulsion of French Canadians from what became British territory after the French and Indian War allies the experience of the Cajuns with the historical experience of American Anglo-Protestants during the Revolutionary era, but the phrase "*Ça disait l'esclave*" [They said we were enslaved] attempts to align the experiences of Cajuns with the experience of people of African descent in the New World.

The romanticized, fictionalized account of the Acadian expulsion was given national FM radio play through the Band's "Acadian Driftwood," written by Robbie Robertson, whose wife was French-Canadian. The song described an Acadian population that had experienced a history of forced exile and hard labor congruent with the historical experiences of people of African descent in the New World: "They signed a treaty and our homes were taken ... The government had us walkin' in chains ... We worked in the sugar fields up from New Orleans." Greil Marcus described it as "a tale of people who dream of northern lights as they bear a southern cross" and of an ethnic culture that held together while keeping to itself, "though a black Cajun culture, the Zydeco, grew up alongside the white." In Robertson's narrative, the exiled Acadians "don't accept America, its weather or its government; they don't really make a new home. They don't make peace with the new land or with themselves," but instead are sickened with longing for a return to their Canadian homeland.[22] Senator Allen J. Ellender of Terrebonne Parish, lecturing his colleagues on the occasion of the Acadian Bicentennial, introduced his request for a commemorative three-cent postage stamp by claiming that the expulsion of the Acadians from Nova Scotia was "a deep scar on the Anglo-Saxon world. Its only counterpart in modern times can be found in the concentration camps of the Gestapo and the Communist secret police."[23] Southwest Louisiana place names still appeared in French Louisiana music, but new more distant place names were written into the songs: Nova Scotia, Saskatchewan, Montreal, Paris. "No French, No More" is the story of a Cajun who was chastised by school teachers for speaking French, and fears the loss of his ancestral language: "Once it is gone, it ain't never coming back no more," the singer warned, and "Nowadays, it's getting so you can't/Tell the Cajuns from *Américains*." In "*Chansons pour les enfants d'Acadie*," Richard is a poor fisherman far from his homeland, protesting the tyranny and exile he suffered: "*L'Acadie, je t'appelle/peux tu m'entendre/crier*" [Acadia, I'm calling you/Can you hear me yelling your name, Acadia?] "In those days, we were looking for an identity," Richard told folklorist Barry Ancelet.[24] Richard first became interested in French Louisiana music as a way to set himself apart in a crowded world of performing musicians, and then became intoxicated with the rhetoric of militant allegiance—"*Solidarité et Fierté*" [Solidarity and Pride]—to the cause of Grand Dérangement history.

Zachary Richard's cousin, Michael Doucet, who had grown up playing Bob Dylan and Pete Seeger songs on guitar, developed a committed interest in the history and myths of Acadia on a trip to France in 1974, when he heard a group of French musicians playing an old familiar song: "In France, I saw eight fiddlers playing '*Jolie Blonde*' the old way, accompanied by a hurdy-gurdy ... I began to understand what we had and what we stood for," Doucet said. He was struck by the realization that French Louisiana music had become "the new folk music, something really beautiful," and that there were serious young French musicians who were devoted to performing it.[25] Doucet, who had grown up on a farm near Lafayette, returned to Louisiana determined to learn to play fiddle and to play old-time French Louisiana songs. He named his new band Beausoleil, after the legendary Joseph Broussard, a leader of the Acadian resistance to the 1755 *Grand Dérangement*. In "*Recherche d'Acadie*," Doucet recounted Broussard's resistance to British persecution, and the founding of a Louisianan Acadia: British soldiers mercilessly burned down family homes, took the old and the young captives on ships, then drowned them as friends and neighbors watched in helpless anguish. Beausoleil appears like a vision guiding the exiled and God-abandoned people of Acadia to a strange new land, and shows them by example how to make Southwest Louisiana their new Acadia. "*Ici en Louisiane/Tous ensemble, bien fiers mais aussi beaucoup pauvres*" [Here in Louisiana/All of us together/So proud but also so poor].

Doucet studied the classics of the French Louisiana canon and performed and recorded dozens of old-time songs, with the hard-drinking, broken-hearted ballads of the French Louisiana canon making way for a new repertoire of songs about the dignity and perseverance of ancestors and the extended family. In "*La terre de mon grand-père*" [The Land of My Grandfather], Doucet lauded his Cajun grandfather's work ethic and forbearance: "*Travaillait toute la journée/En printemps jusqu'à l'hiver/Et il a jamais dit un mot au contraire/C'est ça l'esprit de ma famille cadienne*" [He worked all day long/From spring to winter/And he never one complained/That's the spirit of my Cajun family]. Although Doucet had grown up in Southwest Louisiana, he had never heard of the region's two most famous Cajun fiddlers until he went to Paris: "I came back to Louisiana ... went out and met some of the people I had heard of in

France, like Dewey Balfa and Dennis McGee." Doucet received a National Endowment for the Arts Folk Arts Apprenticeship to learn Cajun fiddle styles. "Dennis McGee really did it for me," he said. "And his songs were so old. Anything after 1940 was a new song to him." Doucet abandoned his plans to go to graduate school in New Mexico to study Romantic poetry so that he could immerse himself in Cajun French music and the Cajun French language instead. "I traded Blake for Balfa," as he put it.[26]

Beausoleil, invited to record for the French label Pathé Marconi, was then asked to perform at the *Louisiane Bien-Aimée* American Bicentennial Celebration in Paris in 1976, where he played under the Arc de Triomphe.

Back in Louisiana, Doucet studied the field work of Lomax and Oster to find "the real songs" and "the black origins of Cajun music ... the whole black French scene which greatly influenced Cajun music at the turn of the century,"[27] and went to work with Dewey Balfa in Balfa's Schools of Tomorrow program, which was funded by a Folk Artists in the Schools grant from the National Endowment for the Arts and sponsored by the Southern Folk Revival project. Balfa worried that if there was nobody to come back from working in the fields to sit on the porch and pick up the fiddle, traditional music would disappear with his generation, along with the understanding of racial solidarity that was the foundation of French Louisiana music. "When you sit at a table and you eat your good gumbo, that's not from your ancestors ... the black people brought this type of culture into our part of the country, and I'm just as proud of eating gumbo as they are. I respect them for who they are," Balfa said. But he faced resistance from one parish superintendent who objected to Balfa's description of French Louisiana music as having been developed by "a mixture of white and black people." The superintendent replied, "How in the world are you gonna make a Cajun with a negro?"[28] Balfa, who continued to play in local bars and drove an Acadia Parish school bus for twenty years, remained an indefatigable cultural activist in Southwest Louisiana and an ambassador of old-time music nationally, performing at the inaugurations of Presidents Richard Nixon and Jimmy Carter and carrying on as a musician and activist even after enduring the deaths in 1978 of his brothers Rodney and Will, who, like so many other talented musicians in the French Louisiana music story, died in a highway accident.

In 1962, construction had begun on Interstate 10 through the coastal prairie land of Southwest Louisiana, creating the major Gulf Coast transportation corridor linking New Orleans to Houston. By 1973 it was nearly complete, cutting straight through the Acadian parishes, crossing the

Atchafalaya River swampland, skirting past Breaux Bridge, cutting through Lafayette, with its small "look French" downtown, transforming the music towns of Rayne and Crowley into names on exit signs off a highway where, day and night, loud trucks barreled past strip malls toward oil refineries. That year, French ethnographer Claudie Marcel-Dubois of the *Musée National des Arts et Traditions Populaires* in Paris, the leading scholar of the folk music of France, contacted Rinzler at the Smithsonian regarding her own research on French folk songs in Louisiana. Rinzler planned a trip in which he, Harry Oster and Marcel-Dubois would start in New Orleans and travel to Basile, Lafayette and Breaux Bridge, first visiting the home of Creole vocalist Alma Barthelemy in Diamond, then going "to the western part of the state and record cajuns (most of them are white), who are great instrumentalists, but many of whom are fine singers with interesting though less sizeable repertoires." They recorded sixty-six songs at Barthelmey's house, and Marcel-Dubois snapped photos of Barthelemy singing as she served coffee at her kitchen table.

Rinzler took down a set of oral histories, asking musicians some of the same questions he'd posed a decade earlier, including what the music was being called. "*La musique 'cadienne*,*" "la musique de fais-do do,"* and "*la musique créole*" were the answers. In his field notes, he jotted down inquiries about television, literacy, the suicide rate, and religion. Visiting "Bois Sec" Ardoin's home, Rinzler was moved by the plain intimacy of the Ardoins' domestic life: "We sat on the porch exchanging small talk until the last light of the day faded and the mosquitos became unbearable. Inside, the walls were covered with dark paneling which was plastered over by photographs of family members and religious artifacts; a tapestry of the Last Supper, Martin Luther King, Jr. and an anguished but humble Jesus displaying the bleeding heart of his bosom," Rinzler wrote. Waiting for Ardoin to pull up to the house in his dilapidated Ford, Rinzler watched the plaid-aproned Mrs. Ardoin scuffling about in bare feet patiently preparing a dinner of fiery gumbo for the couple's fourteen children, a meal that the oldest daughter and the boys would eat first, followed by Mrs. Ardoin and the rest of the girls.

Rinzler thrived in the fieldwork setting, with an eye for detail and an ear for the antiquarian tune. He talked excitedly to Oster and Dubois about the large body of oral literature and folk art Southwest Louisiana musicians had maintained through music. The three musicologists headed for Mamou to stay with Paul Tate and his family, and of course they went to Fred's, which, with its overflowing ashtrays and rickety chairs and dark interior, and walls covered with framed photos of old-time musicians, was an important place in the story.

French researchers from the *Haut Comité de la Langue Française* who had traveled to Mamou in 1970–1971 to report back to the French government on the "survivals of the French language and culture" in Louisiana expected to find very little evidence that Louisiana had ever been a French territory, and to write a report stating that any artifacts of the French language and culture had long since disappeared. Their first impressions, on arriving in New Orleans, bore out that expectation. But they were astounded to hear in the Acadian parishes a "rugged old dialect of French, often Anglicized, enriched with Indian words and idiomatic expressions," a language spoken by tens of thousands of Louisianans, and to observe authentic Francophone traditions. The researchers lamented the fact that the French had almost completely neglected "this chapter of American history," and they struggled to give what they witnessed in Southwest Louisiana a name: "It's not a nation. It's not its own state. A minority, but its people are heterogeneous. And this population does not have a name: we sometimes call them Acadians, sometimes Cajuns … Cajuns just as often call themselves Creoles, or French. Neither a country, nor a state, nor an official identity, but an ethnic reality just the same: all you have to do is go to Mamou, or Carencro or Pierre Part to find yourself in a different America." Nor could the music, in its canon, style, and performance, be separated into Cajun or Creole, or black or white, the researchers concluded, since it was a genre that had developed from ancient French ballads and French Canadian dance music mixed with blues melodies and New Orleans jazz.[29]

On her field work around Southwest Louisiana with Rinzler, Marcel-Dubois, whose academic specialization was the unaccompanied ballad tradition, was intrigued to discover a third version of a *"Les metamorphoses,"* a song she knew well from two recordings, one made in Vendeé, France, and the other in Francophone Guadeloupe. Metamorphosis, which was precisely what Fred's Lounge in Mamou had not done, what it did not represent, and what it would not do. Just like on every other Saturday morning, Revon Reed's show was still broadcast over KUEN, the dancers began to crowd the dance floor early, and the band was still just an accordion and a couple of fiddles.

Before leaving Mamou that summer, Rinzler interviewed the Cajun fiddler Aubrey DeVille, and captured a story that poignantly distills the experience of a single French Louisiana musician while echoing the ques-

tions and musings of ethnomusicologists, anthropologists, and music historians. Answering Rinzler's question about how he had learned to play
"*Le vieux boeuf et le vieux chariot*" on the fiddle, DeVille recounted: "My
daddy's grandpa used to be a fiddle player and it come from him. I don't
know if it's original that he made a copy. My daddy would sing it and I
caught the words and play it on the fiddle. My daddy used to drink a few
drinks and he'd come back home and sing that. So it stayed in my mind.
He'd work the fields..." Rinzler recorded DeVille on vocal and fiddle,
Isom Fontenot on harmonica and vocal, and Preston Manuel on guitar,
and included the haunting melody on "Louisiana Cajun and Creole Music,
The Newport Field Recordings, Recorded 1964–1967" released by
Rounder Records. Rinzler wondered whether DeVille had composed any
original music, and where he'd heard the body of songs he played, and
Rinzler wisely set down DeVille's exact words, which not only capture his
experience, but also distill ethnomusicologists' and folklorists' fundamental inquiries about the genesis, transmission, circulation, and regeneration
of folk music:

> How can somebody make a song without being a copy? There had to be
> somebody to invent that. ... It all comes from somewhere, but that's what
> I'd like to know about, is where. I'd like to have a book and read about it—if
> I could get a book about the songs, how they started. Who invented that?
> What's his name and where he's from? I been in the fifth grade, that's all,
> and I never study about music, I just learn it from each other. I'm just a
> copy, you know.[30]

"Bois Sec" Ardoin had talked about Canray Fontenot's memorized catalog of old-time songs in the same fashion: "*Jug au plombeau*," Ardoin
said. "It's some people he don't even know who make that song. He was
small when he hear that." In Rinzler's unpublished liner notes for the collection, he lamented that the recordings had been done under far-from-
studio conditions in people's homes, and that the performances did not
"capture the genius and galvanizing vigor" of the music, but he hoped the
listener could get a sense of "impressive range, depth, historicity, variety,
and subtlety of Cajun texts, tunes, and performance styles." Rinzler chose
to record Austin Pitre at the crowded Lakeview Park dance hall, where
Pitre played, on an electrically amplified fiddle, "an intricate cascading
obligato within the chord structure" as a crowd mobbed the dance floor
all the way back to the two massive bars, dancing to the electric bass until

two o'clock in the morning, and again back at his home, where he played "*T'as fini de me voir*" [You'll never see me again] on unaccompanied fiddle "in archaic fashion," illustrating his ability to move from public performer to home soloist: "The self-styled public image of the folk/professional and its effect on repertoire and musical style has not yet been studied and is deserving of attention," Rinzler wrote. He included only the oldest songs in each musician's repertoire, explaining that Cajun and Creole musicians had a large general repertoire in common, but that, as for the tune family built around the "*Bombucheur—Jug au plombeau—bataille*"—those songs have distinctive and attractive variants, and "jamming" on one variant or another is dependent on the ability or willingness of musicians to follow one leader's version. In the case of some songs, for example, "*Hack a 'tit Moreau,*" it is unlikely that the average Cajun musician, however skilled, could fit into the continual give-and-take dialogue between Ardoin and Fontenot, Rinzler said: "This is a performance style which seems particularly characteristic of Afro-Americans and African Musicians in its sensitive communicative interlock and obvious improvisational nature."

Reflecting on the relationship between modernization and the romantic folk movement, Richard Blaustein has argued that although folklorists once feared that modernization would lead to cultural homogeneity, the reality has been that "the pressures towards hegemony generate regional, ethnic, and nationalistic separatism."[31] Likewise, musicologists and commercial patrons' determination to catalog, classify, and advertise a style and repertoire of French Louisiana music and popularize a set of leading performers promoted the division of French Louisiana music into two distinct genres. Old-time Cajun and old-time Creole musicians were like fraternal twins who, raised by the same parents, would separate, their common history yielding to the dynamics of marketing. In the commercial promotion of traditional French Louisiana music, the terms "Cajun" and "zydeco" would be used loosely, sometimes interchangeably, beginning in the 1970s, while the cover art told a narrower story. Swallow's 1987 release of Alan and John Lomax's 1934 field recordings, titled "Louisiana Cajun and Creole Music," features a photograph of Cajuns seated on the benches at a *fais do do*; many Cajun CD covers depict musicians performing in dance halls. The photographs create a narrative of rural Southwest Louisiana life: Cajun children stand in a boat as it slowly drifts away from a shoreline dotted with shacks; stern-looking fiddlers sit expressionless as barefoot children dance to their tunes; horse-drawn carriages circle the lawn in Church Point. "Iry LeJeune, Cajun's Greatest, The Definitive

Collection" includes a black and white photo of LeJeune walking down a dirt and gravel road carrying a rocking chair over his head, his mother-in-law beside him walking with a cane, a dog at his heels. These images tell a story about the way traditional music was shared among poor Cajun families on the bayous and prairies. The history of Creole musicians playing French Louisiana music is, visually, part of a different story: the cover of Canray Fontenot's recordings with Bébé and Eraste Carrière, labeled "Cajun Fiddle Styles—Vol. 1.—The Creole Tradition," an Arhoolie release, shows the Carrière brothers at home, and on the cover of "La La, Louisiana Black French Music," Eraste Carrière is seated next to a small wood stove playing the accordion. "*Allons Danser*," a 2009 Rounder Records release featuring "Bois Sec" Ardoin and Balfa Toujours, led by Dewey Balfa's daughter Christine, features a photo of Ardoin in suit, tie, and Sunday hat, seated in a chair beside a woodpile, holding his accordion. Such images convey the history of French Louisiana music within the framework of Creole domestic life and the intimacies of small performance spaces. Record companies rarely depicted Cajun and Creole French Louisiana musicians together on any cover art. In 1976, Rounder Records released Ralph Rinzler's field recordings from his 1964–1967 trips to Southwest Louisiana, using photos of Creole musicians "Bois Sec" Ardoin and Canray Fontenot alongside photos of Cajun musicians Adam and Cyprien Landreneau, Isom Fontenot, Aubrey DeVille and Preston Manuel, and Australia's Sonet label used a nearly full-cover photo of Dewey Balfa and "Bois Sec" Ardoin laughing together on its 1981 "The Ardoin Family Orchestra with Dewie Balfa, A Couple of Cajuns," but these images were the exception, not the rule.

The images that music consumers learned to associate with a genre or musician began to matter even before the advent of television, when post-World War II record companies needed a way to package the new vinyl albums to protect the soft plastic from being damaged during shipping. Columbia Records' art director, the modernist graphic designer Alex Steinweiss, invented not only the cardboard record jacket but the concept of cover art design, convincing Columbia executives to replace the plain brown paper LP wrapper with imagery and graphics that would "illustrate the guts of the music."[32] Visually engaging album covers that told a story about the music's history, style, or impresarios revolutionized the marketing of records, with Columbia's product sales increasing by as much as 800 percent once album covers featured vivid graphic designs and images.[33] The recording industry has been guided by this innovation in marketing ever since. Cover art images direct a listener's attention to the origins, style, and meaning of the music, and invite a genre's fans to dwell on, and privilege, particular associations and histories. Every record company that promoted French Louisiana old-time music showed music consumers what to envision when they heard that regional sound, and although the album titles acknowledge the complexity and richness of the music's genesis and development with phrases that reference Cajun and Creole performers, the cover images depict one or the other half of the story, either the Cajun or the Creole narrative. Arhoolie's 1981 Old-Timey LP of Amédé Ardoin recordings from 1928 to 1938, half of which are solo recordings and half duets with McGee, is titled "Louisiana Cajun Music Vol. 6, The First Black Zydeco Recording Artist," and the cover photo is a small cropped photo of Ardoin. Arhoolie's 1995 "Amédé Ardoin, Pioneer of French Louisiana Blues 1930–1934, I'm Never Comin' Back," more than half the recordings of which feature Ardoin and McGee playing together, depicts Ardoin, holding his accordion, standing in a field of sharecroppers who are being watched by an overseer on horseback. Yazoo's "The Complete Early Recordings of Dennis McGee 1929–1930" collects McGee's recordings with Ernest Frugé and Sady Courville, with photos of McGee and Courville on the cover. But nowhere do Ardoin and McGee appear together, despite their status as the most influential performers in French Louisiana music history. The commercial patrons of French Louisiana music saw, and reproduced for music consumers, a segregated music history in a manner congruent with Karl Hagstrom Miller's analysis of the way that the early twentieth-century recording industry segregated American sound: images and marketing categories "masked the long history of southern musical interaction across the color line." Although southern music was characterized by commonalities, stylistic borrowings, and collaborations between black and white audiences, the commercial compartmentalizing of genres created the impression and conveyed the message that "the music of black and white southerners was defined by their differences from each other rather than through their common histories, sounds, and relationships to American popular music."[34]

There is simply no way to talk about American music history without talking about and across racially demarcated genre categories, yet the commercial patrons of French Louisiana music, perhaps skeptical about their audience's ability to hold a conversation about music that traversed racial histories, found a way, through images, to direct the conversation into and within bounded categories of racial and ethnic identity, guaranteeing that discussions of French Louisiana music would be routed into discussions of Cajun musicians seeking ancestral musical forms in the Canadian northlands, and Creole proto-zydeco performers seeking a separate past. Harry Smith imagined a world in which we wouldn't think about race at all when we talked about music. Ralph Rinzler wanted to see a world in which we felt we could talk companionably about the histories of black, white, ethnic, and rural America. Perhaps we still cannot imagine such a world. But music history, above all other American histories, invites us to imagine, see, and make just such a world.

NOTES

1. Broven, *South to Louisiana*, 102–104.
2. Sara Le Menestrel, "The Color of Music, Social Boundaries and Stereotypes in Southwest Louisiana French Music," *Southern Cultures* 13.3 (2007): 93.
3. Chris Strachwitz, interview with author, Arhoolie Records, El Cerrito, California.
4. Tisserand, *Kingdom of Zydeco*, 132–133.
5. Tisserand, *Kingdom of Zydeco*, 133.
6. Clifton Chenier, in an interview with Ben Sandmel in *Cajun Music*, Savoy, 381.
7. Tisserand, *Zydeco Kingdom*, 32.
8. Savoy, *Cajun Music*, 313.
9. Sara Le Menestrel, *La Voie des Cadiens: Tourisme et identité en Louisiane* (Paris: Éditions, 1999), 331.
10. Savoy, *Cajun Music*, 375.
11. Nicholas Spitzer, "Zydeco and Mardi Gras: Creole Identity and Performance Genres in Rural French Louisiana" (dissertation, The University of Texas at Austin, 1986), 342–343.
12. John Minton, "Houston Creoles and Zydeco: The Emergence of an African American Urban Popular Style," *American Music*, Vol. 14, No. 4, New Perspectives on the Blues (Winter, 1996): 515.
13. Tisserand, *Zydeco Kingdom*, 105.
14. Nicholas Spitzer, "Zydeco and Mardi Gras: Creole Identity and Performance Genres in Rural French Louisiana" (dissertation, The University of Texas at Austin, 1986), 338; 351.
15. Minton, "Houston Creoles and Zydeco," 477–478.
16. Minton, "Houston Creoles and Zydeco," 505.

17. Peter Watrous, "Canray Fontenot, 72, a Singer and Violinist in Creole Style," *The New York Times*, August 2, 1995.
18. Jon Pareles, "Bois Sec Ardoin, Musician and Nurturer of Creole Tradition, Dies at 91," *The New York Times*, May 20, 2007.
19. George P. Bible, *An Historical Sketch of the Acadians: Their Deportation and Wanderings* (Philadelphia: Ferris & Leach, 1906), 135.
20. Ron Emoff, "A Cajun Poetics of Loss and Longing," *Ethnomusicology*, Vol. 42, No. 2 (Spring–Summer, 1998): 285.
21. Ancelet, Cajun and Creole Music Makers, 99.
22. Greil Marcus, "The Band: Northern Lights – Southern Cross," Creem, March 1976. http://www.rocksbackpages.com/Library/Article/the-band%2D%2Dnorthern-lights%2D%2D-southern-cross
23. Bernard, "Acadian Pride, Anglo Conformism," 164.
24. Zachary Richard, interviewed by Barry Ancelet, The Makers of Cajun Music (Austin: University of Texas Press, 1980), 93–95.
25. Ancelet, *Cajun and Creole Music Makers*, 143.
26. Ancelet, *Cajun and Creole Music Makers*, 145–148.
27. Ancelet, *Cajun and Creole Music Makers*, 145–148.
28. Dewey Balfa, interview with Ancelet, AN1.94, 1981 Basile, University of Louisiana at Lafayette Archives. Audio recording.
29. Patrick Griolet, *Cadjins et Créoles en Louisiane, Histoire et Survivance d'une Francophonie* (Paris: Payot, 1986), 9–10; 116.
30. Aubrey Deville, August 10, 1973 interview with Ralph Rinzler, Ralph Rinzler Papers, Fieldwork Box 4 Louisiana, Correspondence 1–3, Ralph Rinzler Folklife Archives and Collections, Smithsonian Center for Folklife & Cultural Heritage, Washington, D.C.
31. Richard Blaustein, "Rethinking Folk Revivalism: Grass-roots Preservationism and Folk Romanticism," in Transforming Tradition, Folk Music Revivals Examined, edited by Neil V. Rosenberg (Urbana: University of Chicago Press, 1993),
32. Kevin Reagan and Steven Heller, Steinweiss, *The Inventor of the Modern Album Cover* (Berlin: Taschen, 2015), 463.
33. Steve Heller, "An Eye for Music," *Print*, Mar/Apr 2005, 57.
34. Miller, *Segregating Sound*, 240.

BIBLIOGRAPHY

Ancelet, Barry. *Cajun and Creole Music Makers*. Jackson: University Press of Mississippi, 1999.
Balfa, Dewey. Interview by Barry Ancelet, Basile, Louisiana. AN1.94, University of Louisiana at Lafayette Archives. Audio Recording.

Bernard, Shane. "Acadian Pride, Anglo Conformism: The Acadian Bicentennial Celebration of 1955." *Louisiana History: The Journal of the Louisiana Historical Association* 41.2 (Spring 2000): 161–174.

Blaustein, Richard. "Rethinking Folk Revivalism: Grass-roots Preservationism and Folk Romanticism," in *Transforming Tradition, Folk Music Revivals Examined*, edited by Neil V. Rosenberg. Urbana: University of Chicago Press, 1993.

Bible, George P. *An Historical Sketch of the Acadians: Their Deportation and Wanderings*. Philadelphia: Ferris & Leach, 1906.

Broven, John. *South to Louisiana, The Music of the Cajun Bayous*. Gretna: Pelican Publishing Company, 1983.

DeVille, Aubrey. Interview with Ralph Rinzler, Mamou, Louisiana, August 10, 1973. Ralph Rinzler Papers, Fieldwork Box 4 Louisiana, Correspondence 1–3, Ralph Rinzler Folklife Archives and Collections, Smithsonian Center for Folklife & Cultural Heritage, Washington, DC.

Emoff, Ron. "A Cajun Poetics of Loss and Longing." *Ethnomusicology* 42.2 (Spring–Summer, 1998): 283–301.

Griolet, Patrick. *Cadjins et Créoles en Louisiane, Histoire et Survivance d'une Francophonie*. Paris: Payot, 1986.

Heller, Steve. "An Eye for Music," *Print*, Mar/Apr 2005.

Le Menestrel, Sara. "The Color of Music, Social Boundaries and Stereotypes in Southwest Louisiana French Music." *Southern Cultures* 13.3 (2007): 87–105.

———. *La voie des Cadiens: Tourisme et identité en Louisiane*. Paris: Éditions Belin, 1999.

Marcus, Greil. "The Band: Northern Lights – Southern Cross," *Creem*, March 1976.   http://www.rocksbackpages.com/Library/Article/the-band%2D%2Dnorthern-lights%2D%2D-southern-cross

Miller, Karl Hagstrom. *Segregating Sound, Inventing Folk and Pop Music in the Age of Jim Crow*. Durham: Duke University Press, 2010.

Minton, John. "Houston Creoles and Zydeco: The Emergence of an African American Urban Popular Style." *American Music* 14.4 (Winter, 1996): 480–526.

Obituary of Bois Sec Ardoin, *New York Times*, May 20, 2007, national edition.

Obituary of Canray Fontenot, *New York Times*, August 2, 1995, national edition.

Reagan, Kevin, and Steven Heller. *Steinweiss, The Inventor of the Modern Album Cover*. Berlin: Taschen, 2015.

Richard, Zachary. Interview by Barry Ancelet in *The Makers of Cajun Music: Musiciens Cadiens Et Creoles*. Austin: University of Texas Press, 1984.

Rosenberg, Neil V., ed. *Transforming Tradition, Folk Music Revivals Examined*. Urbana: University of Chicago Press, 1993.

Savoy, Ann Allen. *Cajun Music: A Reflection of a People, Vol. 1.* Eunice: Bluebird Press, 1984.

Spitzer, Nicholas R. "Zydeco and French Mardi Gras: Creole Identity and Performance Genres in Rural French Louisiana." PhD diss., The University of Texas at Austin, 1986, ProQuest (8700283).

Tisserand, Michael. *The Kingdom of Zydeco.* New York: Avon Books, 1998.

CHAPTER 9

Postscript

In 2000, Revenant Records released Volume 4 of Harry Smith's Anthology of American Folk Music, a compilation of fiddle music, gospel, and blues. Two French Louisiana groups are included in the collection: the Hackberry Ramblers playing "*Dans le Grand Bois*" [In the Forest], and the Four Aces performing "Aces' Breakdown," both recorded at the St. Charles Hotel in New Orleans in 1938. In the liner notes, guitarist John Fahey, who had been so inspired fifty years earlier by the release of Volumes 1–3, poses the question, "Why did Harry Smith choose to end the set with Cajun? Did Smith sympathize or idealize with the agrarian, Acadian French farmers who refused to move to cities and become urbanized and English and turn their backs on their religion?" Thus the story of French Louisiana music as having developed from the exile experiences of Acadians, idealized as principled resistors of empire, is told again. "Did [Smith] want to tell us something," Fahey asks, "like perhaps here and there, hidden from the scrutiny of the intelligentsia and the stock market a folk society still exists, in many ways undisturbed?"[1]

That folk society more than found its way into the society of the stock market in the decades after Dewey Balfa first took the stage at Newport.

Acadiana's heritage tourism industry, which once had trouble competing with Louisiana's plantation tours, now draws tourists looking for "the cultural shock of exotic Frenchness"[2] at the rural Mardi Gras celebrations and music venues of the prairie parishes. A visitor's guide to Acadia Parish explains that the first settlers were "exiled Acadians who were induced by

© The Author(s) 2019
P. Peknik, *French Louisiana Music and Its Patrons*,
https://doi.org/10.1007/978-3-319-97424-8_9

the Spanish government to come to this area with gifts of large tracts of land, cattle and agricultural implements," exchanging the portrait of cast-out exiles for one that depicts Cajuns as highly sought-after recruits who were enticed into settling in Southwest Louisiana.[3]

Although Creoles still hold the annual *courir* (in only one community, LeBleu Settlement, do blacks and whites hold Mardi Gras together), Mardi Gras is treated in tourist literature as a "uniquely Cajun-French cultural institution" obscuring the fact that for most of its history in Southwest Louisiana, Mardi Gras was a cultural activity that saw the participation of a racially mixed population. Many Cajuns are at best "only vaguely aware" that rural Mardi Gras was a longstanding tradition among Creoles as well, and the state and national media that cover rural Mardi Gras describe it as a Cajun event. In the mid-1980s, the organization CREOLE (Cultural Resources Educational Opportunities toward Linguistic Enrichment) dedicated itself to preserving Creole culture and attracting tourists to Creole cultural events in Southwest Louisiana, in an acknowledgment that Creoles had been effectively disinherited from joint proprietorship of French Louisiana cultural traditions.[4] The genuine traditions of Southwest Louisiana were not perpetuated in their original forms as events and ceremonies that were celebrated by diverse inhabitants of the region, and instead reimagined as the unique traditions of the people of one cultural group, the Cajuns.

That cultural group even had its day in court. In a 1980 discrimination suit filed by Calvin Roach, a "native born American of Acadian descent," against his employer, Dresser Industrial Valve and Instrument Division, Dresser was accused of terminating Roach's employment based on his status as a Cajun and his association with other Cajun employees. Dresser argued that had Roach been terminated because his ancestors came from England, Poland, Spain, Germany, Russia, Mexico, or any other country, then Roach would have had a valid legal claim, but Acadia was not a country, and thus Cajuns did not constitute a national or ethnic group. The judge, citing James Domengeaux's description of a Cajun as anyone whose ancestry includes someone who once lived in Acadia, pointed out that the seventeenth-century Acadians were a "multi-national group" that included settlers from Scotland and Ireland, and that they considered themselves to be "a new people." Likewise, in Louisiana, people of many ancestries considered themselves to be Cajun, because in its "openness," Southwest Louisiana had assimilated non-Cajuns into Cajun culture. Agreeing with Roach's claim that he was a member of an ethnic minority, the judge wrote: "The Louisiana Acadian is alive and well. He is 'upfront' and 'main stream.'"[5]

The Southwest Louisiana heritage tourism industry is premised on this folkstream, this mainstreaming of an old-time "outsider" cultural identity and the music, cultural traditions and cuisine associated with that identity. But the idea of folk music in America is no longer tied to the rural origins or self-taught musicianship of the performer. Rather, it has become a presentation style, an indicator of an apparently (though perhaps not actually) modest production budget, a few acoustic numbers, and an attitude toward music that is decidedly not oriented toward commercial pop, even if the music is commercially lucrative and popular. One of the legacies of the folk revival movement was its insistence that the simply dressed, casual-mannered musician is the truly "authentic" American performer.

If the "authentic" French folk music of Southwest Louisiana entered the mainstream through the legacy of local activists like Revon Reed, the advocacy of national folklorists like Ralph Rinzler, and the work of commercial label owners like Chris Strachwitz, it entered the realm of modern art through Harry Smith's still-remarkable *Anthology*, which integrated French Louisiana music into the canon of folk music, with its narratives of poverty, its confessions of desire and depictions of violence, its humor and melancholy, its stories of the American outsider. Although the cultural and racial politics of the decades that followed unhinged Cajun music from Creole music, one slowing down to recapture the old-time sounds of the ancestral rural past, one speeding up to keep up with the fast-tempo pace of modern urban culture, Smith's compilation still has a haunting beauty, juxtaposing as it does the sounds of the black and white rural South, and dramatizing for every listener "what it might be like to live in a town, or a country, where everyone you meet has a point of view and nobody ever shuts up."[6] In other words: to live in the America we have always lived in.

In 2016, Smithsonian Folkways Recordings acquired the Arhoolie catalog. Reflecting on the improvisations and collaborations between Cajun and Creole musicians over decades and decades of American music history, Strachwitz said it was "like Croats and Serbs playing music together although they didn't mix socially." Strachwitz valued the discrete and singular quality of regional and ethnic cultures, and in his recording and promotion of French-language music, made an argument about the vitality and endurance of regional, ethnic, and rural culture in a nation that still entertained a fiction about its own cultural homogeneity. Strachwitz "cut the flame underneath the American melting pot," as one Southwest Louisiana musician put it.

The endurance of traditional French Louisiana music showed to a young generation of Louisianans that despite our necessary orientation in a culture of media technology that accelerates and compresses our sense of time, we also live in historical and ancestral time, and that is the arc of time in which music is played. Songs seemed to connect the Canadian Maritime provinces to the Caribbean islands and the rice fields of Louisiana. The popularization of those songs showed Americans that, despite the standardizing drive of national media culture and the constancy of the world's gaze upon the country's politics, iconic cities and mass-produced consumer goods, there are still moments when, hearing the music of some other part of the country whose landscapes we will never see and whose inhabitants we will never know, we have the sense that parts of the country are profoundly unfamiliar and exist in precarious relation to the dominant, mainstream whole. Marian Leighton Levy, co-founder, along with Ken Irwin and Bill Nowlin, of Rounder Records in 1970, said it was this sense of the vulnerable state of non-majority artistic culture that drove her interest in folk music. Having studied modern European history in graduate school, Levy was "motivated by and concerned for the fate of the creative practices of minority cultures," and wanted to support folk music without romanticizing or manipulating it: "You were harming it if you were trying to stage it a certain way."[7]

The popularization of French Louisiana music was driven by unusual characters with vastly different lives who ended up in the same recording studios or the same bars, people whose histories and experiences separated them sharply, but who all cared about the same thing at the same complicated historical moment. Chris Strachwitz believed he could find the real America in its rural music, just as Ralph Rinzler believed that America's old-time music would help Americans better comprehend their own history. Harry Smith, whose three-volume *Anthology* fascinated a generation of musicians, had envisioned volumes four and five, but by the time Folkways was ready to issue the rest of Smith's collection, he had sold the albums to the New York Public Library. Harry Smith disappeared, in his itinerant, eccentric, confounding way. He was the only one who could name the people on the recordings, so although the library duplicated some of the albums, there was no documentation about the singers. Many of the boxes were destroyed.

In the years just before Smith was nominated for a Grammy for the advancement of American folk music, he was starving in a Franciscan flophouse in the Bowery, where he was recording the sounds of other men dying, their incessant coughing and their prayers. Smith had knocked around with Charlie Parker and Dizzy Gillespie, and one of his last friends was the goddaughter and great-grandniece of a far more famous collector, Isabella Stewart Gardner, an early acquirer of French impressionist paintings whose home, designed to look like a Venetian palace, became Boston's charming Gardner Museum. The second Isabella Stewart Gardner had a mercurial life almost as interesting as Smith's, and Smith knew her because, after four husbands, her final paramour was the doorman of Manhattan's Chelsea Hotel, where Smith spent the last years of his life, dangling a microphone out the window to record the sounds in the alley.

At the Grammy Awards, Smith was lauded for his "ongoing insight into the relationship between artistry and society, and his deep commitment to folk music as a vehicle for social change"; accepting the award, Smith said that his dreams had come true, that he had seen America changed through music. He spent his last Fourth of July recording the sounds of street vagrants on the Lower East Side, of junkies talking and city songbirds and the jump-rope rhymes of children playing in Tompkins Park, listening, as he had throughout his lifetime, for the sounds and the emotions and the human expressions that "link all of us humans together."

The popularization of French Louisiana music was effectuated by a cohort of musicologists, folklorists, collectors, and commercial producers who sought to promote the music for a range of philosophical, social, political, and economic reasons that transcended their interest in the music as pure sound. They were highly successful at bringing the music out of Southwest Louisiana to new audiences, and at launching local musicians into national and international recording and performing careers. Like other folk music forms, French Louisiana music was transformed by its popularization, moving from an old-time home and dance hall genre to an internationally appreciated commercial sound.

The local Mamou, Louisiana movement to preserve and maintain the traditional music of the region was an outcome of a desire shared by Paul Tate and Revon Reed to protect a particular way of life from the cultural alterations wrought by the changing demographics of the state as Anglophone Texans moved across the border, bringing the sounds of commercial country music with them. Fred's Lounge now has a weighty guest book, kept under the bar, filled with the names of French Louisiana music fans who have come from much farther away than Texas to listen to the fiddlers and accordionists and watch couples dance in the narrow space in front of the amps and microphone cords. Tourists from Germany, France, and Australia show up at the bar early on Saturday mornings, studying the photographs and drawings of French Louisiana musicians framed and crowded

together along the dark pink walls, lounging on the faux-leather tan ban-
quette, and drinking Schlitz and cinnamon schnapps, two of the signature
drinks served at Fred's. Ashtrays overflow with cigarette butts. *Esquire*
named Fred's Lounge one of the best bars in America, in a category that
included the swanky bar at the Nomad Hotel on Broadway in Manhattan,
the tropical Lou's Beer Garden in Miami Beach, the Velvet Tango Room, a
Cleveland jazz lounge, the Cat and Fiddle on Sunset Boulevard in
Hollywood, and bars in Portland, Indianapolis, Seattle, and Houston.[8]

Paul Tate is mentioned only briefly in most accounts of the popularization of French Louisiana music, but the esteemed American photographer
Lee Friedlander had the eye to see Tate's central role in the French
Louisiana music story. The New York-based Friedlander, considered one
of the greatest living American photographers and often compared to
Diane Arbus and Garry Winogrand because of the stark geometries of his
depictions of urban social life, spent decades photographing jazz and blues
musicians for Atlantic Records, capturing many of the greats of twentieth-
century music history: Miles Davis, Aretha Franklin, Thelonious Monk,
Billie Holliday, John Coltrane, Coleman Hawkins, Count Basie, Ray
Charles, Chet Baker, Johnny Cash, Tammy Wynette, Ruth Brown, Mahalia
Jackson, and Ella Fitzgerald. Friedlander first visited New Orleans in 1957
to shoot album covers during the jazz revival movement, and in that storied music city, he paired jazz patrons with the traditional jazz musicians
whose work they were promoting: Allan Jaffee, who turned Preservation
Jazz Hall into the French Quarter's most storied jazz venue, next to gospel singer Sister Gertrude Morgan; Richard Allen, founder of Tulane
University's Archive of New Orleans Jazz, beside baritone horn player
Joseph "Red" Clark; and musicologist and jazz historian William Russell
with Louis Keppard, a guitarist and brass band tuba player who had performed with King Oliver.[9] Friedlander then traveled into Southwest
Louisiana, following the music to Mamou, where he took a striking black-
and-white photograph of Paul Tate. In 2001, the National Gallery of Art
purchased the photograph, which is now part of its permanent collection.
Though Tate is standing near Fred's Lounge in front of the law office he
shared with his brother Donald J. Tate at the corner of 6th and Chestnut,
the photograph is mistitled "Paul Tate, Lafayette, Louisiana, 1968." Tate
is wearing a white linen suit with white shirt and black bowtie, and white
leather shoes with pointed black tips. The suit is slightly rumpled, the
linen wrinkled by the humidity, and Tate stands framed in the doorway, his
shadow cast at an angle in the bright afternoon sun. Looking at the pho-

tograph, it's easy to imagine the heat radiating up from the sidewalk; at the edge of the frame, a Creole teenager leans against the wall under the shaded alcove, gazing off in another direction. Tate looks at the camera with an expression that is at once bemused, serene and slightly skeptical, as if he is not yet sure what kind of story the photographer wants to tell.

NOTES

1. John Fahey, "Harry Smith's Anthology of American Folk Music, Volume Four," Revenant Records #211, 2000, compact disc, liner notes, 90.
2. Carolyn E. Ware, "Heritage Tourism in Rural Acadiana," *Western Folklore* Volume 62, No. 53 (Summer, 2003): 182.
3. "Louisiana Cajun Prairie, Acadia Parish, A Visitor's Guide" (Crowley: Acadia Parish Tourist Commission, 2010), 28.
4. Sexton, "Cajun Mardi Gras: Cultural Objectification and Symbolic Appropriation in a French Tradition," *Ethnology* Vol. 38, No. 4 (Autumn, 1999): 297–311.
5. Calvin J. Roach vs. Dresser Industrial Valve and Instrument Division, 494 F. Supp. 215. United States District Court for the Western District Louisiana, Alexandria Division, 1980.
6. Greil Marcus, "Uncle Dave Macon: Agent of Satan?" in Perchuk, *Harry Smith: The Avant-Garde*, 184.
7. Marian Leighton Levy, interview with author, May 2018, Newburyport, Massachusetts.
8. David Wondrich, "Best Bars in America," *Esquire*, Vol. 157, Issue 6/7 (Jun/Jul 2012), 99–116.
9. Nathaniel Rich, "Authenticity All Right: Lee Friedlander's New Orleans," *The New York Review of Books*, May 16, 2014. http://www.nybooks.com/daily/2014/05/16/lee-friedlander-new-orleans/

BIBLIOGRAPHY

Perchuk, Andrew. "Struggle and Structure." In *Harry Smith, The Avant-Garde in the American Vernacular*, edited by Andrew Perchuk. Los Angeles: Getty Publications, 2010.

Rich, Nathaniel. "Authenticity All Right: Lee Friedlander's New Orleans." *The New York Review of Books*, May 16, 2014.

Sexton, Rocky L. "Cajun Mardi Gras: Cultural Objectification and Symbolic Appropriation in a French Tradition." *Ethnology* Vol. 38, No. 4 (Autumn, 1999): 297–313.

Ware, Carolyn E. "Heritage Tourism in Rural Acadiana." *Western Folklore* Volume 62, No. 53 (Summer, 2003): 157–187.

Index[1]

[1]Note: Page numbers followed by 'n' refer to notes.

© The Author(s) 2019
P. Peknik, *French Louisiana Music and Its Patrons*,
https://doi.org/10.1007/978-3-319-97424-8

Printed by Printforce, the Netherlands